LEADERSHIP AND CHANGE IN THE MULTILATERAL

TRADING SYSTEM

STUDIES IN INTERNATIONAL INSTITUTIONAL DYNAMICS

Amrita Narlikar

(Editor-in-Chief)

University of Cambridge

VOLUME 2

LEADERSHIP AND CHANGE IN THE MULTILATERAL TRADING SYSTEM

Edited by Amrita Narlikar and Brendan Vickers

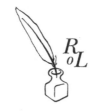

MARTINUS
NIJHOFF
PUBLISHERS

DORDRECHT • LEIDEN • BOSTON
2009

Cover illustration / Design:

Photograph: Atomically resolved images of high temperature superconductors using a Scanning Tunnelling Microscope (Courtesy Professor A. V. Narlikar)

This book is printed on acid-free paper.

Library of Congres Cataloging-in-Publication Data

ISSN   1874-2025
ISBN 13   978-90-8979-010-1 – hardbound
ISBN 13   978-90-8979-020-0 – paperback

ACKNOWLEDGEMENTS

The idea for this book stemmed from a conference that was organised on 4–5 August 2008, by the Institute for Global Dialogue in partnership with the Friedrich Ebert Foundation, in Pretoria, South Africa. The conference was a great success, and the vociferous discussion and debate that it triggered amongst speakers and audience convinced us that there was a real necessity for a book that took stock of developments in the Doha negotiations, and their implications for the multilateral trading system as a whole, particularly under the shadow of an evolving balance of power and leadership.

We would like to express our sincere gratitude to the Executive Director of the Institute for Global Dialogue, Prof Garth le Pere, the Director of the Multilateral Programme, Dr Francis Ikome, and the members of the Institute's Board of Directors (particularly Professor Maxi Schoeman of the University of Pretoria) for their invaluable support and guidance on this project. We are also very grateful to Professors Martin Daunton, Andrew Gamble, Christopher Hill, Brendan Simms, Willy Brown, and Harry Bhadeshia, all at the University of Cambridge, for their constant interest and stimulating conversations. In addition, the project was made possible through the generous financial support of the Friedrich Ebert Foundation. We also thank all the contributors on this project for their splendid cooperation and camaraderie.

Finally, a special note of thanks is due to our families. Amrita Narlikar thanks her parents Dr Aruna Narlikar and Professor Anant Narlikar for providing much intellectual inspiration and moral support throughout, and Batasha for his friendship. Brendan Vickers thanks his mother Elsa Vickers for her support and encouragement over the years, and the triplets Dean, Kyle and Neil Roux for providing many pleasant distractions from work.

CONTENTS

AUTHOR BIOGRAPHIES

Gregory Chin is Assistant Professor, Department of Political Science and Faculty of Graduate Studies at York University, Canada, and Senior Fellow, Centre for International Governance Innovation, Waterloo, Canada.

Manfred Elsig is Assistant Professor, World Trade Institute, University of Bern and Visiting Lecturer at the Graduate Institute of International and Development Studies, Geneva, Switzerland.

Faizel Ismail is the Head of the South African Delegation to the World Trade Organisation in Geneva, Switzerland, and Associate Editor of the *Journal of World Trade*.

Amrita Narlikar is University Senior Lecturer in International Relations, Department of Politics and International Studies, University of Cambridge, and Official Fellow of Darwin College, Cambridge, UK.

Maria Lucia Padua Lima is Professor and Director of International Affairs at São Paulo Law School, Fundação Getúlio Vargas, São Paulo, Brazil.

Geoffrey Allen Pigman is a Member of the Faculty lecturing in Political Economy at Bennington College, Vermont, and is a Visiting Research Fellow, Center for Global Change and Governance, Rutgers University, Newark, USA.

Amit Shovon Ray is Professor of Economics (presently on leave) at the Centre for International Trade and Development, School of International Studies, Jawaharlal Nehru University and Chair Professor of Trade, Technology and Competitiveness at the Indian Council for Research on International Economic Relations, New Delhi India.

Sabyasachi Saha is a researcher at the Indian Council for Research on International Economic Relations, New Delhi, India.

Brendan Vickers is Senior Researcher for Multilateral Trade at the Institute for Global Dialogue in Johannesburg, South Africa, and a Research Associate of the Department of Political Science, University of Pretoria, South Africa.

BRENDAN VICKERS AND AMRITA NARLIKAR

1. INTRODUCTION:

GLOBAL TRADE GOVERNANCE IN A MULTIPOLAR WORLD

Why should the WTO be 'led' by just a few rich white countries? It was that way for years, but the developing countries have fundamentally changed the WTO.[1]

Pascal Lamy, Trade Commissioner of the European Union (1999-2004)

Developing countries like India, Brazil and South Africa are at the forefront of countries defining the parameters of the WTO's future work programme – their ministers, ambassadors and officials are among the most effective and influential trade-policy practitioners in the world today.[2]

Mike Moore, Director-General of the WTO (1999-2002)

Fifteen years after the establishment of the World Trade Organisation (WTO) on 1 January 1995, the organisation and its maiden round of multilateral trade negotiations – the Doha Development Agenda (DDA) – stand at a crossroads. In the view of many observers, the once-ambitious Doha Round suffers from the mutually reinforcing ills of credibility and consistency.[3] Since the outset of the negotiations in November 2001, a dual discourse has evolved, namely that of reconciling multilateral trade liberalisation with diverse developmental priorities. After eight years of negotiations amid proliferating regional trade accords and the sharp decline of world trade following the 2008 global financial crisis,[4] it is a fair

---

[1] Lamy 2002.

[2] Moore 2003, 172.

[3] Evian Group 2006.

[4] The World Bank on 9 December 2008 forecast a 2.1 per cent fall in world trade in 2009, after an overall 6.2 per cent rise in 2008 (World Bank 2008). This was the first contraction in global trade since 1982. Three months later, on 30 March 2009, the World Bank updated its projections: world trade is expected to drop 6.1 per cent in 2009, with significantly sharper contraction in trade volumes of manufactured products (World Bank 2009). WTO economists have also revised further downward their forecast for 2009 world *(continued)*

A. Narlikar, B. Vickers (eds.), Leadership and Change in the Multilateral Trading System, 1–20.

argument that: 'Support for an open, liberal trading system is neither consistent nor unambiguous'.[5] The spectre of global protectionism[6], the revival of Keynesian state capitalism, and fears of a return to the 'low dishonest decade' of the 1930s (in the words of English poet W. H. Auden) further compound Doha's troubled fortunes in an increasingly multipolar trading world. These recent developments all cast a penumbra of doubt over the future of the DDA, as well as the purpose and efficacy of the WTO as a key institution of global economic governance. Although the food, finance and energy crises of the past decade have all generated debate and calls to speedily conclude the Doha Round to stabilise and stimulate the world economy[7], the *Financial Times* has offered its own prognosis: 'It is time to be brave, swallow hard and accept that the Doha round in its present form has failed'.[8]

Launched in November 2001 in the wake of the 9/11 terrorist atrocities, the DDA is today the longest running trade round since the institutionalisation of the post-war rules-based trading system. An objective assessment of the Doha record reveals a pattern of recurrent negotiating drift and deadlock between developed and developing countries, with few developmental dividends.[9] The latter has been punctuated by episodic moments of 'post-crisis politics' and renewed 'development-speak', as was reflected in the July Package of 2004 and the Hong Kong

---

merchandise trade from a decline in volume of 9 per cent to a decline of 10 per cent (WTO 2009a).

[5] Higgott 2009, 39.

[6] The Director-General of the WTO, Pascal Lamy, has to date issued three reports to the Trade Policy Review Body (TPRB) on recent trade and trade-related developments associated with the financial and economic crisis. The first report, released in January 2009, noted only 'limited evidence' of increased trade barriers in response to the global crisis. However, the second report, released in April 2009, stated that there had been 'significant slippage', with increases in tariffs, new non-tariff measures and more resort to trade defence measures, such as anti-dumping actions. The third report, released in July 2009, noted 'further slippage' towards more trade-restricting and distorting policies. However, resort to high-intensity protectionist measures had been contained overall, albeit with difficulties (WTO 2009b-d).

[7] See for example Baldwin and Evenett 2008; Birkbeck and Meléndez-Ortiz 2009. For an alternative perspective on the value of concluding the DDA (and for the international community to rather concentrate on trade gains in other areas), see Meyn et al 2009.

[8] *Financial Times*, 30 July 2008.

[9] Over the course of the DDA negotiations, a number of not unimportant development-related reforms have been implemented or proposed, inter alia: Trade-Related Intellectual Property Rights (TRIPS) and Public Health flexibilities, the elimination of export subsidies in agriculture, specific attention to the cotton issue, aid-for-trade to strengthen production and supply capacities in the developing world, some deviations for least-developed countries (LDCs) under their Trade-Related Investment Measures (TRIMS) obligations, and duty-free quota-free market access for all products originating from LDCs (with caveats at the margins).

Ministerial Conference in December 2005.[10] Certainly, trade diplomats have recorded very limited progress in some technical areas of the Doha negotiations. But while the WTO majors claim slight convergence around a considerably downscaled trade agreement, members have not been willing to make the requisite concessions to formally secure even a face-saving 'Doha super-lite' package. Instead, WTO members have further signalled their effective disengagement from the DDA by turning to alternative regional and bilateral trade agreements.

In sum, developing countries have been able to celebrate the symbolic 'triumph' of a commitment of good faith to development in multilateral trade. However, negotiations to realise those ambitions, including implementing the unfulfilled promises and imbalances created by the previous Uruguay Round (1986-1994), have seriously lagged. This situation partly reflects the weight of changing global and domestic landscapes and the new globalisation challenges that confront trade diplomats in Geneva and national capitals. Simultaneously, the rising powers, despite their increasing and improved participation, have still not shown themselves willing to take on the role of leaders.

In this introductory chapter, we explore the rise of developing countries as major new actors in the multipolar trading system and what this nascent balance of power portends for the WTO as a key institution of global economic governance. The chapter proceeds in four steps. In the first section, we sketch the new geopolitical realities of the twenty-first century global economy and trace the heightened voice and agency of the rising powers Brazil, China and India – flanked by South Africa as the largest and most industrialised economy on the African continent – in the WTO. The second section explores the deep political crisis that confronts modern global trade governance. Among the multiple causes for the stasis in the WTO is a leadership vacuum: neither the established leaders nor the emerging ones are willing to take on the responsibilities of leadership and contribute to the provision of the public good of free multilateral trade. Instead, in the evolving balance of power in the WTO, both the old guard and the new pass the buck of leadership to each other. The third section more fully addresses this agency conundrum from empirical, theoretical and normative perspectives. Ultimately, we make the case that Brazil, India, China and South Africa – the BICS – must assume the mantle of leadership at the High Table of the Doha negotiations – plus

---

[10] Wilkinson argues that the Hong Kong Ministerial Conference in December 2005 was a quintessential instance of post-crisis politics: 'The collapse of the Cancún meeting and the political settlement reached in the July 2004 package ensured that despite a general negotiating sloth, each of the principal protagonists approached the meeting [in Hong Kong] in an optimistic and willing fashion' (Wilkinson 2006:137).

the WTO more generally. The chapter concludes with the purpose and structure of the book, before turning to the country case studies.

1   THE 'RISE OF THE REST' IN A MULTIPOLAR DOHA WORLD

Set against the tectonic and temperamental power shifts of the twenty-first century global economy, the DDA was never going to simply replicate the scripted transatlantic trade rounds of the past. It is indeed significant that the Doha Round negotiations have unfolded against the recent bumptious cycle of global growth from 2002 to 2007. These heady years presaged the phenomenal rise of such (re)emerging powers as Brazil, Russia, India and China (BRICs) to the status of 'new titans'[11] of the world economy. These emerging powers are the producers, consumers and innovators of the future, while their contribution to world output and their share in the growth of world trade has been disproportionately large (as the country chapters in this book demonstrate). A recent report by Goldman Sachs notes that since 2001 and the start of the DDA, the share of the US in world gross domestic product has fallen from 34 per cent to 28 per cent, whilst the BRICs' share has risen from 8 per cent to 16 per cent. During the same period, China's reserves have rocketed from US$200 billion to US$1,800 billion; Brazil's from US$35 billion to US$200 billion; and India's from US$50 billion to US$300 billion.[12]

Equally impressive is their assertive agency to rebalance global power dynamics and refashion the status quo more in favour of the world's underdeveloped majority. The recent leaders' summits of the Group of 20 (G20)[13] that have sought to manage the global financial crisis, the first BRIC summit in Yekaterinburg in June 2009 (which, inter alia, has sought to lessen dependence on the US dollar as the world's reserve currency), and continuing work to transform and expand the Group of 8 (G8) under the Heiligendamm L'Aquila Process[14] have all formally presided over the geopolitical 'rise of the rest'[15] and the twilight of an

---

[11] *The Economist*, 14 September 2006
[12] Goldman Sachs 2007.
[13] The G20 (as opposed to the G20 in the WTO) consists of the world's nineteen largest national economies, plus the EU. These countries are Argentina, Australia, Brazil, Canada, China, France, Germany, India, Indonesia, Italy, Japan, Mexico, Russia, Saudi Arabia, South Africa, South Korea, Turkey, United Kingdom and the US.
[14] See Cooper and Antkiewicz 2008.
[15] Fareed Zakaria refers to the growth of China, India, Brazil and Russia (among others) as 'the rise of the rest' (Zakaria 2009). However, Alice Amsden seminally coined this phrase to describe the late-industrialising countries (Amsden 2001).

epoch of international relations dominated by 'blue-eyed blond men'.[16] Even the smallest of the BICS, South Africa, has regularly punched above its weight in international relations. Not only has the country acquired unprecedented influence as a 'norm entrepreneur' and active global reformer, but also as the de facto (if sometimes reluctant) spokesman for the African continent.[17] South Africa has also sought to exercise middle power leadership as an interlocutor between the advanced developed countries of the North and the poorer developing nations of the South (a bridge-building role that China has also played in the WTO, see Chapter 6).

In this book, besides presenting case studies of the EU and the US, we also focus on the BICS – Brazil, India, China and South Africa – which represent the key new players at the High Table of WTO negotiations.[18] We argue that developing countries – from the rising powers of Asia and Latin America to the more indigent nations of the world, including the least-developed countries (LDCs) and the small vulnerable economies (SVEs) – have acquired unprecedented voice and agency in the WTO. This not only reflects the impressive economic performance, vast capital accumulation and sizeable 'market power'[19] of the tiger and dragon economies, but also the effective bargaining coalitions that their smaller peers have formed in the DDA negotiations (as explored by Amrita Narlikar in Chapter 8). Donna Lee and Nicola Smith make the point that developing countries have shifted from being mere 'objects' of trade talks to being 'subjects' of trade negotiations, even within the WTO's broader reciprocity dynamic.[20] Harnessing their newfound power to influence outcomes, developing countries, which constitute over two-thirds of the WTO's 153-country membership, have actively sought greater voice, influence and participation in the WTO and other global governance fora.

As both system-supporters and change-agents in multilateral trade, developing countries are exercising a major impact on the future of the rules-based trading system, the WTO as its institutional custodian, and the DDA as the first – and given its proclivity to deadlock – arguably the last 'single-undertaking' omnibus trade round of the organisation.[21]

---

[16] Prior to the G20 London summit in April 2009, Brazilian President Luiz Inacio Lula da Silva suggested that the global financial crisis had been caused by the irrational behaviour of 'white people with blue eyes' (*Financial Times*, 27 March 2009).

[17] Vickers 2008.

[18] Note that Russia is not a member of the WTO, and hence is not included in our study.

[19] Peter Drahos lists four sources of effective bargaining power in trade negotiations, viz. market power, enrolment power, commercial intelligence networks and domestic institutions (Drahos 2003).

[20] Lee and Smith 2008; see also Narlikar 2003.

[21] See Warwick Commission 2007; Wolfe 2008.

Since the time of the Cancún Ministerial Conference in September 2003, Brazil and India have been particularly strident in their trade diplomacy; more recently China, which for long appeared to be somewhat detached and aloof from the round's discordant politics following its own arduous accession process (notwithstanding US and European exhortations to play a greater leadership role), has entered the fray. The stand-off in Geneva in July 2008 between the US, China and India over a special safeguard mechanism (SSM) to protect developing country farmers was the fourth time in at least seven years that the DDA negotiations had ended in impasse (see Faizel Ismail's chapter for the reasons for the breakdown, Chapter 9). While each successive failure to reach an agreement has been a major setback for the Doha Round, it has galvanised the resistance of the developing country majors and incrementally shifted the balance of power in the WTO – and globally. Flush with evident 'victory' following the July 2008 ministerial-level conclave, the Brazilian and Indian Foreign and Trade Ministers proudly proclaimed that: 'One thing we can celebrate is that rules here are no longer made by the rich countries. That's the difference with the Uruguay Round'.[22]

Less appreciated in developing country capitals is that greater voice in the WTO also carries the weight of additional responsibilities for maintaining and strengthening the systemic trading regime, including the equitable delivery of its public goods (e.g. open markets). Dani Rodrik correctly argues that the financial crisis will see both the US and Europe weakened as economic actors and upholders of the policy and intellectual orthodoxy. They will be unwilling to provide the kind of leadership that sustained multilateralism in the decades following the Second World War. The corollary to this will be the growth in importance of developing countries, particularly the capital-exporting countries of Asia and the Gulf region.[23] Since the future focus of multilateral trade rules will be among developing countries, it is therefore imperative that they assume greater leadership. As the contributors to this book suggest, the interactions of the developed and developing worlds in the DDA, and the diversity of interests and competing visions of 'development' that they represent, pose both a challenge to the sixty-year-old multilateral trading regime as well as possible solutions.

In the decade since the failure of the Seattle Ministerial Conference in 1999 to launch the Millennium Round, the international trading regime has become ever more politicised and strident. This reflects the realities of a more multipolar world economy, which has dispersed power and complicated collective action. In the WTO, this has seen the emergence

---

[22] Quoted in *Bridges*, 7 August 2008.
[23] Rodrik 2009.

of a 'new politics of confrontation'[24] between the North and the South. Since the time of Seattle, a series of desultory attempts aimed at keeping the Doha bicycle on track have collapsed following a show of strength by the South. At Cancún in 2003, developing countries led by Brazil, China, India and South Africa (see country chapters in this volume) blazed a new trail of resistance politics to the North with the formation of the G20[25], which has demanded greater equity in global agriculture.[26] The emergence of the latter was an important moral and political victory for developing countries: it significantly strengthened their bargaining power, while fundamentally shifting the terms and terrain of the agriculture negotiations (which subsequently stabilised around the G20's 'middle ground' position).

Similar to the Cancún outcome, the Group of 6 (G6)[27] ministerial in Geneva in July 2006 and the Group of 4 (G4)[28] ministerial in Potsdam in June 2007 – held a month prior to the expiry of the US President's Trade Promotion Authority – also ended in deadlock. The breakdown of the Group of 7 (G7) negotiations in Geneva in July 2008 moreover followed short on the heels of the DDA's six month suspension in July 2006. With developed and developing countries still far apart in their positions, the ministerial gathering scheduled for December 2008 was also postponed. Set against the global recession, the Geneva Ministerial Conference in November 2009 – the first regular ministerial gathering since Hong Kong in 2005 – will focus more on organisational matters and the global economy than the DDA. Nonetheless, several factors underpin a new impetus to revive the Doha Round and conclude the negotiations by mid-2010, before US mid-term elections and elections in Brazil. These include the G20 summit declarations from Washington, London and Pittsburgh (as well as the need to discipline protectionism, whether WTO-legal or not); the strong support of WTO member states who 'net gain' from the conclusion of the round (particularly Brazil); the reappointment of Pascal Lamy as the WTO's Director-General and his quest for a 'deal'; and the new leadership in the US and India following their respective electoral cycles in 2008 and 2009.

It is, however, sobering to recall that Doha's protracted difficulties are not without historical precedent. Brinkmanship, crisis and collapse

---

[24] Hurrell and Narlikar 2006.

[25] The G20 in the WTO consists of Argentina, Brazil, Bolivia, Chile, China, Cuba, Egypt, Guatemala, India, Indonesia, Mexico, Nigeria, Pakistan, Paraguay, Philippines, South Africa, Thailand, Tanzania, Uruguay, Venezuela and Zimbabwe.

[26] Narlikar and Tussie 2004.

[27] The G6 comprises the EU, US, Japan, Australia (representing the Cairns Group), Brazil and India.

[28] The G4 consists of the EU, US, Brazil and India.

have indeed been endemic to all multilateral trade rounds since the Allied nations first negotiated the General Agreement on Tariffs and Trade (GATT) in 1947.[29] The previous Uruguay Round, negotiated during the heyday of neoliberal globalisation and the era of market fundamentalism, took seven years to conclude, with even fewer parties than Doha. As we discuss below, there is no shortage of explanations for the failure of the Doha Round to conclude its business.

2   DEVELOPING COUNTRIES AND THE CRISIS OF GLOBAL TRADE GOVERNANCE

Scholars and practitioners have diagnosed a plethora of proximate causes and deeper historical or structural discontents with the multilateral trading system to account for Doha's perpetual inertia. Amrita Narlikar and Pieter van Houten, for instance, attribute the deadlock to uncertainty, particularly heightened uncertainty caused by the emergence of strong coalitions from the developing world whose intentions and ability to withstand external pressures were unclear to their negotiating counterparts.[30] Alasdair Young emphasises the importance of 'transatlantic intransigence' and uses the lens of domestic politics, and better alternatives available to the EU and the US, as the main explanations for the Doha deadlocks.[31] As Druckman and Narlikar go on to argue, the two sets of explanations are complementary: while the uncertainty explanation works better for the first phase of the negotiation, domestic politics and better alternatives for the EU and the US acquire greater relevance for the latter phases of the DDA.[32]

Simon Evenett offers another candidate explanation for why the traditional tool of reciprocity has yielded such few dividends. He cites a combination of four factors, viz. the choice of negotiating agenda; specific political economy forces; the extent of unilateral trade reform that occurred over the last decade; and the fast growth of the leading emerging markets (see country chapters in this volume). Evenett argues that with the widespread tendency of WTO members to engage in unilateral trade reform, and with the impact of a booming world economy that might have led some political leaders to conclude that the benefits forgone from a Doha Round impasse (or even failure) are minimal. According to the latter, China effectively loses an amount equivalent to just three days growth; India loses approximately three weeks growth; and Brazil would

---

[29] Wilkinson 2006.
[30] Narlikar and van Houten 2010.
[31] Young 2010.
[32] Druckman and Narlikar 2010.

forgo the equivalent of one to three months of growth, at least twice as much as India.[33] However, these estimates ignore the dynamic effects of trade policy reform, which are often more consequential than static changes. They also overlook the very significant institutional benefits (such as the Dispute Settlement Mechanism) that the system provides, and are jeopardised by recurrent deadlock and resulting crisis in the organisation.

Importantly, as the multiple explanations for the Doha deadlocks show, the crisis of the WTO is not only technical but deeply political. A symptom of this crisis is a palpable absence of leadership to steer the round to a successful conclusion – and related to this, the silence of consumer and producer groups (e.g. private corporations in the intellectual property, manufacturing and service sectors) that stand to gain.

As this book illustrates, developed countries have both proved unable and unwilling to provide strong guidance, while developing countries with dominant future stakes have shown little incentive to act as unifying drivers. The EU and the US insist that they have made sufficient commitments in liberalising their protected agricultural markets and now seek 'payment' for these domestic trade policy reforms through new commercial flows in non-agricultural market access (NAMA) and services. Developed countries have therefore been the main *demandeurs* for low coefficients, tightened flexibilities and anti-concentration provisions in NAMA, as well as mandatory participation in zero-for-zero industrial tariff liberalisation initiatives. In services trade, the EU has long sought to open markets for its exporters by negotiating bilateral, regional or multilateral accords. The latter included its sponsorship of a deep trade agenda in the DDA. However, with the bulk of its regulatory agenda jettisoned from the DDA (with the exception of trade facilitation), the EU has increasingly negotiated with diminished expectations and diminished enthusiasm.[34] Chapters 2 and 3 by Manfred Elsig and Geoffrey Pigman analyse the reasons behind the abdication of leadership of the DDA by both the EU and the US.

The developing world – usually fractious in its trade interests – has remained largely united in the DDA advancing its own cause. Their point of reference remains the hortatory 2001 Doha Ministerial Declaration, which promised to place the needs and interests of developing countries at the heart of the negotiations. The G20 led by Brazil (whose farming industry stands to benefit substantially from the DDA, as is evident from Maria Padua Lima's analysis in Chapter 4) has held firm to the principle that agriculture, where the greatest trade distortions lie, remains

---

[33] Evenett 2007.
[34] Young 2007.

the locomotive at the front of the negotiating train. By implication, an ambitious outcome in agriculture will calibrate the level of ambition for NAMA and services, and the speed for the round as a whole.[35]

Critics argue that this brand of negotiating brinkmanship (even 'UN-style infantilism'[36]) has created excessive and unfair expectations from the Doha Round, resulting in a lack of willingness – and leadership – of the developing country majors to make any meaningful concessions until these expectations are met. Jeffrey Schott writes that developing countries misinterpreted the Doha mandate as an 'entitlement policy' whereby industrialised countries would make concessions to developing countries. There was no clear understanding of what the latter needed to contribute to the DDA exercise to benefit themselves, other developing countries, and the Organisation for Economic Cooperation and Development (OECD) world.[37]

The obverse view holds that developing countries are prepared to make concessions to help steer the DDA to its conclusion, but not at the expense of their policy space for future industrial development (according to the NAMA-11[38]) or by jeopardising the livelihoods of small farmers and rural communities (according to the Group of 33 (G33))[39]. In its most egregious expression, developing countries 'should be prepared to see the Doha Round fail, and then to put their weight behind another Round on terms fairer to them'.[40] In another variant, this view holds: 'When understood in terms of the contribution of the DDA to multilateral trade regulation already laid, we can see that anything less than an agreement that markedly favours developing countries over their industrial counterparts (and even then, the most vulnerable of their number, not their largest, most notable constituents) will merely perpetuate existing imbalances'.[41] Developing countries have tended to reflect this position by calling upon their more industrialised peers to commit to an equitable, proportional and balanced 'developmental' outcome as mandated by the

---

[35] Ismail 2007.

[36] Sally 2008, 119.

[37] Schott 2008.

[38] The NAMA-11 consists of Argentina, Brazil, Egypt, India, Indonesia, Namibia, Philippines, South Africa, Tunisia and Venezuela.

[39] The G33 consists of 44 countries: Antigua and Barbuda, Barbados, Belize, Benin, Botswana, China, Cote d'Ivoire, Cuba, Democratic Republic of Congo, Dominican Republic, El Salvador, Grenada, Guyana, Guatemala, Haiti, Honduras, India, Indonesia, Jamaica, Kenya, Laos, Mauritania, Madagascar, Mongolia, Mozambique, Nicaragua, Nigeria, Pakistan, Panama, Peru, Philippines, Saint Kitts and Nevis, Saint Lucia, Saint Vincent and the Grenadines, Senegal, South Korea, Sri Lanka, Suriname, Tanzania, Trinidad and Tobago, Turkey, Uganda, Zambia and Zimbabwe.

[40] Wade 2005; see Rodrik 2008.

[41] Wilkinson 2007, 259.

2005 Hong Kong Ministerial Declaration.[42] Set against this measure, the NAMA-11 has, for instance, routinely raised procedural and substantive concerns that the rate of exchange between agriculture and NAMA (within the texts and between them) remains highly imbalanced and skewed, as Brendan Vickers and Faizel Ismail discuss in their respective chapters (see Chapters 7 and 9).

This climate of all-round defensiveness suggests that without renewed political will and leadership on the part of major developed and developing countries, there is virtually no chance of seeing an ambitious and successful conclusion to the Doha Round (and, some would add, a rather parlous future for the WTO). Whether for reasons of politics, principle or pragmatism, the strict distributive bargaining strategies of the North and South have 'claimed' value rather than attempting, to some degree, to 'create' value and mutual gain through more integrative negotiations.[43] This leadership vacuum has plagued the round since its inception, and has led to various calls for the WTO membership to develop a new model of leadership, define a clearer mission for the organisation, and pursue domestic policies that buttress its role.[44] The Sutherland Report on the future of the WTO recognised this as far back as 2004, when it likened the organisation to 'a vehicle with a proliferation of backseat drivers, each seeking a different destination, with no map and no intention of asking the way'.[45] Individually, members are not always the best guardians of the system, the commissioners concluded.

3   PERSPECTIVES ON LEADERSHIP AND CHANGE IN THE DDA

In this book, our contributors explore the changing dynamics of leadership, voice and agency in the WTO's Doha negotiations. This agenda raises two concerns: first, political leadership in the WTO and the current trade round, since the WTO as an inter-governmental organisation is member-driven (although trade rounds are, to varying degrees, conducted in the 'shadow of power'[46]); and second, institutional custodianship of the trading regime's norms, rules and public goods. The latter involves active participation in the rule-making and rule-enforcement processes of the WTO. In recent years, developing countries have played an important role on both fronts. For example, developing countries (including LDCs)

---

[42] See WTO 2005, paragraph 24.
[43] Odell 2000.
[44] Sutherland 2004; Warwick Commission 2007; de Jonquières 2008; Wolfe 2008.
[45] Sutherland 2004, 76-77.
[46] Steinberg 2002; see also Jawara and Kwa 2005.

increasingly act as plaintiffs or third parties to trade disputes against those developed country majors that flout the rules.[47] They have scored some significant victories under the WTO's dispute settlement process (e.g. Brazil against the US in the Uplands Cotton Ruling in September 2004).

The evolving multipolarity of the trading system and the emergence of new centres of power and leadership in the Doha negotiations may be studied from different perspectives: empirical, theoretical and normative. Empirically, it is evident that developing countries – acting alone through their actual or potential market power or in coalitions that pursue collective gains (as Amrita Narlikar explains in Chapter 8) – exercise a major impact on the form, content and process of the Doha negotiations. Unlike the GATT, the WTO is no longer the rich nations' club from which developing countries could afford to maintain a studied aloofness. Developed countries have learnt that they can no longer treat their poorer peers with the same high-handed attitude that they had used in the GATT, since these countries are no longer afraid to act as credible veto-players under the WTO's consensus rules. Admittedly, this countervailing agency is still largely 'negative' (i.e. the ability and willingness to block an agreement). Notwithstanding their recent proactive role in global trade politics, developing countries are unlikely to enjoy significant 'positive' bargaining power – or transform their veto-player status into that of agenda-setters – in the foreseeable future. Nonetheless, the old Quad group (i.e. US, EU, Canada and Japan) that led the decision-making process in the GATT has come to be replaced by a much more representative grouping that has take various forms: the G4; the 'Five Interested Parties' (FIPs) or the Quintet; the G6; and most recently at the July 2008 talks, the G7. Brazil and India, along with the US and the EU, have consistently constituted all permutations of this core consensus-building group.

These recent dynamics and developments, reflecting the ground reality of increasing multipolarity, are indeed a boon for the WTO. The transformation of the old Quad into a new core group that includes the developing country majors guarantees an organisation that reflects the reality of changing power balances in the dynamic twenty-first century. Paolo Subacchi also makes the important point that the inclusion of these new 'power centres' in the inner locus of bargaining demonstrates a surprising flexibility and adaptability of the multilateral trading system,

---

[47] Chad and Benin's participation as third parties to the cotton dispute was the first time an African country had been a party in a WTO dispute either as plaintiff or defendant (Lee and Smith 2008). South Africa later joined Brazil and Canada as a third party in a maize dispute against US; while Brazil previously indicated that it would challenge US ethanol tariffs.

particularly when contrasted with the rigidity of the International Monetary Fund (IMF) and the World Bank (vis-à-vis voice and quota reforms) as well as the UN Security Council with respect to its permanent membership.[48] But there is also the downside, as Faizel Ismail argues in this book (see Chapter 9). These series of informal, small group conclaves appear to have resurrected the old Principal Supplier Principle and the power politics of the GATT, further marginalising key developing country issues from the High Table of the negotiations. This happened during the endgame at Geneva in July 2008.[49] While critical mass plurilateral negotiations are increasingly touted as one possible solution to the challenges posed by consensus-based bargaining[50], Ismail argues that exclusive small groups do not help the cause of a multilateral trading system that already chafes under serious participatory, transparency and legitimacy concerns. Others are more perturbed by the apparent 'cooptation' of Brazil and India into the steering club that governs the WTO and are sceptical that this will presage a more development-friendly trading architecture. Following the 2005 Hong Kong Ministerial Conference, Walden Bello raised this concern: 'It is paradoxical that the G20, whose formation captured the imagination of the developing world during the Cancún ministerial, has ended up being the launching pad for India and Brazil's integration into the WTO power structure'.[51] Brazil's decision to accept the agriculture and NAMA compromises proposed by the Lamy package in July 2008, which threw the unity of the G20 into question, was seen as vindicating these fears.

There is also a neat symmetry between our theoretical and normative perspectives on the evolving multipolarity of the trading system. The 'new politics of confrontation'[52] that has emerged in the post-Cancún period has seen the North and South by-and-large trading places in their support for greater openness. Through their own social learning and adaptation vis-à-vis liberalism, several developing country majors have emerged as key *demandeurs* in the WTO and its Doha Round negotiations for more open markets in areas of their commercial interest. Brazil has shifted to pole position in demanding greater free trade for its agricultural exporters (see Chapter 4); India has pushed for

---

[48] Subacchi 2008.

[49] Issues of concern for developing countries and LDCs – inter alia cotton, bananas, duty-free and quota-free market access, and preference erosion – were not addressed by the proposed Lamy package. Instead, these issues were deferred and placed on the Director-General's 'to-do' list, but the meeting collapsed before they could be discussed (see Chapter 9).

[50] See Warwick Commission 2007.

[51] Bello 2005.

[52] Hurrell and Narlikar 2006.

mode four (i.e. cross-border movement of temporary workers) in services (see Chapter 5); and China – still new to the game of trade politics – has a strong interest in liberalised manufacturing markets (see Chapter 6). While South Africa has joined the G20 in pressing for ambitious liberalisation of global farm trade, the country has adopted more defensive positions in NAMA and services (even though South Africa has clear services export interests in Africa and elsewhere; see Chapter 7). Although a classical liberal vision of development is not wholly shared by the developing world (e.g. the G33 and G90 advance more defensive community claims on agriculture), in Taylor's view: 'It is an interesting sign of the times – as well as the hegemonic status of liberal norms regarding economics – that the elites from key developing countries are demanding greater liberalisation, not less'.[53]

The rise of Brazil, China and India has led to growing anxieties in OECD countries about the costs and benefits of globalisation, which has diminished their appetite for further trade liberalisation. This means that industrialised countries are no longer willing to alone underwrite the costs of further multilateral reform. Subacchi underscores this new dynamic: 'The shift to a multipolar order does mean that the provision of collective goods is no longer in the hands of the hegemon, but has become a matter of collective goodwill'.[54] The question is whether the new poles of the world economy are able and willing to provide leadership and share the task of exercising a global geopolitical role – or whether their domestic issues and challenges will take priority. In this regard, Arthur Stein has argued that if states perceive an international organisation such as the WTO to be in need of reform, their interest in multilateralism must be sufficiently great to exceed the expected costs of reform; otherwise unilateralism or ad hoc multilateralism will be the result.[55] Leadership may thus be gauged by the extent to which WTO members are prepared to underwrite the costs of maintaining and strengthening the multilateral trading regime, including the public good of open markets.

As the BICS acquire greater prominence in the international economic system, it is patent that further multilateral trade reform is dependent on greater systemic leadership from the developing world. The report of the first Warwick Commission on the future of the multilateral trading system succinctly summarises this challenge:

> Simply put, the fast-growing emerging economies must assume constructive leadership roles in the global trading system while steps are needed to ensure that the originally dominant economic actors,

---

[53] Taylor 2007, 155.
[54] Subacchi 2008, 497.
[55] Stein 1990.

above all the United States and the European Union, do not disengage. At the same time, the smallest and poorest WTO Members must retain a valued stake in the system.[56]

What does this practically mean for the WTO membership, and particularly the BICS? Amrita Narlikar has argued that the transformation of veto-player status into positive influence and leadership involves two steps.[57] As a first step, political leadership for the BICS in the WTO involves a demonstration of firmness and commitment on certain values and goals. Developed countries have seldom had a problem doing this, given their large markets and greater bargaining power. But developing countries have also shown great success in demonstrating firmness of intent (rather than simply cave in to pressure in the early stages of the negotiating game), especially through coalitions such as the G20, G33 and the NAMA-11. However, standing firm on its own does not make a WTO leader.

The second and crucial step of political leadership in the WTO requires the courage and willingness to make some concessions, and to be able to return to domestic constituencies with the reassurance that the package thus obtained will be of benefit to all members and society. This may require national policies of redistribution and welfare, where necessary. This means that ascendant developing countries – the BICS – must reciprocate concessions and bear the costs of providing greater equity of outcomes for their less-developed, smaller and more vulnerable peers. This principle is implicit in the 2005 Hong Kong Ministerial Declaration, which enjoined developed countries – as well as developing countries in a position to do so – to grant LDCs duty-free quota-free market access for all their products.[58] This would be complemented by an aid-for-trade package to strengthen production and supply capacities.

Developing countries will also have to shoulder broader responsibilities in the wider system of global economic governance. Under a new global governance compact – suggestively called 'Bretton Woods II' by British Prime Minister Gordon Brown – capital-exporting developing countries should accept greater transparency in the operation of their sovereign wealth funds and pledge not to use them for political purposes. In return, developed countries should refrain from investment protectionism. The largest emerging economies, such as China, India and

---

[56] Warwick Commission 2007, 10.
[57] Narlikar 2007; also see Narlikar, Chapter 8.
[58] Countries that could not immediately meet this commitment would provide at least 97 per cent market access to LDC exports. However, the 3 per cent carve-out allowed the US to continue protecting its textile and garments sectors, and Japan to support its rice, fish, and leather goods and footwear industries.

Russia, will also need to carry some of the burden of reducing greenhouse gas emissions to mitigate climate change.[59] In another view, the complex political and economic realities of the modern world economy demands that industrialised and developing countries should adopt more nuanced and cooperative approaches towards the notion of policy space in the WTO, to the benefit of both.[60]

4   PURPOSE AND STRUCTURE OF THE BOOK

This book and its insights aim to contribute to the growing scholarship on the multilateral trading system and the challenges that it confronts today. A major contribution of our collection is its country-specific analysis: with six of the ten chapters focusing on the motivations driving the behaviour of the key players, we are able to offer new insights into explaining the negotiation strategies of the established and emerging leaders of the organisation, and further how their actions have brought the WTO to a point of stasis today. Not only do we try to better understand the reasons and causes of disengagement of the EU and US, but also the reluctance of Brazil, India, China and South Africa – the BICS – to assume leadership and act as unifying, rather than backseat drivers of the Doha Round.

Part I of the book focuses on the EU and US. Both countries represent traditional Great Powers in the WTO: they used to constitute the old powerhouse of the Quad in the GATT and continue to be major players as members of the 'new' Quad and its variations in the WTO. Part II presents case studies of Brazil, India, China and South Africa. These four countries have played a leading role in the Doha process, both individually and as leaders of Southern bargaining coalitions. The interactions between the BICS on the one hand, and the EU and US on the other hand, help us to better understand existing power vacuums and alternative balances of power in the WTO.

Besides the individual countries that are major players in the WTO, we also need to examine the role of coalitions in the WTO. Coalitions are a crucial source of empowerment for the BICS as well as other developing countries, but also a source of deadlock in the organisation. And while our central focus in the book is on the major players in the WTO, and the leadership they offer (or fail to offer), we are also interested in the role of LDCs and other small players, especially in their role in coalitions. Indeed, to some extent, LDCs and other smaller players in the WTO may be seen as key constituencies to whom the leading players must sell their competing visions and thereby improve the

---

[59] Mattoo and Subramanian 2009; Rodrik 2009.
[60] Rodrik 2009.

accountability of the system. Part III therefore presents a theoretical investigation of bargaining coalitions in the WTO, and also an empirical account of the strategic and tactical lessons for these developing country coalitions from the Geneva talks in July 2008. Our concluding chapter summarises and culls together the findings of our case studies in Parts I, II, and III, and suggestions some solutions whereby the problem of leadership in the WTO might be addressed.

REFERENCES

Amsden, Alice H. 2001. *The Rise of 'The Rest': Challenges to the West from Late Industrializing Economies.* Oxford: Oxford University Press.

Baldwin, Robert and Simon Evenett (eds). 2008. *What world leaders must do to halt the spread of protectionism.* London: Centre for Economic Policy Research (VoxEu.org).

Bello, Walden. 2005. The Real Meaning of Hong Kong: Brazil and India Join Big Boys' Club. *Focus on the Global South.* 22 December.

Cooper, Andrew F. and Agata Antkiewicz (eds). 2008. *Emerging Powers in Global Governance. Lessons from the Heiligendamm Process.* Waterloo, Ont.: Wilfred Laurier University Press.

De Jonquières, Guy. 2008. After the Doha débâcle. What next for the global trade system? Briefing Paper IEP/JEF BP 08/05 (September). London: Chatham House.

Drahos, Peter. 2003. When the Weak Bargain with the Strong: Negotiations in the World Trade Organization. *International Negotiation* 8(1):79-103.

Druckman, Dan and Amrita Narlikar. 2010. Conclusion. In *Deadlocks in Multilateral Negotiations: Causes and Solutions,* edited by Amrita Narlikar, Cambridge: Cambridge University Press.

Evenett, Simon J. 2007. Reciprocity and the Doha Round Impasse. Lessons for the Near-Term and After. Policy Insight 11 (August). London: Centre for Economic Policy Research (CEPR).

Evian Group. 2006. Can the Doha Drift be Stopped? Preliminary Report and Position Paper of an Evian Group Exceptional Meeting, 11 February. At: http://www.eviangroup.org/p/1210.pdf

Goldman Sachs. 2007. *BRICs and Beyond.* Goldman Sachs Global Economics Group.

Higgott, Richard. 2009. The demand for global governance: containing the spread of the financial crisis to the trade sector. In *Rebuilding Global Trade: Proposals for a Fairer, More Sustainable Future,* edited by Carolyn D. Birkbeck and Ricardo Meléndez-Ortiz. Geneva and Oxford: International Centre for Trade and Sustainable Development (ICTSD) and University College, Oxford.

Hurrell, Andrew. 2006. Hegemony, liberalism and global order: what space for would-be great powers? *International Affairs* 82(1):1-19, January.

Hurrell, Andrew and Amrita Narlikar. 2006. The New Politics of Confrontation: Developing Countries at Cancún and Beyond. *Global Society* 20(4):415-433, October.

Ismail, Faizel. 2007. *Mainstreaming Development in the WTO. Developing Countries in the Doha Round.* Jaipur and Geneva: CUTS International and Friedrich Ebert Stiftung.

Jawara, Fatoumata and Aileen Kwa. 2003. *Behind the scenes at the WTO. The real world of international trade negotiations.* London: Zed Books.

Lamy, Pascal. 2002. Leadership, the EU and the WTO. Speech delivered at the Evian Group, Montreux, Switzerland, 13 April. At: http://trade.ec.europa.eu/ doclib/docs/2004/september/tradoc_118804.pdf

Lee, Donna and Nicola J. Smith. 2008. The Political Economy of Small African States in the WTO. *The Round Table* 97(395):259-271, April.

Mattoo, Aaditya and Arvind Subramanian. 2009. From Doha to the Next Bretton Woods. A New Multilateral Trade Agenda. *Foreign Affairs,* January/February.

Meyn, Mareike et al. 2009. Pursuing a Doha trade deal is a low priority. Opinion 126. London: Overseas Development Institute (ODI).

Moore, Michael. 2003. *A World Without Walls. Freedom, Development, Free Trade and Global Governance.* Cambridge: Cambridge University Press.

Narlikar, Amrita. 2007. All that glitters is not gold: India's rise to power. *Third World Quarterly* 28(5):983-996, June.

Narlikar, Amrita and Diana Tussie. 2004. The G20 at the Cancun Ministerial: Developing Countries and Their Evolving Coalitions in the WTO. *The World Economy* 27(7):947-966.

Narlikar, Amrita and Pieter van Houten. 2010. Know the enemy: Uncertainty and deadlock in the WTO. In *Deadlocks in Multilateral Negotiations: Causes and Solutions,* edited by Amrita Narlikar. Cambridge: Cambridge University Press.

Odell, John S. 2000. *Negotiating the World Economy.* Ithaca and London: Cornell University Press.

Rodrik, Dani. 2008. Don't cry for Doha. Project Syndicate, 5 August.

Rodrik, Dani. 2009. Let Developing Nations Rule. In *Rebuilding Global Trade: Proposals for a Fairer, More Sustainable Future*, edited by Carolyn D. Birkbeck and Ricardo Meléndez-Ortiz. Geneva and Oxford: International Centre for Trade and Sustainable Development (ICTSD) and University College, Oxford.

Sally, Razeen. 2008. *Trade Policy, New Century: the WTO, FTAs and Asia Rising.* London: Institute of Economic Affairs.

Schott, Jeffrey J. 2008. The future of the multilateral trading system in a multi-polar world. Discussion Paper 8. Bonn: German Development Institute. At: http://www.iie.com/publications/papers/schott0608.pdf, accessed on 4 November 2008.

Steinberg, Richard H. 2002. In the Shadow of Law or Power? Consensus-Based Bargaining and Outcomes in the GATT/WTO. *International Organization* 56(2):339-374, Spring.

Subacchi, Paola. 2008. New power centres and new power brokers: are they shaping a new economic order? *International Affairs* 84(3):485-498.

Sutherland, Peter et al. 2004. The Future of the WTO: Addressing Institutional Challenges in the New Millennium. Geneva: World Trade Organization.

Stein, Arthur. 1990. *Why Nations Cooperate: Circumstance and Choice in International Relations*. Ithaca, NY: Cornell University Press.

Taylor, Ian. 2007. The periphery strikes back? The G20 at the WTO. In *The WTO after Hong Kong. Progress in, and prospects for, the Doha Development Agenda*, edited by Donna Lee and Rorden Wilkinson. London and New York: Routledge.

Vickers, Brendan. 2008. South Africa: Global Reformism, Global Apartheid and the Heiligendamm Process. In *Emerging Powers in Global Governance. Lessons from the Heiligendamm Process*, edited by Andrew F. Cooper and Agata Antkiewicz. Waterloo, Ont.: Wilfred Laurier University Press.

Wade, Robert H. 2005. Doha Failure Would Not Amount to Disaster. *Financial Times*. 4 November.

Warwick Commission. 2007. *The Multilateral Trade Regime: Which Way Forward?* Coventry: University of Warwick. At: http://www2.warwick.ac.uk/research/warwickcommission/report/uw_warcomm_tradereport_07.pdf, accessed on 27 April 2008.

Wilkinson, Rorden. 2006. The WTO. Crisis and the governance of global trade. London: Routledge.

Wilkinson, Rorden. 2007. Building asymmetry. Concluding the Doha Development Agenda. In *The WTO after Hong Kong. Progress in, and prospects for, the Doha Development Agenda*, edited by Donna Lee and Rorden Wilkinson. London and New York: Routledge.

Wolfe, Robert. 2008. Can the Trading System Be Governed: Institutional Implications of the WTO's Suspended Animation. In *Can the World Be Governed? Possibilities for Effective Multilateralism*, edited by Alan S. Alexandroff. Waterloo, Ont.: Wilfrid Laurier University Press.

World Bank. 2008. Global Economic Prospects 2009. Washington, DC: World Bank, 9 December.

World Bank. 2009. Global Economic Prospects 2009. Forecast Update. Washington, DC: World Bank, 30 March.

World Trade Organization (WTO). 2009a. *World Trade Report 2009. Trade Policy Commitments and Contingency Measures.* Geneva: WTO.

WTO. 2009b. Report to the TPRB from the Director-General on the Financial and Economic Crisis and Trade-related Developments. Job(09)/2, 26 January.

WTO. 2009c. Report to the TPRB from the Director-General on the Financial and Economic Crisis and Trade-related Developments. WT/TPR/OV/W/1, 20 April.

WTO. 2009d. Report to the TPRB from the Director-General on the Financial and Economic Crisis and Trade-related Developments. Job(09)/ 62, 1 July.

Young, Alasdair. 2010. Transatlantic intransigence in the Doha negotiations. In *Deadlocks in Multilateral Negotiations: Causes and Solutions,* edited by Amrita Narlikar. Cambridge: Cambridge University Press.

Zakaria, Fareed. 2009. *The Post-American World.* New York: W. W. Norton and Co.

Part I

The Established Powers

MANFRED ELSIG[1]

2. THE EU IN THE DOHA NEGOTIATIONS: A CONFLICTED LEADER?

The European Union (EU) is a key actor in global trade politics and lends itself to the study of leadership and change.[2] This chapter traces the role of the EU during the Doha Round and addresses in particular the European Commission's change of attitude towards the multilateral trade agenda.[3] The European Commission (thereafter the Commission) initially played a leading role in attempting to launch trade negotiations in the second half of the 1990s. More recently, it has exhibited less leadership in the negotiations and signs of disengagement have multiplied. This chapter discusses this process of positional change from an exit-voice-loyalty perspective.[4] It is shown that EU-internal politics have contributed to an observed pattern of increasingly conflicted leadership in relation to the negotiations within the World Trade Organisation (WTO). Finally, the EU has not been able to successfully adapt to new forms of decision-making within the WTO or to the challenges related to the emergence of a multipolar trade world.

Students of EU foreign policy have shown great interest in exploring the expected as well as the observed role of the EU as an international actor (actorness). In particular, the question of what type of power the Community represents has been discussed at length.[5] Notions of soft power or normative power have become commonly accepted for describing the nature of the EU. The realist angle has been largely overlooked. The realist concept of power has predominantly focused on individual Member States' foreign policies, in particular in the area of

---

[1] I would like to thank Eugénia da Conceição-Heldt, Carsten Daugbjerg, Amrita Narlikar and Brendan Vickers for valuable comments. Thanks also go to Susan Kaplan for editorial assistance. Financial support from the Swiss National Science Foundation through the NCCR trade regulation (http://www.nccr-trade.org) and from ISD is gratefully acknowledged.
[2] In this chapter, I use the term European Community (EC) when specifically referring to the times prior to ratification of the Maastricht Treaty, otherwise I use the general term European Union.
[3] I use the term Doha Round as it describes the process of negotiations better than the term Doha Development Agenda.
[4] Hirschman 1970.
[5] Duchêne 1972; Bull 1982; Manners 2002.

security policy, where material or coercive power can be observed.[6]
While in many areas of foreign policy the EU has often failed to speak
with a strong and unified voice, trade policy marks an important
exception. With the Treaty of Rome, the governments of the six
founding European states defined the delegation tools to empower the
Commission to negotiate trade relations on behalf of the EC and its
Member States. The Commission has been managing the EU's common
commercial policy since its inception.[7] One puzzle that has emerged is
the EU's reluctance to use its 'hidden power' (defined by the sheer size of
its market) in significant ways.[8] Meunier and Nicolaïdis have argued that
the EU is a sort of hybrid power in trade policy, combining elements of
dominance and replication; dominance in the form of dictating the terms
of (bilateral) trade agreements and replication by way of exporting 'a
system of market liberalization'.[9] They introduced the notion of 'conflicted
power' to capture the tensions between intra-EU politics, the preference
heterogeneity among actors in using trade as a vehicle for foreign policy
goals, and the existence of conflicting principles.

This chapter focuses on the EU in a 'conflicted power' reading.
Translated to the multilateral trade venue, we observe how internal EU
tensions define a 'conflicted leadership' and have an impact on the
performance of the Commission at the negotiation table. The EU has
attempted to lead by way of introducing a 'deep trade agenda'. This
agenda has developed as a result of increased market integration following
a number of successful trade rounds that brought tariffs down.[10] As a
consequence, new behind-the-border challenges were moving up on
Brussels' priority list for regulating trade, illustrated by the initiative at
the Singapore Ministerial Conference in 1996 to tackle competition and
investment-related obstacles.[11] However, the EU was not capable of
building a strong coalition for its cause; on the contrary it faced significant
resistance from various groups, new coalitions and the US. Given these
difficulties, the EU has clearly lowered its ambitions to regulate these
issues through the global trade institution.[12] The failure to shape the

---

[6] This applies in particular to those EU states holding a permanent seat in the UN Security
Council and to larger EU states that actively support UN or NATO peace keeping and
peace building operations.

[7] Elsig 2002.

[8] Neo-realists have some difficulties in explaining EU trade policies within a *realpolitik*
framework (Drezner 2007).

[9] Meunier and Nicolaïdis 2006, 912.

[10] Young and Peterson 2006.

[11] Young and Peterson 2006. The so-called Singapore Issues call for further multilateral
regulation in the areas of investment, competition, public procurement and trade
facilitation.

[12] Young 2007a-b.

agenda towards addressing more behind-the-border obstacles has also led the EU to turn some of its political and diplomatic resources away from the multilateral venue for trade regulation and to join the bandwagon of negotiating preferential trade agreements.[13]

The chapter is organised as follows. First, I sketch the changing attitude of the EU (and in particular the Commission) towards the Doha Round. Second, inspired by Hirschman's framework on exit-voice-loyalty, I analyse attitudinal change and partial exit from the system. Third, domestic factors and mechanisms that have had an impact on the Commission's position are discussed: agricultural policy reform, enlargement and lack of support by the export industries. Fourth, the concluding section speculates about factors that might shape the future of EU trade policy in relation to the multilateral trading system.

1   LOSING ENTHUSIASM AND GIVING UP LEADERSHIP

The EC rose during the Uruguay Round to achieve the status of a co-sponsor of the multilateral trading system. Together with the US an ambitious Community (characterised by growing membership and strengthened by a liberal-inspired programme to create the single European market) started to replace the Quad as the inner circle of decision-making and pushed for a conclusion of the negotiations.[14] After the Uruguay Round and in the fading days of a liberal constitutional moment[15], the EU advocated the launching of a new trade round. This initiative orchestrated by Trade Commissioner Sir Leon Brittan was influenced by a number of factors, including a group-think type of post-Uruguay Round triumphalism among trade diplomats, the successful conclusion of various sector agreements in trade in services, and the in-built agenda of the Uruguay Round that mandated continued negotiations in agriculture and services. The EU, and in particular the Commission, was fairly enthusiastic about the idea of sponsoring a new round. The prospect of starting new negotiations advanced at the 50-year celebration of the GATT/WTO system in Geneva in 1998, when President Bill Clinton invited the trade community to the US for a ministerial. In the run-up to this ministerial conference in Seattle in 1999, European diplomats pushed strongly for the launch of a new round following the single-package approach.[16] Commissioner Brittan coined the term 'Millennium Round' to set high expectations in terms of ambitions and coverage.

---

[13] European Commission 2006.

[14] Steinberg 2002. The Quad comprised the US, the EC, Japan and Canada.

[15] Fukuyama 1992.

[16] Kerremans 2005.

The attitude of the EU towards the round changed considerably over time. After initial enthusiasm, the EU has mutated to a less active party to the negotiations. Its expectations have not been met and its capacities to lead through granting concessions have been limited. Currently, the EU flies the flag half-heartedly and stays engaged in negotiations in order to avoid complete failure. It has strategically positioned itself in such a way as not to be blamed for a possible collapse of the round and an immediate crisis for the multilateral trading system. If the round delivers in terms of trade liberalisation, it will not be because of EU leadership in the end. This position is a far cry from its initial ambitions, its influence on the evolving agenda and activism in early negotiations. Below, the attitudinal change is sketched.

The Commission started planning new negotiations operating with the single-package approach at the end of the Uruguay Round. It was willing to continue negotiating for the liberalisation of agricultural markets (as part of the in-built agenda) and attempted to add new elements to design a larger package.[17] This package reflected the interests of the Commission, in particular growing ambitions to 'export' its own model of regulation (e.g. Singapore Issues, intellectual property rights). The EU over time has accepted a deep trade agenda due to its own experience in regulating economic integration. Thus, strong consensus emerged within the EU to prioritise 'behind-the-border' issues.[18] Based on this ideational turn, the Commission with support of member states called for designing global rules to address the challenges of economic globalisation.[19] The export of regulation is at the same time interest-based as European firms will profit from global trade rules that are equivalent or similar to European regulation. Thus, the EU engages in 'seeking multilateral agreements on the making of domestic rules'.[20] From the very beginning of the Doha negotiations, the push for exporting the EU model was tied to a call for more market access in emerging developing countries (in services and a wide array of goods sectors).[21]

In addition, the proposed size and composition of the negotiation package was deemed necessary to attract the interest of key European exporters in order to counter pressures from import-competing groups, in particular from influential interest groups within the agricultural and

---

[17] In addition to the need to re-open negotiations in agriculture based on Article 20 of the Agreement on Agriculture, the expiry of the peace clause by 2003 risked a high number of subsidy cases in agriculture being brought against the EU (Kerremans 2005, 8).

[18] Young and Peterson 2007.

[19] Meunier 2007.

[20] Young and Peterson 2007, 795.

[21] See Young 2007a, 123-6. Two other issues of interest (i.e. environment and core labour standards) had already been sidelined in the Singapore Ministerial Conference.

traditional industry sectors. The first awakening occurred during the Seattle Ministerial Conference in December 1999.[22] The newly appointed Trade Commissioner, Pascal Lamy, attempted without success to persuade other members, including the US and key developing countries, to support the broad EU agenda. Two years later at the Doha Ministerial Conference, the Commission acted on the basis of the same mandate as internally negotiated in the run-up to Seattle. Its strategy changed insofar as it signalled to developing countries that their developmental concerns would be addressed.[23] Overall, its objective remained to launch negotiations on a substantial package that included key elements of a deep trade agenda. While the Commission was able to introduce some wording on the relationship between multilateral environmental treaties and the WTO and the consideration of non-trade concerns in agriculture (e.g. multifunctionality), it had to make partial concessions on the Singapore Issues.[24] In relation to addressing the concerns of developing countries, the Commission pushed for the 'Everything But Arms' initiative and played a constructive role in bringing about an agreement on Trade-Related Aspects of Intellectual Property Rights (TRIPS) and public health.[25] The US, which until Doha had been reluctant to push for a big round, changed its position in the months prior to the ministerial in Qatar's capital. The George W. Bush administration estimated that the EU would open up its agricultural markets to a larger degree within a bigger package that allowed for concessions across issue areas.[26] In addition, the events of 9/11 seem to have facilitated the Doha deal as the US administration strove to signal strongly to the rest of the world that the US intended to support this multilateral venue for cooperation.

Notwithstanding a partial setback in Doha (e.g. Singapore Issues), in the run-up to the 2003 ministerial conference in Cancún the Commission attempted to revive the negotiations. It tabled jointly with the US an agreed text to address the modalities of the agriculture negotiations.[27] The Commission signalled potential concessions on eliminating export subsidies and lowering tariffs for agricultural products.[28] In Cancún, the emergence (and blocking strength) of the Group of 20 (G20) on

---

[22] Elsig 2002.

[23] The EU accepted the 're-branding' of the round to help agree on a ministerial declaration to launch negotiations: the Doha Development Agenda.

[24] At India's insistence the decision on the Singapore Issues was postponed to the next ministerial conference (Young 2007a).

[25] Young 2007a.

[26] Kerremans 2005, 10.

[27] The transatlantic initiative was somewhat surprising given that the transatlantic relations were experiencing the worst crisis for decades.

[28] Kerremans 2004.

agriculture and the Core Group (on the Singapore Issues) left a lasting impression on the EU negotiators.[29] The Singapore Issues did not survive as an entire sub-package the ministerial conference. Two issues (investment and competition) were abandoned in the form of a bargaining chip towards the end of the negotiations. The EU offered to drop its insistence on including these issues in exchange for receiving commitments from other parties in other areas and in order to save the ministerial from failure. The strategic offer by the EU Trade Commissioner Lamy, however, did not produce the type of final hours' dynamics (and negotiations did not go into overtime) anticipated by Lamy's team. The decision by the chairman of the ministerial to close the conference without attempting a last round of negotiations following the major EU concession drew sharp criticism.[30] This was a hard blow for the Commission, as investment and competition policy were now off the table without the EU having gained anything in return. Thus, the package was curtailed further and the Commission started to become concerned about selling a balanced deal at home. The Cancún failure had a considerable impact on the EU's enthusiasm about the round. This could be interpreted in retrospect as a turning point in relation to the EU's leadership role. There was considerable disappointment with the Cancún outcome. Commissioner Lamy told the European Parliament shortly after Cancún that: '[C]ancun is a political shock, we must go back to basics... ask ourselves some questions about the Union's international trade policy in order to confirm whether the foundations... remain, or do not remain, unchanged'.[31] In addition, the Commission started to flirt with the idea to push bilateral agreements as witnessed in a speech by Commissioner Lamy in Washington DC later that year.[32] The Commission also attempted to limit the potential losses from signalling too many concessions. It re-emphasised that commitments put forward would only materialise if others started to move as well.[33]

After the Cancún ministerial, the attention of negotiators increasingly turned towards addressing agriculture. Parties prioritised farm policies over other business (which the EU had wanted to avoid).[34] In light of growing

---

[29] Narlikar and Tussie 2004.

[30] Patricia Hewitt, UK Secretary of State for Trade and Industry, lamented after the decision by the chairman, Minister Luis Ernesto Derbez, to close the meeting that this was 'utterly unexpected' and 'premature' and 'there was a deal to be had' (*BRIDGES Daily Update*, 15 September 2003).

[31] Lamy 2003a.

[32] Lamy 2003b.

[33] European Commission 2003.

[34] In 2002, the Commission had already objected to pressures from other contracting parties to draft modalities for the agricultural negotiations before modalities on other *(continued)*

demands from other contracting parties to move on agriculture, the EU attempted to revive negotiations in June 2004 by signalling potential concessions on its farm policies.[35] It offered to eliminate agricultural export subsidies and to reduce trade distorting subsidies. In addition, the Commission proposed a round for free for least-developed countries (LDCs). This helped to keep the round alive. The offer brought additional momentum to the negotiations that led to the conclusion of the so-called July 2004 package, which offered a framework on agriculture for continuing talks. There was also general agreement to phase out export subsidies. This was communicated as a breakthrough. However, as BRIDGES predicted correctly at the time: 'negotiations on modalities of substance, much of which has been left undetermined, will be a "real challenge" that Members have yet to confront'.[36]

Some progress in the agricultural negotiations seemed to develop in July 2005, when the Commission accepted de facto the G20 framework for cutting agricultural tariffs. In the run-up to the Hong Kong Ministerial Conference in December 2005, the Commission came under increasing pressure from the US and the G20. As a consequence, it improved its offer on farm tariffs and agreed to an end date (2013) to phase out export subsidies.[37] The Hong Kong Ministerial Declaration urged members to continue bargaining with high 'ambitions' to achieve substantial progress, but it did not include tangible new concessions. Following the Hong Kong Ministerial Conference, the Commission signalled on various occasions additional willingness to move on agricultural market access.[38] It improved its offer to cut farm tariffs up to 50 per cent (the G20 demanded 54 per cent, the US 66 per cent), and at the same time insisted that the G20 lowered the projected ceilings for industrial goods tariffs.[39] The WTO Director-General, Pascal Lamy, supported the EU's call for reciprocity by stressing the need for parallel progress on the triangle of priority issues on the table: US domestic farm support, the EU's agricultural market access and the stance of the developing countries (in particular

---

issues were negotiated. The Commission pushed for a simultaneous approach (Kerremans 2005).

[35] European Commission 2004.

[36] *BRIDGES Weekly Trade News*, 3 August 2004.

[37] *Financial Times*, 31 October 2005; *Financial Times*, 26 December 2005; Young 2007b. 'Pascal Lamy, the head of the World Trade Organisation... described the EU's proposal as "a serious offer which merits serious discussions". He added: "Europe and the United States are moving on farm issues. This is what allows the rest of the negotiations to be unblocked"' (*Financial Times*, 31 October 2005).

[38] Less attention was paid to internal support (and the various boxes). The Common Agricultural Policy (CAP) reform of 2003 and the further use of decoupling seem to have curbed the most vocal critics related to the EU's internal support schemes.

[39] *Financial Times*, 19 May 2006.

India and Brazil) on lower industrial tariffs. In the talks held in Geneva in July 2006, incoming Trade Commissioner Peter Mandelson reiterated the EU's offer to cut farm tariffs.[40] But once again the proposal did not produce the hoped-for momentum. The talks broke down. The round was officially suspended after the failure to agree on how to find a magic formula for the triangle.[41] After the talks resumed in late 2006, the focus moved gradually away from the EU offer on agriculture and more towards the flexibility mechanisms to protect sensitive products, an approach supported by the EU. In addition, more attention was directed towards tariff cuts for the industrial products of emerging developing countries. There was, however, no real progress in a number of rapidly following small group meetings. After such a negotiation session among the Group of 4 (G4) in Potsdam in June 2007, Commissioner Mandelson argued that 'it emerged from the discussion on (industrial goods) that we would not be able to point to any substantive or commercially meaningful changes in the tariffs of the emerging economies as a reasonable return on what we are paying in the round'.[42] In summer 2008, the most recent push to move the package forward resulted in another failure. The draft text on agriculture included a reduction in the top band of tariffs between 66 per cent and 73 per cent.[43] Given some movement on market access in agriculture, the EU was not singled out as the laggard and blame went to others.[44]

The key challenge the Commission has faced in providing leadership in the Doha Round was that its ambitious agenda was substantially reduced over time. Given the demand on the EU to move first on agriculture, the EU Trade Commissioners attempted to offer the

---

[40] Mandelson 2006.

[41] The US and the EU blamed each other for the failure in making concessions on farm subsidies and agricultural market access. However, the chief negotiators for India and Brazil recognised movement on market access by the EU getting closer to the G20 proposal of 54 per cent. Attention focused on pushing for larger cuts for the highest tariffs. Both countries hinted 'that Washington's refusal to move on domestic support was the principal reason for stalemate'. Indian Minister of Commerce and Industry Kamal Nath was quoted as saying that 'everybody put something on the table, except one country which said "we can't see anything on the table"' (*BRIDGES Weekly Trade News*, 26 July 2006).

[42] Mandelson 2007. The G4 comprised the US, EU, Brazil and India.

[43] The US offered to cap overall trade-distorting support (OTDS) at US$15 billion. WTO Director-General Lamy further suggested that developing countries could designate up to 4 per cent of their tariff lines in agriculture as sensitive and thus subject to lower tariff cuts (*BRIDGES Daily Update*, 25 July 2008).

[44] *Financial Times*, 9 October 2008. The negotiations broke down over Special Safeguard Measures and opposed India and China to the US. A 'landing zone' on other agricultural issues was within the members' grasp.

maximum concessions acceptable to the majority of its Member States.[45] However, as long as uncertainty remained as to what the EU would get in return on non-agricultural market access (NAMA) and services, the Commissioners' hands were tied. In light of absence of linkages (and few observable efforts to form a coalition with other contracting parties interested in market access), the Commission's various moves to offer concessions seem more important than often portrayed.[46] As the concessions on NAMA and services anticipated by the Commission officials did not materialise, Directorate-General (DG) Trade started to lose interest and directed more attention towards gaining market access through bilateral and inter-regional trade agreements. Growing discontent and calls for protectionism within the EU led DG Trade to further downgrade its ambitions for a market-liberalising round. Officials in Brussels increasingly pictured the round as a tool for controlling increasing signs of protectionism and locking in existing reforms. A member of the Mandelson Cabinet explained: 'We see increasing signs of protectionism and a Doha deal could serve as a risk insurance against this development'.[47] This was reflected in a reaction by Commissioner Mandelson following the failure of the Geneva negotiations in summer 2008 when he argued that 'we have lost for now the insurance policy that would have bound in the openness of the global economy'.[48]

2   EXIT, VOICE AND LOYALTY: THE COMMISSION'S PARTIAL EXIT

Albert Hirschman offered a general framework for analysing the relationship between exit, voice and loyalty in a variety of organisations, including social groups, markets and political systems.[49] Can we capture the EU's fading enthusiasm and new embracement of bilateralism by applying this framework? Hirschman argues that actors dissatisfied with

---

[45] Commissioner Mandelson was constantly criticised by the French government and the governments of like-minded Member States (*BRIDGES Weekly Trade News* 2 November 2005; *Financial Times* 30 May 2007). French President Nicolas Sarkozy put a great amount of pressure on Commissioner Mandelson. In June 2008, he associated the Commission's stance on agriculture with Ireland's rejection of the Lisbon Treaty (*Financial Times* 20 June 2008). He also demanded an immediate meeting with the Commissioner during the July 2008 negotiations in Geneva. Commissioner Mandelson responded that his negotiation commitments had to come first (*Financial Times* 29 July 2008).

[46] The Commission took occasional risks by tabling proposals that were opposed by a large number of Member States.

[47] Interview with member of the Mandelson Cabinet, Brussels, 23 June 2005.

[48] Mandelson 2008.

[49] Hirschman 1970.

the quality of certain products or outputs have two main options: they can raise voice (signalling discontent) and/or exit (disengage). Voice and exit are complementary elements. Exit depends largely on the success of using voice to influence the future provision of goods or organisational performance in a preferred direction. Simultaneously, the success of voice depends on the likelihood to find alternative products, groups or organisations. The more credible the alternatives are, the greater the likelihood of exit if voice fails to bring about change. In some organisations (e.g. state or family) the exit option is largely constrained by the existence of a quasi monopoly. Other organisations are embedded in more competitive markets where exit is an often observed phenomenon. Loyalty enters the equation as the greater the loyalty to an organisation, the more reluctant actors are to take the exit option, as exit will generate certain emotional and social costs.[50] Loyalty usually 'holds exit at bay and activates voice'.[51]

Analysing the EU's attitude in the current multilateral trade negotiations directs our attention to the Commission's use of voice, its threat of exit and the existence of loyalty towards the WTO. There is sufficient evidence to argue that in particular the chief negotiator on behalf of the EU States (the Commission) has tried to demonstrate leadership since the late 1980s. The Commission has treated the GATT/ WTO regime as its preferred international platform to regulate trade. Over time, a high degree of loyalty developed towards the GATT/WTO system, boosted by the creation of the WTO in 1995. The WTO was the key regulatory venue for the EU to export its own logic of supranational coordination of liberalising and regulating markets. Loyalty (and also leadership) was in particular manifested by the so-called Lamy Moratorium starting in 1999. Under the guidance of Trade Commissioner Lamy, the EU created a de facto hierarchy among various venues for negotiating trade and placed a moratorium on engaging in new preferential trade agreements of a bilateral nature while multilateral negotiations were ongoing.[52] The Commission was largely satisfied with the performance of the WTO. The success of the sector agreements after the Uruguay Round cemented this attitude throughout the second half of the 1990s. The EU (the Commission and the Member States) was actively engaged in shaping a new round (a new product). Its 'voice' translated into a number of attempts to provide additional leadership, such as offering concessions on agriculture

---

[50] The costs of disengagement vary considerably from one organisation to another. These are higher in social groups (e.g. family or sports team) than in the market (switching from one product to another).

[51] Hirschman 1970, 78.

[52] Elsig 2007.

and helping to address development concerns (e.g. TRIPS and Public Health, Everything but Arms initiative and aid-for-trade).

Over time, however, voice did not translate into sufficient influence. This can be largely explained by the mounting pressures from other trading nations and the changed negotiation context. In the current trade negotiations, we have witnessed the emergence of a strong group of developing countries, which reflects increasingly a multipolar trade world in the making. The Commission was pushed by other contracting parties to offer more on agriculture and drop its insistence on including the Singapore Issues. The EU's role within the negotiations was further weakened by an increasingly opaque coalition-based decision-making system, in which it was no longer sufficient for the EU to agree with the US to push the agenda forward.[53] The EU also had difficulties in finding coalition partners to support its broad agenda and its direction.[54]

The conflicted nature of the EU in attempting to sponsor trade negotiations became more and more visible over time. There was little observable support from domestic constituencies and critical voices within the EU were mounting. The Commission came under growing internal pressure as the concessions it had signalled on agricultural market access were not resulting in tangible offers from other trading partners. Given growing criticism from member states (organised by France), the Commission was increasingly reluctant to lead. Against this background, alternative options (partial exit) became more and more appealing, not least after the Cancún failure and the meagre output of the Hong Kong Ministerial Conference. Thus, the Commission started to study alternative means of gaining access to important markets.

In 2006, the incoming Commission pushed for the implementation of the new Lisbon economic agenda based on 'competitiveness'. The new Commission, which was campaigning on a liberal programme, was far less constrained by past loyalty to the WTO and started a gradual process of disengagement. With its Communication 'Global Europe', the new Commission sketched a strategic change that amounted to a partial exit.[55] In this document, the Commission presented a pragmatic forum-shopping approach actively using various platforms to negotiate trade. This new policy abandoned the moratorium on launching new bilateral trade negotiations. A new focus on bilateralism and Asian markets replaced the Lamy doctrine of giving preference to the WTO.[56] The policy

---

[53] Steinberg 2002.
[54] With the exception of support from the G-10 group (the group of multifunctionalists in agriculture) and at times from the G-33 (friends of special products).
[55] European Commission 2006.
[56] European Commission 2006.

shift was also supported (yet not directly influenced) by the majority of EU Member States and large parts of European business interest groups.[57] Partial disengagement by Commissioner Mandelson and his team became even more apparent when, after the failed negotiations in July 2006, he suggested an 'early harvest' package for developing countries in a number of areas.[58] This proposal, born out of frustration with the lack of progress in Geneva, was puzzling for many observers. An early harvest would have made selling the rest of the round's outcome at home more difficult. Some elements of an early harvest package (e.g. trade facilitation) would have been important to accept further steps towards liberalising agricultural markets and would have garnered support from export industries. In addition, it would have decreased the pressure on developing countries to improve market access. Thus over time, enthusiastic leadership turned towards a partial exit in the form of a pragmatic forum-shopping approach vis-à-vis other venues to regulate trade.

3   DOMESTIC FACTORS AND THE CONFLICTED NATURE OF LEADERSHIP

While the Commission's overall experience with the Doha Round negotiations helps explain its decision to partially exit, internal developments have further affected the Commission's ability to display leadership. Three factors from internal EU politics stand out: first, the role and timing of agricultural policy reform; second, the enlargement process and its implications; and third, lack of support by export-oriented industries. These factors have contributed to the perception of conflicted leadership and have had an impact on the Commission's loyalty towards multilateralism.

The reform status of the Common Agricultural Policy (CAP) has been a key determinant of the degree of leadership the EU can offer at international trade negotiations. Three elements stand out: market protection, internal subsidies and export subsidies. While the Commission has difficulties in making concessions in WTO negotiations that go beyond internal decisions on CAP reform, the negotiation mandate is often formulated vaguely to leave the Commission some wiggle room.[59]

---

[57] Elsig 2007.

[58] Mandelson suggested short-term measures to rescue the development agenda. In particular, his call to include a new agreement on Trade Facilitation and de-linking it from the round drew considerable criticism (see *BRIDGES Weekly Trade News*, 26 July 2006).

[59] In addition, it is not always clear what effects CAP reform will have on technical issues in the WTO negotiations (e.g. market access, various boxes for support). This degree of uncertainty, the Commission's use of asymmetric information and its expertise as chief negotiator increase the Commission's autonomy to some degree.

In addition, the Commission can use the international pressure to induce internal reform. The Commission sets the agenda by tabling reform proposals and influences the outcomes by strategically using timing, finding compromise solutions and managing scope.[60] Not surprisingly, the Commission's signalling of concessions (in market access and export subsidies) in the current negotiations has also been linked to the internal reform process. Key drivers for CAP reform in 2003 were financial concerns strongly shared by net contributors to the EU budget, the shadow of Eastern enlargement and the ongoing Doha negotiations.[61] As the budgetary implications seemed too important not to be addressed, the Commission had some leverage to propose reform steps. Already in 2002, head of state and governments agreed on a budgetary framework that included the definition of a ceiling on overall spending for the period of 2007 to 2013. Given this constraint, the reform led to a reduction and a further decoupling of direct payments.[62] This setting of an upper limit on aggregate financial support to farmers and the agreed shift towards more indirect support was an important signal to trading partners. This partly explains why the EU was less pressured by its trading partners to make offers on domestic support (here the US was singled out) and why focus turned increasingly towards market access measures (tariffs). In addition, given a predefined ceiling on EU spending on CAP (and a growing number of beneficiaries of farm subsidies due to enlargement), a consensus emerged that export subsidies needed to be tackled.[63] It became obvious that the EU was likely to show flexibility on this issue. The Brussels compromise on the direction of CAP reform had a direct effect on the Doha negotiations as well, as it helped in designing the US–EU proposal on agriculture that was put forward in Cancún.[64] The flip-side of the CAP 2003 reform was that other contracting parties understood that the Commission had strong incentives to lock-in these reforms and thus the concessions offered would be received by other partners quasi automatically. This paradox partially explains the lukewarm responses to the Commission's attempts to offer additional concessions on market access.

---

[60] Daugbjerg 1998; Coleman and Tangermann 1999. In contrast, Paarlberg (1997) finds little evidence of a link between the WTO/GATT system and internal reform.

[61] Swinbank and Daugbjerg (2006) focus in particular on the WTO as a key driver.

[62] The Commission argued that this move away from direct market support and further aid to rural development 'would provide a major advantage in the WTO' (as it would allegedly improve green box compatibility) and 'facilitate the integration of new Member States into the CAP' (European Commission 2002:19, in Swinbank and Daugbjerg 2006).

[63] There was widespread consensus that the effects of export subsidies on world prices in particular hurt the market shares of developing countries.

[64] Young 2007a.

Another element that shaped the EU's position in the Doha Round was Eastern enlargement. This could be modelled as an external shock that had three important effects in relation to the aggregation of EU-internal preferences and the EU's standing in the negotiations. First, it had a notable effect on limiting CAP spending and strengthened the Commission's proposals for further decoupling as discussed above. Second, the accession of 10 new members in 2004 and of Bulgaria and Romania in 2007 made the EU the most powerful trade actor measured in terms of trade flows in goods and services. In principle, this should have positively affected leadership in the EU context. Third, the enlargement processes had an impact on the internal balance of interests on agricultural liberalisation. This affected leadership in subtle ways. Let us focus on this third point below.

The majority of new Member States have shown great reluctance to support additional concessions in agriculture and have been less than eager to push for market opening in NAMA and services. For all new Member States, accession to the EU meant that they secured access to their formerly most important export markets.[65] In addition, new members faced the prospect of gradual erosion of preferences though liberalising vis-à-vis the rest of world. This limited their interest to engaging in across-the-board liberalisation in trade in goods and services. In particular, three of the larger new Member States (Poland, Hungary and Slovak Republic) have shown little enthusiasm for offering additional concessions that could have an impact on their competitiveness within the EU single market.[66] The new Member States have also shown a vigorous interest in the new market access approach and new bilateralism; however, they favoured the prioritisation of special bilateral relationships with the closer EU neighbourhood.[67] On the aggregate, Eastern enlargement led to a slight shift in the balance of membership interests resulting in additional reservations about further liberalisation within the WTO context.

The third internal factor that has contributed to the Commission's diminishing 'loyalty' and the EU's shift away from the multilateral trade

---

[65] The proportion of intra-EU export flows in relation to all exports is around 75 per cent for the eight central and eastern European countries that joined in 2004 (Elsig forthcoming).

[66] An interesting case is Hungary. Before joining the EU, Hungary was a member of the Cairns group advocating liberalisation in agricultural markets. Today, it supports a group of members within the EU that is reluctant to engage in further liberalisation within the agricultural sector.

[67] Most of the new Member States were also unwilling to follow the Commission's proposal to change the existing practices in anti-dumping procedures to allow for a more 'liberal' application and interpretation of trade remedies (Elsig forthcoming).

venue is the absence of vocal support from export industries. One important variant of the standard trade theory explaining trade liberalisation relies on a simple argument in which export industries (from all countries involved in negotiations) counterbalance – and eventually override – the pressure from import-competing industries.[68] The crucial support of export industries largely explains why the EU and the US were able to overcome domestic veto players in earlier trade rounds. These explanations further suggest that over time the import-competing interests are weakened vis-à-vis exporters and this should lead to a sort of domino-effect towards liberalisation that will be difficult to stop.[69] However, there is growing empirical evidence to suggest that export industries have been less engaged and vocal in this round than in previous trade rounds. WTO Director-General Lamy lamented on various occasions that export industries (that were among the beneficiaries of liberalised markets) were largely silent. On the EU side, the Commission has negotiated without the necessary support from its export industries. Exporters have lost interest in the negotiations as little movement was visible on NAMA and services. This leaves much of the lobby action (and thus voice) to the import-competing industries that often lack credible exit options.[70] Although their influence has decreased over time, import-competing interests still show disproportionate representation, and this is magnified if export interests remain passive.[71] This applies in particular to farm interests. A more parallel negotiation approach would have brought about more support of export industries in the early stages of the negotiations.

At the same time, it seems that multinational firms have learned to live with the spaghetti bowl of regulations.[72] They have adapted to find ways to secure market access, be it through tariff-jumping, acquisitions, lobbying activities, or support for bilateral trade and investment deals. All these measures provide for more timely outcomes to respond to business interests. The abovementioned activities that produce quicker solutions to regulatory concerns stand in contrast to a long drawn out trade round in which the prospects of opportunities through market-opening initiatives seem less certain. Not surprisingly, most of the important business and industry representations in Brussels have welcomed the Commission's new market access approach to trade negotiations and have not shown worries regarding a downgrading of the

---

[68] Bagwell and Staiger 2002; WTO 2007.

[69] Baldwin 1994.

[70] Drezner 2007.

[71] Young 2007b.

[72] The spread of different rules of origin is one factor that increases transaction costs for exporters. Small exporters have not the same opportunities as multinational firms to adjust to regulatory challenges.

Doha negotiations.[73] In other words, many of the domestically active market actors that have a credible exit option have so far abstained from using their resources to lobby strongly for a new round.

4   STRENGTHENING THE EU'S LOYALTY TOWARDS THE WTO?

What might affect the current equilibrium of lukewarm support shown by the EU towards the WTO? The final section speculates about the EU's future use of the multilateral trading platform. Five factors will most likely have an effect on the future direction of EU trade policy vis-à-vis the WTO: the aggregate degree of loyalty of leading WTO members, dealing with a changed negotiation environment, the effects of new regionalism, impacts of the current financial crises, and EU internally established leadership.

First, the EU will closely observe the loyalty and leadership of other key sponsors in the trading system. Given its own experiences, the EU will continue to stress the classical advantages of international organisations including instruments to locking-in domestic reforms, lowering transaction costs, and overcoming domestic pressures to gradually liberalise markets.[74] In particular, the rising powers explored in this volume – namely Brazil, China and India (see country chapters) – will be increasingly invited to play a leading role in the system. In the case of China, there is still a predominant perception among the Chinese trade community that negotiators had offered sufficient concessions during accession negotiations. Thus, as a newly-acceded member they should receive special treatment in this round. As a consequence, it will take some time for Chinese leaders to provide additional leadership (Gregory Chin suggests that since 2008 Beijing has played a more active leadership role – see Chapter 6). India for its part has only recently discovered its true potential for playing a more active role in the trading system. Given the current political-economy landscape in India (explored by Amit Ray and Sabyasachi Saha in Chapter 5), there might exist an external misconception of India's short term leadership capacities. Brazil has been the most active emerging economy over the past 20 years within the WTO context. Given the difficulties within Mercosur to create a common market, a strong existing loyalty towards the WTO and high competitiveness in agricultural export markets (discussed by Maria Lima in Chapter 4), it seems more a question of timing than substance for Brazilian leadership to materialise. In addition, other trading nations that benefit greatly from

---

[73] European Commission 2006; Elsig 2007.
[74] WTO 2007.

an open trading system need to play a more active role (such as South Africa, discussed by Brendan Vickers in Chapter 7). A new constituency beyond the G4 needs to be built to support multilateralism.

Second, the new balance of trade powers is a challenge to which old-style trade diplomacy has to adjust. In addition, greater use of coalition-building and more active membership makes processes less predictable. In particular, the EU's negotiators found it difficult to engage in coalitions and to garner sufficient support within a number of key negotiation areas. However, incremental institutional adjustment will not be enough as the necessity of design change can no longer be ignored. In this respect, reform discussions on decision-making should focus on the triangle that has led to a dysfunctional system: the undifferentiated use of the consensus rule, the single-package approach, and the member-driven nature of the organisation. Relying on incremental change will not suffice to overcome various decision-making traps.[75]

Third, other venues to regulate trade are *à la mode*. It remains to be seen, however, whether the current enthusiasm that has led to a surge in bilateral trade agreements will last. There are a number of regulatory issues, including subsidies, competition rules, investments, dispute settlement, and rules of origin that need to be addressed in a multilateral setting. In addition, within the WTO, weaker parties can empower themselves by engaging in coalition-building and are not trapped in an asymmetrical power situation. With respect to the EU, difficulties in achieving significant market access through new bilateralism will automatically increase calls to return to Geneva in order to manage the emerging patchwork of overlapping preferential trade regimes.[76] This could lead to stronger support to 'multilateralize regionalism'.[77]

Fourth, present bargaining positions of the leading players are affected by the state of the world economy itself. The financial crises, the weakening of liberal ideas, a newly defined role of the state in running the economy and in particular the bleak economic outlook in many of the Organisation for Economic Cooperation and Development (OECD) markets will put pressure on the WTO. In times of global recession, additional multilateral cooperation could have material and symbolic effects on distressed markets. Current pressures within EU to support certain strategic European industries (European champions) and to limit foreign ownership of key firms will further test the strength of the global trading system. Moreover, the abovementioned signals of protectionist forces in OECD countries may increase the willingness of exporting

---

[75] Elsig 2009.
[76] Evenett 2007.
[77] Baldwin and Low 2009.

nations, including emerging developing countries, to lock-in existing market access conditions. These factors call for leadership on the international level to engage in a coordinated effort to address emerging protectionist pressures by making use of the WTO to build a buffer against potential beggar-thy-neighbour policies. The EU can offer leadership due to its experience in tackling sensitive liberalisation projects and in managing country-specific and product-specific protectionist attitudes within the EU. The financial crises could lead to the emergence of such a consensus and eventually create the momentum needed for decision-makers to raise their ambitions, start real negotiations and close a round sooner rather than later.[78]

Finally, leadership starts at home. The EU as a conflicted leader needs a strong and competent Commission to lead the EU Member States and to speak with one unified voice in trade politics. The performance of a new Commission starting at the end of 2009 will be judged according to the Commissioners' will to reinvest in multilateralism to help foster a stable, predictable and fair trading system.[79] There are also positive signs on the other side of the Atlantic. As Geoffrey Allen Pigman argues in Chapter 3 of this volume, the incoming US administration seems to be more inclined to engage in multilateral cooperation than the former administration was. The new US President Barack Obama may be more willing to use various platforms offered by international organisations to regain a leadership position and re-install US soft power.[80] In particular, taming a Democrat-dominated Congress will prove important for offering international leadership. Finally, other state leaders in industrialised and emerging countries need to work hard to find a common 'landing zone' in negotiations in the Doha Round and beyond. For the time being, the trading system is suffering from too many bystanders and forum-shoppers. New forms of leadership by a critical mass of actors are necessary to address the current turbulence in the world economy.

---

[78] At the time of writing, the WTO Director-General Lamy has been trying to persuade negotiators to come back to the negotiation table addressing potential pressures emanating from the financial crises and to lock-in existing policies.

[79] It will be easier to negotiate and conclude a round before the Lisbon Treaty is eventually ratified by all EU Member States. After ratification, the European Parliament will receive additional powers in trade policy-making, which will add a new layer of veto players in the EU.

[80] Nye 2004.

REFERENCES

Bagwell, Kyle and Robert Staiger. 2002. *The Economics of the World Trading System.* Cambridge: MIT Press.

Baldwin, Matthew. 2006. EU Trade Politics – Heaven or Hell? *Journal of European Public Policy* 13(6):926-42.

Baldwin, Richard. 1994. *Towards an Integrated Europe.* London: CEPR.

Baldwin, Richard and Patrick Low. 2009. *Multilateralizing Regionalism – Challenges for the Global Trading System.* Cambridge: Cambridge University Press.

Bull, Hedley. 1982. Civilian Power Europe: A Contradiction in Terms? *Journal of Common Market Studies* 21(2):149-64.

Coleman, William and Stefan Tangermann. 1999. The 1992 CAP Reform, the Uruguay Round and the Commission. *Journal of Common Market Studies* 37(3):385-405.

Daugbjerg, Carsten. 1998. *Policy Networks under Pressure: Pollution Control, Policy Reform, and the Power of Farmers.* Aldershot: Ashgate.

Drezner, Daniel. 2007. *All Politics is Global: Explaining International Regulatory Regimes.* Princeton NJ: Princeton University Press.

Duchêne, Francois. 1972. Europe's Role in World Peace. In *Europe Tomorrow: Sixteen Europeans Look Ahead*, edited by R. Mayne. London: Fontana.

Dür, Andreas. 2007. Avoiding Deadlock in European Trade Policy. In *Dynamics and Obstacles of European Governance*, edited by Dirk De Bievre and Christine Neuhold. Cheltenham: Edward Elgar.

Elsig, Manfred. 2002. *The EU's Common Commercial Policy.* Aldershot: Ashgate Publisher.

Elsig, Manfred. 2007. The EU's Choice of Regulatory Venues for Trade Negotiations: A Tale of Agency Power? *Journal of Common Market Studies* 45(4):927-48.

Elsig, Manfred. Forthcoming. European Union Trade Policy after Enlargement: Larger Crowds, Shifting Priorities and Informal Decision-Making. *Journal of European Public Policy.*

Elsig, Manfred. 2009. WTO Decision-Making: Can We Get a Little Help From the Secretariat and the Critical Mass? In *Redesigning the World Trade Organization for the Twenty-first Century*, edited by Debra Steger. Waterloo: Wilfred Laurier University Press, CIGI and IDRC.

European Commission. 2002. Commission Publishes Indicative Figures on the Distribution of Direct Farm Aid. MEMO/02/198, 1 October.

European Commission. 2003. Reviving the DDA Negotiations- the EU Perspective, 26 November.

European Commission. 2004. WTO-DDA: EU Ready to Go the Extra Mile in Three Key Areas of the Talks, 10 May.

European Commission. 2006. Global Europe: Competing in the World. Commission Staff Working Paper COM(2006)567 final.

Evenett, Simon. 2007. The Trade Strategy of the European Union: Time for a Rethink? Mimeo. Available at http://www.evenett.com.

Fukuyama, Francis. 1992. *The End of History and the Last Man.* New York: Free Press.

Hirschman, Albert. 1970. *Exit, Voice and Loyalty: Responses to Decline in Firms, Organizations and States.* Cambridge, MA: Harvard University Press.

Kerremans, Bart. 2004. What Went Wrong in Cancun? A Principal-Agent View on the EU's Rational Towards the Doha Development Round. *European Foreign Affairs Review* 9(3):363-93.

Kerremans, Bart. 2005. Pro-Active Policy Entrepreneur or Risk Minimiser? The EU's Role in the DDA as a Derivative of the Principal-Agent Relationship between the Commission and the Member States. Paper presented at the Third ECPR Conference, Budapest.

Lamy, Pascal. 2003a. Results of the WTO Ministerial Conference in Cancun. Plenary Session on the Ministerial Conference of the WTO in Cancun, Strasbourg, 24 September.

Lamy, Pascal. 2003b. Trade Crisis. Speech delivered at the European Institute, Washington DC, 4 November.

Mandelson, Peter. 2006. We Need to Look Ahead and to Rebuild. Transcript following the suspension of the WTO Doha negotiations, Brussels, 25 July.

Mandelson, Peter. 2007. Potsdam G4 Meeting Ends with No Agreement on Industrial Tariff Cuts. Discussion with journalists, Potsdam, 21 June.

Mandelson, Peter. 2008. Mandelson Regrets Loss of Doha 'Insurance Policy'. Remarks following the failure of the July 2008 talks, Geneva, 30 July.

Manners, Ian. 2002. Normative Power Europe: A Contradiction in Terms? *Journal of Common Market Studies* 40(2):235-58.

Meunier, Sophie. 2007. Managing Globalization? The EU in International Trade Negotiations. *Journal of Common Market Studies* 45(4):905-26.

Meunier, Sophie and Nicolaïdis Kalypso. 2006. The European Union as a Conflicted Trade Power. *Journal of European Public Policy* 13(6): 906-25.

Narlikar, Amrita and Diana Tussie. 2004. The G20 at the Cancun Ministerial: Developing Countries and Their Evolving Coalitions in the WTO. *World Economy* 27(7): 947-66.

Nye, Joseph. 2004. *Soft Power: The Means to Success in World Politics.* New York: Public Affairs.

Paarlberg, Robert. 1997. Agricultural Policy Reform and the Uruguay-Round: Synergistic Linkage in a Two-Level Game? *International Organization* 51(3):413-44.

Steinberg, Richard. 2002. In the Shadow of Law or Power? Consensus Based Bargaining in the GATT/WTO. *International Organization* 56(2): 339-74.

Swinbank, Alan and Carsten Daugbjerg. 2006. The 2003 CAP Reform: Accommodating WTO Pressures. *Comparative European Politics* 4:47-64.

Young, Alasdair. 2007a. Negotiating with Diminished Expectations: The European Union and the Doha Development Agenda. In *The WTO after Hong Kong: Progress in, and Prospects for, the Doha Development Agenda*, edited by Donna Lee and Rorden Wilkinson. London: Routledge, pp. 119-136.

Young, Alasdair. 2007b. Trade Politics Ain't What It Used to Be: The European Union in the Doha Round. *Journal of Common Market Studies* 45(4):789-811.

Young, Alasdair and John Peterson. 2006. The EU and the New Trade Politics. *Journal of European Public Policy* 13(6):795-814.

WTO. 2007. *The GATT/WTO at 60*. Geneva: WTO.

GEOFFREY ALLEN PIGMAN

3. US TRADE POLICY AND THE RISE OF THE BIG EMERGING ECONOMIES

Over the course of the most recent global economic growth cycle, which can be defined roughly as running from 2002 to 2007, the contribution of the 'big emerging economies' (BEEs) to world output and their share in the growth of world trade has been disproportionately large. Most analysts would include China, India and Brazil in this group of states on the basis of rapid industrial development, significant expansion of productive output and export volumes, and growth of a large consumer middle-class (see country chapters in this volume). Whilst there may disagreement about which additional countries to include in the group – Russia, Mexico, Argentina, Viet Nam, South Africa, Indonesia and Pakistan are often named, amidst others still – their impact on growth and trade is agreed to be significant. The global economy grew at an average 2.9 per cent *per annum* over the decade 1998-2008, but whereas developed countries grew at 2.2 per cent *per annum* (2000-2008), developing countries grew at 5.6 per cent *per annum*. By value, world exports and imports each grew an average 12 per cent *per annum* 2000-2008, but within that Brazil's exports grew 17 per cent and imports 15 per cent, China's exports 24 per cent and imports 22 per cent, and India's exports 20 per cent and imports 24 per cent *per annum* in the same period.[1] PriceWaterhouse Coopers has projected the per capita gross domestic product (GDP) of China, India and Brazil to grow at an average of 5.8 per cent, 4.7 per cent and 3.8 per cent *per annum* respectively over the period 2007-2050, in contrast to 2.4 per cent, 1.6 per cent and 1.5 per cent for the United States (US), Germany and Japan respectively over the same period.[2] The growth of these emerging economies has had a major impact upon their trade with the US. Brazil, Russia, India and China, which Goldman Sachs dubbed the 'BRICs', collectively doubled their exports to the US between 2003 and 2007 and more than doubled their imports from the US over the same period.[3]

---

[1] World Trade Organization 2009.
[2] Hawksworth and Cookson 2008.
[3] *Emerging Business Markets* 1 July 2008.

A. Narlikar, B. Vickers (eds.), Leadership and Change in the Multilateral Trading System, 45–71.

The rise of the BEEs has held particular significance for the US as the largest economy in the global economic system, as the largest consuming nation and as the hegemonic power in the post-Cold War international system of nation-states. The significance of this shift in global trade towards a group of newer players lies primarily in that it has occasioned a notable adjustment in US trade policy, whether consciously intended or as a more reflexive response to conditions on the ground. Three trends in US trade policy over the period of the 2002-2007 economic boom can be seen as linked to the rise of the BEEs. The first, which is clearly not causally linked to the rising powers but which has permitted these countries to have a greater impact upon US trade policy than they might have done otherwise, is the gradual return of US foreign policy from a largely unilateralist approach towards greater multilateralism following the 2003 invasion of Iraq. The second and third trends, each of which can be understood as having been caused by the rise of the BEEs, have moved the US away from its prevailing pattern of trade relations in the era of the General Agreement on Tariffs and Trade (1947-1994) and World Trade Organisation (WTO) (1995-present). Of these trends, one is the re-subordination of US trade policy to broader foreign policy objectives, as had been the case in the immediate post-Second World War period and during earlier periods of US history. The other sees the foreign policy approach to and relationship with each big emerging economy (including trade policy) as becoming increasingly differentiated rather than having much in common, by virtue of the BEEs' status as developing countries or non-strategic allies or other broad policy categories of states. In the sections that follow, each of these trends will be considered at greater length. The concluding sections assess the effects of two more recent developments, the interlocking impacts of the 2008 US presidential election and the global financial turbulence upon US trade policy towards the big emerging economies and upon US-BEE negotiations in the WTO's Doha Development Agenda (DDA) multilateral trade liberalisation talks.

1   INCHING TOWARDS MULTILATERALISM

The first of the three major US policy trends of the past five years affects US trade policy and other aspects of US foreign policy in equal measure. In senior foreign policy circles in the second Bush Administration and in Congress, multilateralism made something of a comeback. In the period following the terror attacks of 11 September 2001, President George W. Bush and his close advisers, including Vice President Dick Cheney and Defence Secretary Donald Rumsfeld, made clear to US allies and other powers that they alone would decide how the US would fight what they titled the 'Global War on Terror' (GWOT), and that it would be for other governments to choose whether or not to participate. President Bush demanded participation, and expected to be it on the US's terms. At a news conference on 6 November 2001 with French President Jacques Chirac, Bush said, '[o]ver time it's going to be important for nations to know they will be held accountable for inactivity. You're either with us or against us in the fight against terror.'[4] This bare-knuckles approach to existing and potential allies led to the US embrace of the notion of a 'coalition of the willing' to undertake an invasion of Iraq to remove Saddam Hussein from power, in the absence of unambiguous United Nations (UN) resolutions of support, and to Secretary Rumsfeld's widely criticised delineation of Europe into 'Old' European countries (mostly in the West) unwilling to assist the US-British invasion coalition and the 'New Europe' of central and eastern European states recently freed from the yoke of Soviet domination and ostensibly eager to participate in the Anglo-American crusade to bring Western-style freedoms to the people of Iraq.

This functional unilateralism brought US-European relations to their lowest point since the end of the Cold War, and arguably to their lowest point since the Second World War. Both Bush administration officials and the leaders of 'Old Europe', French President Chirac and German Chancellor Gerhard Schröder in particular, fearing a multifold series of negative consequences flowing from a further deterioration of relations, wisely pulled back from this precipice after a flight suit-clad President Bush declared 'victory' in the Iraq invasion whilst aboard the aircraft carrier USS Abraham Lincoln in May 2003. Beginning with tentative discussions with the Europeans about their possible participation in rebuilding post-war Iraq, US policymakers began cautiously to rediscover the virtues of multilateral cooperation on issues of global significance. Significantly, this process had not advanced far enough to mitigate the still rather toxic atmosphere in US-European relations that contributed to the failure of the WTO's 2003 Cancún Ministerial Conference, which had been intended to advance the DDA towards a successful conclusion.

Once underway, though, the Bush Administration's gradual creep back towards multilateralism can be seen as moving through two phases. The first, which took root firmly once Condoleezza Rice replaced Colin Powell as Secretary of State in 2005, could be characterised as 'pragmatic' multilateralism. A number of factors can be understood as contributing to the policy shift, including the exceptionally high level of international criticism of Bush administration diplomacy strengthening the hand of senior Bush advisers who were concerned about the impact of negative external perceptions of the US. Rice, who possessed the twin virtues of being a scholar trained in diplomacy and international relations, and of

---

[4] CNN 2001.

having the ear of the president, was pivotal in bringing about this change of direction. As Powell could claim neither virtue amongst his strengths, it had been easier for the unilateralist tactical preferences of close Bush confidantes Vice President Dick Cheney and Defence Secretary Donald Rumsfeld to prevail during the first Bush Administration. Although the administration maintained the tough 'our way or no way' unilateralist discourse on GWOT through the administration's most difficult year in Iraq, 2006, US forces in Iraq under the command of General David Petraeus began consciously to learn from US and British errors in counterinsurgency strategy in past wars (Malaya and Viet Nam), a process strengthened by the appointment of former Central Intelligence Agency (CIA) director Robert Gates to replace Rumsfeld as Defence Secretary.[5]

Rice, for her part, prevailed upon President Bush to adopt pragmatic diplomatic tactics in addressing one of the most serious issues on the US security agenda: potential nuclear proliferation in North Korea and Iran. In Rice's view, the best interests of the US would be served by relying upon the People's Republic of China to take the lead in pressing the North Korean government of Kim Jong Il for a multilateral solution to the long running stalemate over uranium reprocessing facilities, and moreover the US should take a back seat to Germany and France in a European Union (EU)-led push to resolve a similar conflict with Iran concerning Iran's right to construct civilian nuclear power generating capacity. In each case, the negotiating partners of the US had more at stake in the potential conflict than Washington did, and moreover there was less pre-existing hostility between Iran and the EU and between North Korea and China than there was between either 'rogue state' and the US. At the 2005 Group of 8 (G8) summit at Gleneagles, Scotland, the Bush Administration yielded to pressure from G8 allies led by British Prime Minister Tony Blair to elevate the importance on the G8's global issue agenda of debt relief for highly indebted poor countries in Africa and of climate change.[6] On trade, this pragmatic multilateralism translated into more public articulation of US government support for the DDA, even if the link between public support and negotiating tactics may not have been particularly consistent. US Trade Representative Susan Schwab joined with other trade ministers at the World Economic Forum's Annual Meeting in Davos in January 2007 in a resolution intended to 'jump start' the stalled multilateral round. At Davos, Schwab called for an agreement that contained enough gains to satisfy US farmers, other economic interests and their champions in Congress. 'It

---

[5] Nagl 2005.
[6] Pigman and Kotsopoulos 2007.

has to be more than a lowest-common-denominator deal that doesn't generate trade flows', Schwab argued.[7]

Gradually the pragmatic multilateralism of the second Bush term has evolved into what could be characterised as somewhat principled multilateralism: 'somewhat' because adherence to principles can never be allowed to trump what may be perceived as particularly pressing national interests at any given moment. Even before the global financial turbulence of summer and autumn 2008 elevated the urgency of multilateral cooperation to thaw global credit markets and stabilise the balance sheets of major international financial institutions, the presidential candidates of both major parties were extolling the virtues of multilateralism in diplomacy and cooperation with multilateral institutions ranging from the UN to the WTO. Democratic presidential candidate Senator Barack Obama (Illinois) made support for multilateralism a centrepiece of his foreign policy platform. In March 2008 Republican presidential candidate Senator John McCain (Arizona) explicitly rejected the unilateralism of the early Bush Administration, pledging to make the US a model international citizen in terms of multilateral cooperation with allies. McCain also mooted the idea of creating a new 'league of democracies' to address issues not amenable to resolution through the UN or other existing multilateral bodies.[8] By October 2008, US Treasury Secretary Henry Paulson and Federal Reserve Board Chairman Ben Bernanke were so committed to the importance of multilateral coordination to stabilise global financial markets that when British Prime Minister Gordon Brown decided that the best way to encourage major banking institutions to resume lending to one another was for governments to take significant equity stakes in large banks, the American officials forsook their own preferred plan of using government funds to buy distressed assets from banks in favour of Brown's plan.

The history of US multilateralism in trade policy since the Second World War with respect to multilateralism has followed a somewhat different trajectory from the ebb and flow of US backing for multilateral approaches on the broader foreign policy stage, even if there has been a convergence of support for multilateralism in trade and other foreign policy arenas in recent years. Arguably, from the initial Anglo-American negotiations on the shape of the post-war international economic system, the American position was one of greater commitment to multilateralism, in the sense of equality of treatment by and of nations, than the British and French stance. At Bretton Woods American negotiators prioritised the principles of non-discrimination and national treatment for the future international trading system over that of tariff reduction, whereas France

---

[7] Schwab 2007.
[8] See McCain 2008; Gerson 2008; Ward 2008.

and Britain favoured greater tariff cuts but at the same time sought to maintain discriminatory tariff preferences for their colonies and former colonial trading partners. The Americans conceded these issues to their European counterparts (even as the American-backed White Plan for an international monetary system prevailed over the British-backed Keynes Plan), agreeing to greater tariff cuts and accepting the preservation of regional preferential trading areas (PTAs).[9] Less than a dozen years after the trade treaty came into operation, the Europeans used GATT Article XXIV, which permits PTAs provided they be trade creating rather than trade diverting, to launch the trade and economic integration of Europe. In the meantime the American government, finding that tariff cutting benefited US exporters of manufactured goods, was content in a GATT-based trading system dominated by like-minded industrialised countries to press for greater reductions in trade barriers, at least up to a point, on a non-discriminatory basis.[10]

Nearly three decades later American policy makers in the Reagan Administration shifted in a more European direction by deciding to pursue bilateral and regional PTAs as a parallel track to multilateral trade liberalisation for achieving US trade liberalisation objectives, in large part because of the change in the number and type of actors in the international trading system as developing countries emerged as competitors in their own right. The US-Israel Free Trade Agreement (1985), the Canada-US Free Trade Agreement (1988), the North American Free Trade Agreement and the Asia-Pacific Economic Cooperation (APEC) accord (1993) and a series of additional bilateral PTAs followed. Negotiations for a hemispheric Free Trade Area of the Americas, begun at the 1994 Summit of the Americas, continue sporadically. More recently, in 2008 US trade officials began negotiations with the Trans-Pacific Partnership countries (Chile, New Zealand, Singapore and Brunei) on a 'Trans-Pacific Strategic Economic Partnership Agreement' that would include an FTA between the partner countries. Engaging in what trade economist Fred Bergsten has described as 'competitive liberalisation', US President Bill Clinton signalled clearly to the rest of the world by signing the NAFTA and APEC agreements in December 1993 that he remained committed to multilateral trade liberalisation but intended to use the signing of PTAs to bring pressure on US trading partners to make concessions in multilateral trade rounds.[11]

In the 2000s, Bush administration trade officials averred consistently that their commitment to the WTO and the DDA was fully compatible

---

[9] Gardner 1956, 145-161.
[10] Destler 2005, 6-8.
[11] Bergsten 1996.

with the more recent US interest in PTAs, as both the Bush Administration and the Democratic leadership in Congress sought to use trade policy to burnish their image as committed multilateralists only latterly tarnished by the invasion of Iraq. Despite criticisms of early Bush Administration trade policy, in more recent years the US track record of compliance with WTO Dispute Settlement Body (DSB) rulings has been considered to be good. The May 2008 WTO Trade Policy Review (TPR) report observed that the US had 'made progress in implementing several WTO rulings calling for changes to US legislation', with a few rulings yet to be implemented fully. Similarly, US compliance with WTO notification obligations was good, with the exception of notifications on agricultural tariff quotas and government procurement statistics.[12] In May 2006 the US implemented the WTO's DSB ruling on the controversial Foreign Sales Corporation and Extraterritorial Income Exclusion Acts by modifying US legislation that had allowed foreign subsidiaries of American firms to pay lower US taxes than their foreign competitors, resolving a long running dispute that had cast US in high profile opposition to several major trading partners.[13] In 2006 Congress passed legislation to end subsidies paid to upland cotton exporters in order to bring the US into compliance with 2005 DSB panel and Appellate Body rulings in a dispute brought by Brazil, although an 'Article 21.5' dispute over implementation of the ruling was still ongoing at the time of writing.[14] In the same year Congress brought the US into compliance with a 2003 WTO DSB ruling by repealing the 2000 Byrd Amendment, which permitted antidumping duties and countervailing duties collected against subsidised imports collected by the US Treasury to be paid to domestic import-competing industries.[15] In 2007 the US implemented a 2006 WTO DSB ruling that a regulation governing gasoline imports discriminated against imported gasoline from Brazil and Venezuela.[16]

Of arguably equal importance to direct US cooperation with the WTO have been moves by Washington towards greater multilateral cooperation in trade-related areas, such as antitrust regulation and enforcement and harmonisation of banking and other financial regulations. In the area of antitrust cooperation, a process has evolved whereby prospective cross-border mergers of large firms in the US and Europe must clear the twin hurdles of approval by the US Department of Justice

---

[12] WTO 2008, 12.
[13] Odessey 2006.
[14] WTO Dispute Settlement: Dispute DS 267, United States – Subsidies on Upland Cotton; WTO 2008, 87.
[15] Office of the US Trade Representative 2006.
[16] WTO Dispute Settlement: Dispute DS4, United States – Standards for Reformulated and Conventional Gasoline.

and the European Commission's DG Competition. Greater US cooperation on multilateral financial regulation, which included the 2005 Market Risk Amendment to the Basel II Framework standards for capital adequacy for banks, was already accelerating prior to the multilateral regulatory reform measures adopted in late 2008 and early 2009 in response to the 2008 credit crisis and related financial turbulence. As the global recession gathered pace in late 2008, US officials in the outgoing Bush administration called for a speedy conclusion of the WTO's Doha Round to stimulate economic growth, making reference to the disastrous impact on the global economy of the 1930 Smoot-Hawley Tariff, which had been conceived as a response to the 1929 stock market crash.

2   BACK TO THE (PRE-COLD WAR) FUTURE?

The dramatic change in the international system occasioned by the end of the Cold War triggered a fundamental shift in US trade policy and the diplomatic strategy required to achieve policy objectives. Clinton administration officials adopted a series of trade policies that set the US on a course back towards greater politicisation of trade relations, at least on a bilateral basis, between Washington and its many trading partner nations. This change of course can be understood as a move back towards a type of bilateral trade relations that was more the norm over the century and a quarter between the Napoleonic Wars and the Second World War. During the Cold War, a sort of separation was maintained, albeit imperfectly, between the *haute politique* realm of the US-Soviet bipolar security discourse and the seemingly depoliticised realm of economic cooperation amongst the Western powers through multilateral economic institutions such as the International Monetary Fund, World Bank and the GATT. Trade politics amongst the Western allies tended to subordinate bilateral to multilateral cooperation and to subordinate (if not completely to sublimate) trade politics to security politics. Hence more often than not negotiation of trade liberalisation agreements in the GATT during the Cold War turned on economic trade-offs between similar industrial powers. The US was the most powerful but not sufficiently dominant to enforce its will uniformly and consistently over the other major players in the system, in particular the European Communities/EU and Japan. Another effect of the Cold War political climate was that US trade policy officials tended to view developing countries as generally alike and not of great significance except as proxies in Cold War conflicts, passage of GATT Part IV and institution of a Generalised System of Preferences notwithstanding.

The American approach to trade policy began to change significantly following the election of Bill Clinton as president in 1992. Clinton and his new team of economic advisers assessed the impact of the end of the

Cold War on the position of the US in the global economy, and in response drew up foreign policies intended to reflect their conclusion that no longer could economic and security policy be treated as separate realms and no longer could global economic policy be viewed as distinct from domestic economic policy. Under the able leadership of Under Secretary of Commerce for International Trade Jeffrey Garten, administration officials identified ten countries around the world that were emerging as attractive markets for US exports of goods and services and as targets for US investment capital, owing to their large populations of incipiently middle-class consumers and their prospects for stable, democratic governance, rule of law and protection of property rights. This list of countries, named the Big Emerging Markets (BEMs) and also dubbed the 'Big Ten' by Garten in his eponymous 1997 book, contained a range of states extending from former Soviet bloc states such as Poland, which later would enter the EU, to huge rapidly industrialising countries having undertaken economic reform programmes, such as China, India and Brazil (see country chapters in this volume), to democratising mid-tier regional powers such as South Africa, Argentina, Mexico, South Korea, Indonesia and Turkey.[17]

The Clinton administration adopted an ensemble of economic assistance measures designed to assist this group of states in developing fully functioning market economy structures and to prepare to join the WTO (following its launch in 1995), as well as political assistance intended to facilitate stability, democratic institutions, and the rule of law. Clinton strategies intended to capture exporting and investment opportunities in the Big Ten for US-based businesses included creating inter-governmental task forces for each country, as well as an 'Advocacy Center' or 'economic war room' within the Commerce Department to facilitate public-private cooperation in promoting US exports to and investment in the Big Ten. Binational public-private business-government councils were established between the US and most Big Ten countries.[18] One major power notably not named to the Big Ten list was the Russian Federation, but the administration adopted an analogous package of economic and policy measures spearheaded by Vice President Al Gore and administered over a five year period by a high-level binational commission co-chaired by Gore and his Russian counterpart, Prime Minister Viktor Chernomyrdin. Concluding the Uruguay Round itself in 1994, which established the WTO, the membership of which would come to encompass over three quarters of the world's nations, was an equally

---

[17] Garten 1997.
[18] Garten 1997, xiv-xvii.

important leg of Clinton's overall global economic strategy alongside the BEM approach and the Russia policy.

Whilst Clinton's Big Emerging Markets strategy marked a change in US trade policy overall and a shift in the US approach to developing countries, US trade policy still treated the Big Emerging Markets countries as a group. Arguably the US policy package for the BEMs is one of the reasons why their economies began to grow as fast as they did (sometimes with negative consequences, as evidenced by the East Asian and Russian financial crises of 1997-1998). However, Clinton did not manage to integrate US security policy with trade and economic policy objectives uniformly and effectively, which led to policy errors such as the benign neglect of South Asian politics, which resulted in the ratcheting up of tensions and the 1998 nuclear tests by India and Pakistan, an outcome very much not intended by Clinton's Big Ten policy towards India. In what Julian Lindley-French has characterised as NATO's 'strategic vacation', over the period (using US-format dates) 11/9/1989 to 9/11/2001 economic growth policy objectives took precedence over military security objectives to a considerable extent.[19] However, this changed abruptly following the terror attacks of 11 September 2001.

In the post-9/11 period US policymakers had to re-learn how trade policy could be used as an important tool in strengthening bilateral security relations with states that had hitherto not been major security allies of the US. In autumn 2001 Washington rapidly lifted military cooperation sanctions that had been imposed upon India following the 1998 nuclear tests, and in the years that followed the US-India security relationship would be upgraded to a major strategic alliance, culminating in 2008 with a nuclear cooperation accord. Similarly, Bush administration officials came to realise that the importance of maintaining China's cooperation in their GWOT and Beijing's assistance in resolving the stalemate with North Korea over nuclear proliferation meant that conflicts over trade and monetary relations (as well as the long running Taiwan Straits dispute) had to be kept at a manageable temperature, protestations of members of Congress from districts with factories competing with Chinese imports notwithstanding. The 2007-2008 economic roller coaster of a run-up in global resources prices followed by a financial crisis and global recession may have ended the GWOT period of security dominance of the foreign policy discourse once again. Yet if anything it has clarified for US policymakers that trade policy is an essential tool in the large foreign policy toolbox that the President and his advisers have at their disposal for pursuing grand strategy.

---

[19] Lindley-French 2006.

3   DIFFERENTIATING US TRADE POLICY: BRICS, NOT BLOC

When President Clinton signed the North American Free Trade Agreement (NAFTA) in 1993, it marked a turning point for US trade policy towards developing countries in that, for the first time, Washington was recognising that trade policies towards less developed trading partners needed to be tailored to each individual relationship and set of objectives. NAFTA marked the first instance of a regional PTA including both industrialised countries (the US and Canada) and a large developing country (Mexico). US policymakers had for the most part maintained a 'one size fits all' trade policy towards developing countries since the Johnson administration had agreed to GATT Part IV in 1964, an agreement in which industrialised members of the GATT permitted developing countries the right to derogate from GATT principles of national treatment and non-discrimination on a temporary basis in return for developing countries' commitment to adherence to GATT obligations as their economies modernised. US enactment of a Generalised System of Preferences in 1971, which admitted a list of products of developing countries to the US duty free, was consistent with this policy approach.

But as noted above, the end of the Cold War changed how the Clinton administration perceived US global economic policy interests. Alongside the Big Emerging Markets strategy, another approach to achieve those interests was to differentiate hitherto homogeneous trade policies towards developing countries through bilateral and regional approaches tailored to region- and country-specific US interests. Even as the WTO began functioning in January 1995, it was already evident that Clinton would no longer rely upon the traditional postwar US trade policy approach of relying upon the relatively depoliticised GATT trade bureaucracy and the highly politicised US domestic trade bureaucracy to manage trade relations with important emerging economies. Hosting the 1995 Summit of the Americas in Miami, Clinton proposed a Free Trade Area of the Americas (FTAA) that would bring all the countries of the Western Hemisphere except for Cuba into a free trade zone, including Big Emerging Markets Brazil and Argentina. The Administration's objectives fused the trade agenda of opening new markets for US exports with a security agenda of stabilising and strengthening Latin American governments against leftist opposition movements. FTAA negotiations have taken place only sporadically in the years since the Miami summit, owing to opposition to the project within the US and in some Latin American countries. In 2000, Clinton signed the Africa Growth Opportunity Act (AGOA) to promote economic development, democratisation and good governance in sub-Saharan African states. In the same year he signed the US-Caribbean Basin Trade Partnership Act (CBTPA), extending the 1983 Caribbean Basin Initiative into a PTA with 19 Caribbean and Latin American states, and also concluded the important bilateral US-Jordan FTA, using trade liberalisation to anchor Jordan's support for Clinton's push for peace between Israelis and Palestinians.

The administration of George W. Bush further shaped the trend towards using trade policy as one tool in the larger US foreign policy toolkit for managing relations with industrial country allies and developing countries alike. Although the FTAA talks did not gain sufficient traction to lead to a deal, the Bush administration saw PTAs as a vital component of their Latin American security policy. Bush officials agreed a PTA with the four Central American Free Trade Area (CAFTA) countries in 2003 and have pursued bilateral PTAs with several other states, including Peru, which was completed in 2007, and Colombia, which was signed in 2007 but still awaits approval by the U.S. Congress at the time of writing. Economist Jagdish Bhagwati asserts that US officials used both threats and incentives to press Latin American countries to join PTAs. Bhagwati cites a study by Craig Van Grasstek contending that US officials made Colombia's withdrawal from participation in the WTO's Group of 20 (G20), a coalition of developing countries pressing for agricultural trade liberalisation, a condition for negotiating a PTA with Colombia.[20] In 2004 Washington concluded FTAs with key security allies Australia, Morocco, and Bahrain and in 2006 with Oman. In each of these instances US policymakers used bilateral trade liberalisation to achieve trade and security objectives with allies in a complementary way. Neither the level of economic development of the trading partner nor the pure logic of market opening opportunities for US exporting industries was the primary driver of the policy push for these bilateral trade agreements.

The differentiation of US trade policy towards developing countries really came into its own during the administration of Bush the Younger with respect to the Big Emerging Economies, the largest and most powerful of US developing country trading partners: states such as China, India, Brazil, and, in a somewhat different position as a former Socialist 're-industrialising' power, the Russian Federation. These four countries increasingly have been grouped by economists and analysts at investment banks as a new category of nation-state actor having common interests in the global economy, tagged as the 'BRICs'. In her 2006 'Transformational Diplomacy' speech at Georgetown University, Secretary of State Rice declared that the rise in importance of these powers required a sea change in US diplomacy, involving redeployment of staff and resources and building new regional partnerships.[21] But what is argued

---

[20] Van Grasstek 2004 in Bhagwati 2008, 83-84.
[21] Rice 2006.

here is that US foreign policy since the Cold War towards each of these major states has become increasingly differentiated, and that over the same period trade policy has been re-integrated into the bigger toolkit of US foreign policy. A brief review of US policy towards and relations with each of the BRICs should help to clarify this transformation.

The US relationship with the People's Republic of China, arguably the most important of this very important foursome to the US, has evolved from a security relationship focused on managing tensions across the Taiwan Strait into one of mutual (if wary) dependence, even as policy makers on both sides of the Pacific probably wish that it were not so. The security relationship and the economic relationship have become inseparable over the last decade. Following the terror attacks of 11 September 2001, the Beijing government found that, with a large Muslim population in the west of China, its interest in controlling the threat of terrorism on its territory organised by Muslim fundamentalist organisations like al-Qa'eda aligned closely with US counter-terror strategy, so the two nations became allies in GWOT. Both nations also shared an interest in preventing the government of North Korea from acquiring and deploying nuclear weapons. US Secretary of State Condoleezza Rice, as she moved the US back towards multilateralism, recognised that China's interest in preventing the nuclearisation of North Korea was even more immediate than that of the US and secured the agreement of the Bush White House to let Beijing do the 'heavy lifting' in the negotiations with North Korea, which achieved the result that Washington sought whilst giving China the prestige of leading the successful multilateral negotiation process. Later, through carefully calibrated remarks and actions President Bush gave his support to the Chinese government's crucial political need to stage a successful Olympic Games at Beijing in summer 2008 without disruptive protests by human rights and Tibetan autonomy activists.

Integrated into the increasing security interdependence between the two powers is an economic relationship characterised by even more extensive interdependence, as the US has become China's largest export market, and China has become the US's third largest trading partner (behind Canada and Mexico). The US runs a bigger trade deficit with China than with any other country by far (US$266 billion in 2008).[22] The Chinese central bank and private financial institutions have become the largest foreign holders of US debt, holding US$739 billion or over a quarter of foreign-held US Treasury securities in January 2009.[23] US economic policy towards China has been geared towards the reality that were this relationship to be disrupted or to change in a disorderly way, the

---

[22] US Census Bureau
[23] US Department of the Treasury

dislocation would be extensive and mutual. US officials fear a withdrawal of Chinese capital, just as Chinese officials fear a cut-off of US markets for their exports. Hence the Clinton administration worked to bring about China's accession to the WTO, which took place in November 2001, resulting in China's lowering of substantial tariffs and non-tariff barriers to imports from the US and other WTO members (see Gregory Chin's chapter in this volume, Chapter 6). US Treasury Secretaries John Snow and Henry Paulson, responding to domestic political pressures from US industries competing against imports from China, pressed Beijing repeatedly to allow the yuan's value to rise against the dollar so that US exports to China would be more competitive. Once China's central bank ended its hard peg of the yuan to the dollar in 2005, the yuan rose 8 per cent by mid-2008, and US exports to China have grown steadily. The two countries are in process of negotiating a bilateral investment treaty to facilitate further cross-border investment in both directions. Chinese financial institutions have shown willingness to participate in the recapitalisation of troubled US banks in the mortgage-related financial turbulence, with China's sovereign wealth fund CIC agreeing in December 2007 to take a US$5 billion stake in US investment bank Morgan Stanley.[24]

The relationship between the US and India has changed even more rapidly since the end of the Cold War than that between the US and China. In May 1989, US-India relations were still at such a low level of engagement and US-India trade so limited that, when the US named India to a short list of countries targeted by the 1988 Omnibus Trade Act for 'Super 301 ' market-opening trade negotiations under threat of mandatory trade retaliation should the talks fail, India was able to refuse to negotiate on grounds that the potential loss from trade retaliation was insignificant.[25] However, a year later US Trade Representative Carla Hills removed India from the Super 301 list, as India was making concessions in the multilateral format of the Uruguay Round negotiations that pleased US officials (explored by Amit Ray and Sabyasachi Saha in this volume, Chapter 5). The relationship changed swiftly, as India joined the US-led coalition against Saddam Hussein in the 1991 Gulf War, and the US lifted Cold War-era restrictions to enable India to buy US-built supercomputers. The Clinton administration focused on developing the economic relationship to increase trade and investment under their Big Emerging Markets strategy, which bore considerable fruit as India's economy liberalised and bilateral trade and investment expanded rapidly. Yet the 1998 testing of nuclear devices by India and Pakistan exposed US benign neglect of the security relationship and South Asian security concerns in the 1990s and

---

[24] Sorkin 2007.
[25] Pigman 1996.

resulted in a setback to developing US-India security cooperation until the 2001 terror attacks brought Indian and US interests together dramatically in GWOT. In summer 2002 the US played a key role in defusing India-Pakistan tensions over Kashmir. In June 2005 US Defense Secretary Rumsfeld and Indian Defence Minister Mukherjee signed an agreement upgrading the US-India security relationship to a strategic partnership analogous to the long-running post-Second World War US-Japan relationship.[26] Today the US-India relationship is not unlike the US relationships with the EU and Japan, in that trade disputes occur routinely and get resolved, either bilaterally or through the WTO's DSM, all without derailing the overall stability of the relationship. In summer 2008, for example, Prime Minister Manmohan Singh risked considerable political capital by submitting his government to a vote of confidence in India's Parliament in New Delhi in order to secure passage of a major strategic US-India bilateral nuclear cooperation accord, even as Commerce Minister Kamal Nath was at the WTO in Geneva opposing an American proposal to resolve a major bilateral disagreement over the Special Safeguard Mechanism to counter sudden import surges at a moment when a deal to conclude the DDA was reportedly within reach.[27]

The US-Brazil relationship has been transformed less by events flowing from the end of the Cold War than it has by the growth of the Brazilian economy, both in terms of its productive capacity and of its size as a consumer market (discussed in detail in Maria Lima's chapter, Chapter 4). Trade and investment ties grew rapidly in the 1990s, as Brazil was one of the most important countries on the Clinton 'Big Ten' list of BEMs. Following initial anxiety over the prospect of the election of Luiz Inacio Lula da Silva as president in 2003, owing to his populist background, the Bush administration were impressed by Lula da Silva and his foreign policy and economic teams and built a strong working relationship with the Brazilian leadership. The relationship has borne fruit for Washington, in that the US desire to contain the influence of Venezuela's president Hugo Chavez in Latin America dovetails with Lula da Silva's interest in Brazil assuming the leadership role in Latin American politics. On trade policy towards the US, Brazil's main objectives beyond their DDA negotiating stance have been to maximise agricultural exports to the US under existing WTO law and to convince the US not to 'graduate' Brazil from its import tariff preferences under the US Generalised System of Preferences (which normally would occur due to Brazil's level of economic development). Brazilian sugar cane producers lobbied the US hard to lift a tariff on cane ethanol imports that Washington

---

[26] Embassy of India 2005.
[27] Grammling 2008.

imposes to protect American corn ethanol producers. The issue emerged in the 2008 US presidential election, with Republican candidate Sen. John McCain (Arizona) embracing repeal and the winning candidate, Democratic Sen. Barack Obama (Illinois), maintaining support for the corn ethanol producers. Falling oil prices reduced the attractiveness of ethanol as a substitute for gasoline in the short term, so prospects for repeal of the tariff remained uncertain at the time of writing. On the eve of Obama's inauguration in January 2009, Brazilian President Lula da Silva urged the incoming US chief executive to make completing the WTO Doha Round a policy priority.[28]

Of all the sweeping changes that have occurred in US-Russia bilateral relations as a result of the end of the Cold War (and which are well documented elsewhere), what is most significant in this context is the progressive integration of trade issues into the mainstream of the ongoing dialogue, alongside other economic issues and the security discourse. Although the Clinton administration did not make Russia one of the Big Ten, facilitating Russia's transformation to democratic governance and a liberal market economy was their core foreign policy objective for Russia. Clinton Russia policy included a major trade and investment component, not least of which was the yet to be achieved objective of securing membership for the Russian Federation in the WTO. The Gore-Chernomyrdin Commission, a high-level binational commission that met twice annually for five years, took the lead in promoting bilateral economic cooperation in the energy, science and high technology areas. The commission's efforts led to two significant bilateral trade treaties governing commercial satellite launch services, which in turn in turn permitted and encouraged the Russian aerospace industry to be integrated into the global production chain through joint ventures with US firms. The creation of International Launch Services (ILS), a joint venture between US-based Lockheed Martin and Russian firms Energia and Khrunichev to market commercial satellite launch services using the Russian-built Proton and US-built Atlas booster rockets, is one of the most important examples of the successes of the Clinton approach.[29]

Whilst without question the Clinton policy approaches had an impact on the modernisation and privatisation of Russian firms and the liberalisation of Russia's financial markets, Russia's overall economic transformation took its own course. The 'cowboy capitalism' of rapid privatisations and the dominance of a first generation of indigenous financial 'oligarchs' in the 1990s perhaps in retrospect inevitably gave way to a resurgence of state influence in large Russian firms orchestrated

---

[28] Reuters 2009.
[29] Pigman 2004.

by President Vladimir Putin in a global market environment in which Russian energy and commodities companies like Gazprom, TNK, Lukoil and Norilsk Nickel have become major global players. The evolution of the US-Russia security relationship has also followed a similarly convoluted path. The rapid acceleration of security cooperation between the North Atlantic Treaty Association (NATO) and Russia, which saw Russian participation in NATO peacekeeping missions in Bosnia and Kosovo slowed with Russia's opposition to NATO bombing of historical ally Serbia in 1999. Russia under the leadership of Vladimir Putin has become more diffident towards further NATO expansion eastwards and has become strongly opposed to NATO membership for Georgia and Ukraine and to US deployment of an anti-ballistic missile system in central and eastern Europe. Like China and India, Russia found that it shared security interests with the US in the GWOT, which has resulted in substantial cooperation in counter-terrorism operations.[30] However, multilateral negotiations on Russian accession to the WTO have moved ahead only in fits and starts over the past five years. One of the obstacles to Russian WTO membership that remains is US repeal of the Cold War era 'Jackson-Vanik' legislation that conditioned US granting of Permanent Normal Trade Relations (most favoured nation status) to Russia upon Russian enactment of free emigration policies. In the latter years of the Bush administration, momentum in the US Congress to repeal the legislation, long regarded as anachronistic, slowed, owing to the rise in security tensions between the two countries over issues such as the ABM system and Russia's summer 2008 invasion of the Georgian enclave of South Ossetia.[31] President Obama's Secretary of State, Hillary Rodham Clinton, signalled early in 2009 that the Obama administration sought to improve US-Russia ties, raising the prospect of renewed attention to Russia's WTO membership bid.

US-Russia trade relations have not deepened in the same way that US trade relations with the other three BRICs have done. However, the evolution of US-Russia trade relations illustrates the main points about how US trade policy towards the BEEs have changed just as effectively: with respect to each of the BRICs, US trade policy has become one tool in the larger toolkit of US foreign policy instruments, and, despite similarities between the four BRICs, US policy towards each has become increasingly differentiated from its policies towards the others and from US policies towards other developing countries. Although space does not permit a full analysis here, a similar pattern can be observed in US trade policy and foreign policy towards the next tier of BEEs, which

---

[30] MacFarlaine 2006.
[31] Palmer 2009.

includes states such as Mexico, Viet Nam, Indonesia, Argentina, Pakistan and South Africa (see the chapter by Brendan Vickers in this volume, Chapter 7). Observing this continuity in the pattern of evolution of US trade policies towards the BEEs since the end of the Cold War raises the inevitable question of when and how the trend might change. If US trade policies can be understood as emerging from the interaction of exogenous variables (external change) and endogenous political factors, then an examination of the endogenous sources of US trade policy is required.

4   US TRADE POLICY UNDER OBAMA: *PLUS ÇA CHANGE, PLUS C'EST LA MÊME CHOSE?*

The nature of divided government in the United States means that in the passage of trade legislation, whether to implement a multilateral or bilateral trade treaty or to implement a domestically administered trade policy, requires the cooperation of the executive branch and the Congress. Historically, the President, surrounded by his executive office and foreign policy advisory apparatus, has tended to use trade policy primarily to advance the national interest on the global stage, whilst Congress has sought to use trade policy to meet constituent demands. In this endeavour Congress has often been joined by the other Federal departments that have large constituencies of businesses competing with imports, such as the Departments of Commerce and Agriculture. This has resulted in a long running pattern of the White House seeking to use trade liberalisation as an instrument of grand strategy, whereas Congress has remained sympathetic to constituent demands for sectoral protection. As David Lake contends, the president's success in convincing Congress to back trade liberalisation is dependent upon his skills as a negotiator and his ability to mobilise pro-trade constituencies amongst management and workers in exporting industries. The challenge lies in the classic collective goods problem of benefits from trade liberalisation being broad but diffused, whilst benefits from sectoral protection are smaller but concentrated.[32] This divergence of trade policy interests, as Destler has argued, has prompted Congress to delegate overall trade policy leadership to the president for fixed periods of time in return for White House cooperation in meeting particular Congressional needs to limit trade liberalisation in response to constituent demands.[33]

For many decades, the House of Representatives has been fairly finely balanced between supporters and opponents of trade liberalisation, with the US Senate tilted slightly more in favour of trade. The group of

[32] Lake 1988, 66-88.
[33] Destler 2005, 11-37.

House members and senators who usually vote for trade bills is a centre coalition backed by finance, consumers, and managers and workers in exporting industries. The pro-trade coalition cuts across party lines, comprising around one third moderate Democrats and two thirds moderate Republicans. The backbone of the anti-trade coalition consists of managers and workers in import-competing industries. However, many opponents of trade bills are ideology-driven as well, coming either from the left of the Democratic party, viewing trade liberalisation as skewed in favour of business at the expense of labour, environmental and other social interests, or from amongst nationalist right Republicans, who view trade agreements as ceding vital elements of US sovereignty to multilateral bodies like the WTO or, at the least, constraining US freedom to act legislatively as and when necessary. The vulnerability of the pro-trade Congressional coalition requires relations between the White House and Capitol Hill on trade issues to be good if trade legislation needed to meet US commitments to trading partners is to be passed.

The contemporary context for surveying the trade policy horizon in the presidency of Barack Obama is that, in recent decades, more often than not trade relations between the two ends of Pennsylvania Avenue have ranged from mixed to very poor indeed. The first administration of George W. Bush did a very lacklustre job of selling the benefits of trade liberalisation to Congress, much as had been the case with the first Reagan administration in the early 1980s and the second Clinton administration in the late 1990s. The Bush team needlessly politicised trade policy, taking the view, mistakenly in the event, that they did not require the support of any Democrats to pass trade legislation. One particularly problematic result of this intransigence was the unwillingness of Congress to renew 'Fast Track' enabling legislation that facilitates the passage of other trade bills, such as bilateral trade treaties and WTO multilateral agreements. Since the late 1960s, US trade legislation has become increasingly complex as it has had to address non-tariff barriers to trade, so under the Trade Act of 1974 Congress granted to the president the power to submit a trade bill to Congress for an up-or-down vote without amendment. 'Fast Track' (more recently re-named 'Trade Promotion Authority'), which Congress has only granted for fixed periods of time and in return for political concessions from the White House, prevents members of Congress from making innumerable amendments to trade bills, which, in the case of enabling bills for trade treaties, would then have to be taken back to foreign negotiating partners for approval, rendering the treaty making process impossibly cumbersome and time consuming. In part as a result of the Bush administration's partisan trade policy, the 2004 and 2006 elections saw Democrats increase their numbers in both Houses. The pro-trade coalition in the House of Representatives was diminished, with an estimated net increase of 33 elected House and

Senate members committed to the 'Fair Trade' legislative agenda.[34]
Since Fast Track expired in 2007, Congress was unwilling to renew it
during the remainder of the Bush presidency, leaving it to the next
administration to secure renewal if they hope to obtain Congressional
approval for any bilateral or multilateral trade treaties. The lobby group
Public Citizen reports a further net increase of 35 pro-'fair trade'
members of Congress elected in November 2008.[35]

The Obama administration faces a number of domestic challenges
in conducting US trade policy. Obama is much more dependent than Bill
Clinton was upon major trades unions representing (for the most part)
workers in 'sunset' import-competing industries, as well as populist
grassroots voter organisations such as MoveOn.org. These left-leaning
Democratic constituencies are much more aligned with the left sceptics
of trade liberalisation in Congress than with the pro-trade, centre coalition.
However, Obama is also beholden to the Democratic pro-Wall Street
centre represented by figures such as former Clinton Treasury Secretaries
Robert Rubin and Lawrence Summers, New Jersey Governor and former
Goldman Sachs CEO Jon Corzine, and financier Warren Buffett. As
Obama faced the daunting task of mediating between and choosing
amongst the policy preferences of these vying rivals, his early selection of
Illinois Congressman and Democratic Congressional Campaign Committee
chair Rahm Emanuel to serve as his chief of staff portended close
cooperation between the Obama White House and the Democratic Party
leadership on Capitol Hill. Emanuel is highly acclaimed for his work in
increasing the number of Democrats elected to the House of Representatives.
As a former member of President Clinton's inner circle, Emanuel has the
capacity to build bridges effectively between different wings and factions
within the party. Obama's choices of former New York Federal Reserve
Governor Timothy Geithner as Treasury Secretary and former Clinton
Treasury Secretary Lawrence Summers as chairman of the National
Economic Council suggested that he wanted to assuage fears of Wall
Street and the broader business community about the substance of his
economic strategy.

The substance of Obama's trade policy inclinations could not be
discerned easily from his campaign pronouncements, as presidential
candidates during campaigns present different views of their trade policy
in an effort to woo different constituencies. In the run-up to the Ohio
primary, for example, Obama declared to Ohio voters his commitment to
renegotiate NAFTA, even as his campaign's chief economic adviser,
Austan Goolsbee, gave informal assurances to Canadian officials that

---

[34] Tucker and Wallach 2008.
[35] Public Citizen 2008.

they had nothing to fear from this protectionist rhetoric. Obama's first nominee for US Trade Representative was California congressman Xavier Becerra, an outspoken critic of NAFTA supported by the labour left, which raised fears amongst pro-trade constituencies of a significant protectionist tilt to Obama trade policy. Becerra declined the nomination, however, with the indelicate public pronouncement that in his view making trade policy would not be a high priority for the Obama administration. Obama subsequently named former Dallas mayor and avowed free trader Ron Kirk to the post, an appointment that raised eyebrows amongst some labour leaders but was praised by the business community. The stakes surrounding Obama's trade policy have been heightened dramatically by the onset of a global recession in the wake of the financial turbulence of summer and autumn 2008, which has put multilateral trade liberalisation as a tool to stimulate global economic growth in the spotlight, even as pressure for import protection from domestic firms and workers affected by the recession has increased. The Obama administration's first highly visible foray into trade policy, the inclusion of a 'Buy America' provision in the US$800 billion economic stimulus package passed by Congress in February 2009 stipulating that steel used in stimulus package-funded infrastructure projects must be domestically produced, was viewed by US trading partner countries as provocative and WTO-illegal. The stimulus package itself, coupled with the other components of the administration's economic recovery programme, promises to increase the US Federal budget deficit by US$1-2 billion, which the Federal Reserve is monetising by purchasing long-term US Treasury bonds. This creates a significant risk of high inflation, which shifts the real cost of US debt onto foreign creditors, and dollar depreciation, which would function as a backdoor tariff on imports and could touch off a round of competitive currency devaluations. Overall, initial indications of the impact of Obama economic policies on trade are not promising, but at the time of writing it is still early to judge what their final impact will be.

5   CONCLUSIONS: OBAMA TRADE POLICY, THE BEES AND THE DDA

In contrast to the protectionist cast to early economic policy legislation in the Obama administration, the multilateral economic diplomacy of the Obama White House has received high praise for promising and delivering greater international cooperation to counteract the global recession. The global G20 configuration of advanced industrial powers and BEEs, which began meeting in November 2008 to coordinate efforts to promote global economic recovery, has continued to meet with the enthusiastic support of President Obama. The April 2009 London G20 summit was concluded with a strong sense of multilateral agreement on better coordination of global financial regulation and a massive global economic stimulus package aimed at developing countries through creation of US$1 trillion of International Monetary Fund Special Drawing Rights. Yet the WTO was the ghost at this feast of multilateral cooperation and compromise, with conclusion of multilateral negotiations to complete the DDA far from prominent on the London G20 agenda. Moreover, even given the need to promote global economic recovery articulated at London, as of mid-April 2009 there had been precious little in the way of specific commitments from Obama officials to completing the DDA.

The reluctance of the otherwise enthusiastically multilateralist Obama White House to commit to completing the DDA may constitute a recognition of the inevitable outcome of perhaps incompatible diplomatic trajectories: the reintegration of US trade policy into grand strategy, the differentiation of US bilateral relations with the BEEs, and the rise of the BEEs to leadership on behalf of broader developing country interests in the DDA. The DDA has seen the eclipse of the traditional Quad grouping of developed countries (i.e. US, EU, Japan, Canada) steering the multilateral negotiating process in favour of a shifting series of small groups of powerful countries, including both industrial countries and BEEs, meeting to resolve differences and coordinate negotiating positions. In 2005, US and EU ministerial level negotiators began meeting with their counterparts from Brazil and India in a configuration that came to be known as the Group of 4 (G4) to attempt to find a balance of overall concessions required to reach a deal at the WTO's Hong Kong Ministerial Conference in December 2005. Another configuration that met in autumn 2005, known as the FIPs-plus, was comprised of the G4 plus Japan, Korea, Switzerland, China and Argentina. At this phase of the talks and in these configurations the US indicated willingness to make substantial concessions on agricultural subventions, which were sought by many developing countries led by the WTO G20 negotiating group (see Maria Lima's chapter, Chapter 4), and which placed Washington at odds with the EU, whose offer on agriculture was perceived as being significantly less valuable. Following the Hong Kong Ministerial Conference, however, the G4 configuration became a Group of 6 (G6) with the addition of Australia and Japan. In the G6 negotiating group, which began meeting at the World Economic Forum's 2006 Annual Meeting at Davos in January 2006, the EU and US negotiators closed ranks, supported by Australia and Japan, over non-agricultural market access (NAMA) issues and accommodated one another's concerns over agriculture. This evolution led to a breakdown of the G4/G6 configuration at a July 2007 ministerial meeting in Potsdam, with India and Brazil aligned against the advanced industrial powers (explored by Faizel Ismail in his chapter, Chapter 9). A year later, at the 2008 mini-ministerial meeting the Group of 7 (G7) core negotiating group that re-emerged included China as well as India and

Brazil amongst the BEEs, in addition to the US, EU, Japan and Australia.[36] The participation of US negotiators in this series of negotiating groups and alliances is indicative of their willingness to consider trade policy objectives as part of a broader basket of grand strategy objectives in foreign policy and to adjust trade policy objectives and the relative priorities of particular objectives in relation to broader foreign policy needs.

Yet crucially, these shifts in US strategy and tactics have not borne fruit for the US trade agenda, and the administration's lack of emphasis on completing the DDA may be merely an acknowledgement of this reality. Faizel Ismail argues convincingly that the stalemate of the DDA negotiations reflects the increased power of developing countries, which has been concentrated by their increased capacity to work collaboratively through coalitions like the WTO's G20 and the NAMA-11 to defend their welfare interests and articulate a broader sense of agency.[37] The increased negotiating effectiveness of these coalitions is due in large part to the willingness of the BEEs not only to participate, but to lead. If Ismail's argument is correct, the BEEs have prioritised their developing country agency role over opportunities to do bilateral foreign policy trade-offs with the US (and, by extension, with the EU), which has the effect of limiting the effectiveness of the US reintegration of trade policy into grand strategy and differentiation of bilateral relationships with the BEEs.[38] Excluding trade from bilateral diplomatic bargaining between the US and BEEs may or may not benefit a broader range of developing countries' trade objectives, but is almost certain to limit the scope of outcomes of bilateral US-BEE negotiations.

Even were a DDA deal to be done, the prompt renewal of Fast Track would be necessary to secure DDA approval in Congress. President Obama cannot expect an easier time obtaining Fast Track renewal because both houses of Congress have Democratic majorities. The Congressional 'price' to the Obama administration for renewing Fast Track is likely to be higher than it was for prior administrations, including mandatory encoding of labour and environmental provisions into subsequent trade bills. The Obama administration may also have to face the hangover of a raft of trade-related legislation proposed by Democrats in the outgoing 110th Congress, much of which was directed against China and much of which was a result of poor trade relations between the Bush White House and the Capitol Hill of Senate Majority Leader Harry Reid (Nevada) and

---

[36] Grammling 2008.
[37] Ismail 2007.
[38] Grammling 2008.

House Speaker Nancy Pelosi (California).[39] However, given the financial turbulence, global recession and emerging structure of multilateral consultation and coordination to address the global recession, the Obama administration and 111th Congress may find mutual advantage in cooperating with one another on trade issues to an incrementally greater degree than was the case under George W. Bush, which in turn would increase the capacity of President Obama to cooperate multilaterally with US trading partners on stimulating global economic recovery.

---

[39] Various bills proposed, among other things, would have removed PNTR (MFN) status from China, banned new trade agreements with China, mandated bilateral trade balancing with trading partners (a particularly trenchant throwback to the mercantilism of the 1930s), and made currency manipulation a countervailable subsidy. The Democratic leadership in the 110th Congress remained resistant to Bush efforts to secure passage of the pending US-Panama, US-Colombia and US-South Korea FTAs, seeing opportunity in winning votes from workers in import-competing industries, which led one former Bush Treasury Department official in July 2008 to describe the US-Colombia FTA as 'dead' and the US-South Korea FTA as 'deader than dead'. Obama officials in early 2009 indicated willingness to revisit the three PTAs.

REFERENCES

Bergsten, C. Fred. 1996. Competitive Liberalization and Global Free Trade: A Vision for the Early 21st Century. Working Paper 96-15. Washington DC: Institute for International Economics.

Bhagwati, Jagdish. 2008. *Termites in the Trading System; How Preferential Agreements Undermine Free Trade*. Oxford: Oxford University Press.

Van Grasstek, Craig. 2004. Asia Pacific Regional Initiative on Trade, Economic Governance, and Human Development', unpublished manuscript, Kennedy School of Government, Harvard University, June.

CNN. 2001 You are either with us or against us. 6 November, http://archives. cnn.com/2001/US/11/06/gen.attack.on.terror/, accessed 16 October 2008.

Destler, I. M. 2005. *American Trade Politics* (4th edition). Washington, DC: Institute for International Economics.

Embassy of India. 2005. Press release, New framework for the U.S.-India defense relationship, Washington, DC, 28 June, http://www.India nembassy.org/ press_release/2005/June/31.htm, accessed 5 April 2009.

Gardner, Richard N. 1956. *Sterling-Dollar Diplomacy*, Oxford: Clarendon Press.

Garten, Jeffrey A. 1997. *The Big Ten: The Big Emerging Markets and How They Will Change Our Lives*. New York: Basic Books.

Gerson, Michael. 2008. Muddy Multilateralism. *Real Clear Politics*, 25 April, http:// www.realclearpolitics.com/articles/2008/04/muddy_ multilateralism.html

Grammling, Steffen. 2008. Major Setback for WTO's Doha Round: 'Mini-Ministerial' Failed and Future Looks Dim – A Chance for Reclaiming Its 'Development Dimension'? *Dialogue on Globalization Fact Sheet*, Friedrich-Ebert Stiftung, Geneva Office (August).

Hawksworth, John and Gordon Cookson. 2008. The World in 2050; Beyond the BRICs: a broader look at emerging markets growth prospects. PriceWaterhouse Coopers, March.

Ismail, Faizel. 2007. The G20 and NAMA 11: The Role of Developing Countries in the WTO Doha Round. University College, Oxford, and Department of Politics and International Relations, Oxford University, Global Economic Governance Programme, Lecture presented as part of GEG's Seminar Series on Making Globalization Work for Developing Countries, 23 November.

Lake, David A. 1988. *Power, Protection, and Free Trade*. Ithaca, NY: Cornell University Press.

Lindley-French, Julian. 2006. *The North Atlantic Treaty Organization; the Enduring Alliance*. Abingdon: Routledge.

McCain, John. 2008. Speech to Los Angeles World Affairs Council, 26 March.

MacFarlaine, S. Neil. 2006. The 'R' in BRICs: is Russia an emerging power? *International Affairs* 82(1):41-57.

Nagl, John A. 2005. *Learning to Eat Soup with a Knife: Counterinsurgency Lessons from Malaya and Vietnam*. Chicago: University of Chicago Press.

Odessey, Bruce. 2006. Congress Passes Bill Ending WTO Export Tax Break Dispute with EU. The US Mission to the European Union website, 12 May. http://useu.usmission.gov/Article.asp?ID= BF20671F-5ACA-41C3-9AA9-142963220D62, accessed 31 October 2008.

Office of the US Trade Representative. 2006. Congress takes important action: Byrd repeal brings US into compliance with WTO ruling', press release, 1 February, http://geneva.usmission.gov/Press2006/ 0202ByrdRepeal.html, accessed 31 October 2008.

Palmer, Doug. 2009. Russia WTO bid still faces big U.S. obstacles. *Reuters*, 1 April, http://www.reuters.com/article/worldNews/ idUSTRE53084H20090 401? sp=true, accessed 5 April 2009.

Pigman, Geoffrey Allen. 1996. United States trade policies at loggerheads: Super 301, the Uruguay Round and Indian services trade liberalization. *Review of International Political Economy* 3(4):728-762, Winter.

Pigman, Geoffrey Allen. 2004. The New Aerospace Diplomacy: Reconstructing Post-Cold War US-Russian Economic Relations. *Diplomacy and Statecraft* 15(4):1-41, December.

Pigman, Geoffrey Allen and John Kotsopoulos. 2007. 'Do this one for me, George': Blair, Brown, Bono, Bush and the 'Actor-ness' of the G8'. *The Hague Journal of Diplomacy* 2(2):127-145.

Reuters. 2009. Brazil's Lula urges Obama to act on Doha Round, 19 January, http://www.reuters.com/article/politicsNews/idUSTRE50I31U20090119, accessed 4 April 2009.

Rice, Condoleezza 2006. Transformational Diplomacy. Speech to Georgetown University, 18 January, www.state.gov, accessed 28 March 2009.

Schwab, Susan. 2007. Statement by US Trade Representative at panel discussion, 'Frozen Trade Talks and the Need for Progress', World Economic Forum 2007 Annual Meeting, Davos, Switzerland, January www.weforum.org/ en/knowledge/Events/2007/AnnualMeeting/KN_SESS_SUMM_18552? url=/en/knowledge/Events/2007/AnnualMeeting/KN_SESS_SUMM_ 18552, accessed 28 March 2009.

Sorkin, Andrew Ross. 2007. Deal Book; Morgan Stanley Posts Loss, Sells Stake to China. *The New York Times*. 19 December, http:// dealbook.blogs.nytimes.com/2007/12/19/morgan-stanley-to-sell-stake-to-china-amid-4th-quarter-loss/, accessed 5 April 2009.

Tucker, Todd and Lori Wallach. 2008. Fair Trade Victory. *Foreign Policy in Focus: Commentary*, 21 November, www.fpif.org/fpiftxt/5692, accessed 22 March 2009.

US Census Bureau. Foreign Trade Statistics, Top Trading Partners – Total Trade, Exports, Imports, http://www.census.gov/foreign-trade/statistics/ highlights/top/ top0812yr.html, accessed 5 April 2009.

US Department of the Treasury. 2009. Major Foreign Holders of Treasury Securities, http://www.ustreas.gov/tic/mfh.txt, accessed 5 April 2009.

Ward, Andrew. 2008. McCain pledges multilateralism. *Financial Times,* 18 March, http://us.ft.com/ftgateway/superpage.ft?news_id=fto031820081519224520, accessed 20 October 2008.

WTO. 2008. Trade Policy Review Report by the Secretariat, United States, 5 May, WT/TPR/S/200.

WTO. 2009. World Trade 2008, Prospects for 2009; WTO sees 9% global trade decline in 2009 as recession strikes. Press release, Press/554, 23 March 2009, www.wto.org, accessed 28 March 2009.

WTO. Dispute Settlement: Dispute DS 267, United States – Subsidies on Upland Cotton, http://www.wto.org/english/tratop_e/dispu_e/cases_e/ds267_e.htm, ccessed April 2009.

WTO. Dispute Settlement: Dispute DS4, United States – Standards for Reformulated and Conventional Gasoline, http://www.wto.org/english/tratop_e/dispu_e/cases_e/ ds4_e.htm, accessed 31 October 2008.

Part II

Rising Powers in a Multipolar Trading System

MARIA LUCIA L. M. PÁDUA LIMA

4. BRAZIL'S MULTILATERAL TRADE DIPLOMACY IN THE WTO

This chapter explores the positions adopted by Brazil and the Group of 20 (G20) in the Doha Development Agenda (DDA) negotiations of the World Trade Organisation (WTO) and the possibility that this trade round will ensure significant gains for the developing world, especially the least-developed countries (LDCs). The focus is on Brazil's role in the G20 coalition of developing countries. Formed at the time of the Cancún Ministerial Conference in September 2003, the G20 has pressed the case for greater equity in global farm trade.

The chapter is divided into three sections. The first section provides an initial analysis and understanding of Brazil's contemporary development and trade policy. This analysis aims to clarify Brazil's role and interests in global trade and identify the arguments that underpin Brazil's current negotiating strategy in the DDA. The chapter then turns to briefly explore the historic formation of the G20 and Brazil's participation in the agriculture negotiations post-Cancún, with emphasis on the role of the G4 (the US, EU, India and Brazil – see country chapters in this volume). I also reflect on the impact of the global financial crisis on the Brazilian economy and international exchange more generally. Six months after the initial eruption of the crisis in September 2008, it is possible to clearly detect the first negative effects of the global crisis on international trade flows – in general, but also particularly in Brazil. As many analysts suggest, the major risk confronting international trade today is the strengthening of protectionism[1], with extremely negative repercussions for the global economy as a whole. Strengthening the multilateral trading system, which includes concluding the Doha Round, is an important antidote for growing trade protectionism and to guarantee a speedy and less harmful recovery from the global crisis. For this reason, this chapter explores how the Doha Round may be concluded to ensure gains for developing countries (particularly in agriculture) and positively alter the growth pattern and relationship of trade, investment and technology transfer to benefit developing countries and LDCs.

---

[1] Baldwin and Evenett 2009.

A. Narlikar, B. Vickers (eds.), Leadership and Change in the Multilateral Trading System, 75–95.

1   DOMESTIC DRIVERS OF BRAZIL'S MULTILATERAL TRADE DIPLOMACY

For most of the previous century, the Brazilian economy experienced high rates of economic growth. This allowed the country to transform from being a strictly agricultural economy and an exporter of primary goods, to become an industrial nation by the second half of the twentieth century. The industrialisation process that Brazil underwent followed the so-called import-substitution industrialisation (ISI)[2] paradigm. The final goal of ISI was to alter the productive structure of the economy by transferring economic dynamism from the primary to the secondary sectors. In order to achieve this, it was necessary to adopt a combination of economic policy measures that protected infant industries, including import controls. The result of this productive transformation would be mirrored in the trade balance, with modifications to exports (composed mainly of primary products with very little diversification) and imports (comprised of durable and non-durable consumer goods).

By the start of the 1980s, the Brazilian economy ceased to generate the high rates of growth that had characterised previous decades. This loss of economic dynamism was attributed to the ISI strategy, together with protection of the domestic market. This interpretation was corroborated by comparing Brazil to the other newly-industrialised countries (NICs) of that period, namely South Korea, Hong Kong, Singapore and Taiwan. Unlike Brazil, the latter countries had adopted an expressive policy of trade opening as their industrialisation strategy. Towards the end of the 1980s, the conventional analysis of Latin American economies moreover strengthened the thesis that ISI was largely responsible for the mediocre growth experienced by these countries[3]. In the case of Brazil, several scholars[4] diagnosed that ISI, having reached its main goal, had been depleted by the start of the 1960s. Its permanence throughout the following decade was only made possible by the excess of liquidity in the international financial markets. With changes to the international economic and financial conditions, the ISI model totally collapsed.

---

[2] This strategy included an emphasis on economic diversification through import-substitution industrialisation (ISI) for the sake of greater economic autonomy. As part of this strategy, Brazil had since the end of the Second World War adopted rigid trade controls and many industrial promotion schemes (see Furtado 2007).

[3] The so-called 'Washington Consensus' condensed the main criticisms of the ISI model adopted by many Latin American countries. According to this position, unilateral trade reform was an important means for countries to stimulate growth (see Bresser Pereira 1991).

[4] Tavares 1972.

The decade of the 1980s in Brazil was marked by an external debt crisis, followed by an adjustment process in the balance of payments, extremely high inflation rates and the total economic impossibility of sustaining ISI. The strict control of imported goods during this period of adjustment was due to an imperious need for commercial surplus, rather than maintaining ISI. Nonetheless, in the Brazilian case, this industrialisation strategy was successful. One is able, naturally, to question the cost of adopting this model, its extension throughout the decades and the consequences of postponing a change of strategy.

Having resolved the external debt crisis of the previous decade, at the start of the 1990s Brazil was able to resume borrowing in the international financial markets and partake in globalisation processes. Since the dominant diagnosis on the 1980s crisis centred on the old ISI model, the proposition of unilateral trade reform was seen as the best – if not the only – option to develop the country.[5]

It is not difficult to understand the reasons why unilateral trade reform and the other prescriptions of the so-called Washington Consensus were so widely accepted in the country. In general terms, these proposals – based on regaining access to international financial markets – hinted at the possibility that Brazil could reproduce the US strategy of growth based on continuous and growing current account deficits. Allowing for the stabilisation of domestic prices, while incurring eventual deficits in the trade balance and current account without the sanction of the International Monetary Fund (IMF) and starting growth without the need for a national strategy were irresistible.

The Washington Consensus proposals endorsed by the Brazilian government and society promised that pro-market reforms (including unilateral liberalisation) and abandoning a national strategy would deliver development just as in the American case.[6] However, this proved impossible to achieve and by the end of the 1990s, growing disappointment at the outcomes of reform was intensified by the foreign exchange crisis that hit the country in 1999.

The combination of external crisis and weak performance of the Brazilian economy broke once and for all the idea that quick and easy benefits would derive from a trade policy based on unilateral opening. This understanding helped to shape the Brazilian negotiating position

---

[5] The Uruguay Round (1986-1994) was concluded during a period when the benefits of the free trade paradigm were widely accepted within Brazil.

[6] After the recent economic events that took place in the US (especially post-September 2008), it seems that this strategy has also been exhausted by that country. In the American case, this model has lasted for over three decades and has, in general, generated more prosperity for American society than for Brazil or Latin America.

presented since the beginning of the Doha Round, namely that access to the Brazilian market must be based on reciprocity of market openings in developed countries, essentially in agricultural products.

Since then, it was understood that the integration of the agricultural sector into multilateral disciplines (initially started during the Uruguay Round) was a key issue for Brazil and other developing country exporters. Even before the launch of the Doha Round in 2001, Brazil had prioritised the need to actively promote the opening of developed countries' markets for agricultural products, while managing unfair trade practices by these countries.

Brazil's agricultural modernisation started in the 1970s during the military regime, when plantations were extended from the temperate areas of the country (Southeast and South) to the centre-west and northeast tropical zones. This expansion was made possible by the Brazilian Agricultural Research Corporation (EMPRAPA)[7], which successfully conducted research to adapt seeds, develop new products and offered government credit at minimal prices. At the beginning of the 1990s, the food-producing agricultural sector had become one of the most dynamic sectors of the Brazilian economy. This largely reflected the success of economic liberalisation policies, particularly the reduction of state intervention and the country's significant integration into world markets. While on the one hand there was a dramatic change in the forms of intervention (e.g. an abrupt reduction of subsidised credit), on the other hand public investment in research and technology was not only maintained, but also extended. Moreover, access to the international financial markets guaranteed alternative means of finance, in the absence of government credit. In this way, during the period 1990 to 2008, the production of grains more than doubled and the production of meat almost tripled. This rapid growth in agriculture contrasts sharply with other sectors of the Brazilian economy and was largely made possible through exporting, which more than doubled during the same period.

It should be emphasised that the improved competitiveness of Brazil's agricultural exporting industry is linked to several factors: public and private sector investment in research and technology; price stabilisation since 1994; and extensive investment in capital equipment. In Brazil, the estimated annual growth in productivity was 5.7 per cent between 1998 and 2002. The comparable annual rate in the US during the same period was 1.8 per cent.[8]

---

[7] The Brazilian Agricultural Research Corporation (EMBRAPA) is a public company for farming research. EMBRAPA was founded in 1973.

[8] Gasques et al. 2004.

These investments in research and technology not only allowed an improvement in productivity, but also made it possible for modern agriculture to spread to new areas in the interior of the country. This allowed for greater diversification of products compared to the smaller group of tropical commodities that Brazil had previously produced. By the end of the 1990s, this combination of domestic changes with an increase in global demand generated the most significant growth of the past decades in the agricultural sector.

Notwithstanding the success of Brazil's agricultural exports, the expansion of Brazilian agribusiness confronts various obstacles, internally and externally. The internal issues are related to macroeconomic constraints, such as high interest rates, the volatility of the exchange rate and excessive tax loads, among others. There are other domestic concerns too. These include the regulation of genetically-modified products; the reduction of the government's budget on sanitary control and animal disease prevention; and uncertainty that stems from the intensification of social movement campaigns for agrarian reform.

The biggest external obstacle for Brazil is the difficulty of accessing developed country markets. For this reason, Brazilian agribusiness has recognised the Doha Round as an opportunity to improve the international trade conditions for their agricultural exports. Agribusiness holds a special place of prominence in the Brazilian private sector.[9] This sector is highly organised and has established private institutes that engage in deep and detailed studies on different aspects of agribusiness.[10] The industrial and services sectors have also been involved in key initiatives aimed at formulating active policies vis-à-vis the DDA. These have largely sought to reduce or eliminate tariff peaks or to guarantee the possibility of adopting trade defense measures.

2   THE DOHA ROUND: BRAZIL AND THE G-20

The Uruguay Round generally determined the key elements that would constitute the DDA, which was launched as a 'Development Round' in 2001. For developing countries, the euphoria of the 1990s over the benefits of free trade was misplaced and the expected returns from the previous round of trade liberalisation proved disappointing. Although trade liberalisation remained the main objective of the Doha Round, it

---

[9] These include the National Agriculture Association (*Confederação Nacional da Agricultura*); Brazilian Agribusiness Association; National Cooperatives Organisation and many others agricultural associations.

[10] ICONE is the best example of such a private institution dedicated to agricultural research. There is also some collaboration with government authorities on the international negotiation process.

was coupled with a strong development agenda. This recognised that trade liberalisation could intensify asymmetries between developed and developing countries, instead of softening them. In this regard, the sectoral negotiations – namely agriculture, non-agricultural market access (NAMA) and services – became even more complex and interdependent. Since the start of the Doha Round, the economic and social situation of developing countries and LDCs has therefore been central to the discussions.

By the time of the exchange crisis in 1999, there was great disappointment in Brazil with the unfulfilled promises of unilateral trade reform.[11] In this way, the more aggressive Brazilian positions adopted at Doha in 2001 were in a certain way already present at the WTO's frustrated ministerial conference in Seattle two years earlier. Nonetheless, this new Brazilian positioning was consistent with the view of other developing countries, who were equally frustrated with the inadequate outcomes from the previous Uruguay Round. Even before the launch of Doha Round in 2001, developing countries started to demonstrate an intense activism based on a growing technical knowledge and a capacity to articulate their own interests.

An example of the developing world's proactive approach to multilateral trade was their involvement in the Cairns Group.[12] As foreseen in article 20 of the Uruguay Round's Agreement on Agriculture (AoA), agriculture negotiations commenced in 2000. In these negotiations, the Cairns Group presented a proposal to reduce tariff peaks and escalation; establish maximum tariff levels; expand tariff-quotas; and perfect administration methods for these quotas.[13]

As is well-known, agriculture was subjected to multilateral disciplines the first time during the Uruguay Round. However, both the AoA and its implementation were insufficient to promote an effective improvement to the economic conditions of developing countries, where the world's rural population is mainly concentrated. Developed countries are the main users of export subsidies and tariff and non-tariff barriers to protect agricultural markets. By contrast, Brazilian agriculture – the world's third largest exporter in this sector – operates free of trade-distorting practices and instruments. This largely explains Brazil's leadership position among developing countries and LDCs. It is also important to

---

[11] To a large degree, the second term of President Fernando Henrique Cardoso (1999-2002) was concerned with the need to adjust the balance of payments in the face of the exchange crisis, which had derived from the rationing of international credit.

[12] The Cairns Group was created in 1986 and includes the following exporters of agricultural goods: South Africa, Argentina, Australia, Bolivia, Brazil, Canada, Chile, Colombia, Philippines, Guatemala, Hungary, Indonesia, Malaysia, New Zealand, Paraguay, Thailand and Uruguay.

[13] See WTO 2000.

recall that agriculture is the point of convergence among all WTO members, except for developed countries.[14]

By the time that the Doha Round was launched in 2001, Brazilian negotiation authorities were clear that the agriculture tripod (i.e. increasing market access, reducing levels of domestic support and eliminating export subsidies) was an 'absolute priority' for Brazil.[15] It was equally important that Brazil construct a wide arc of alliances to elevate the level of ambition for the Doha mandate.[16] The concept of 'agribusiness' has been central to the construction of the Brazilian position in agriculture, which is more connected to the current realities of the country. This concept better portrays modern agriculture, which is not only restricted to the direct producer but encompasses the whole value-chain: the inputs, the agriculture itself, the agro-industry and the distribution channels. These front-and-back linkages to agribusiness include activities from the primary, secondary and tertiary sectors of the economy and demand continuing technological development, sophisticated management capacity and clearly a negotiating vision that reflects this contemporary notion.

The Doha mandate established a level of expectations. Paragraph 13 of the Doha Ministerial Declaration (DMD) contains an explicit commitment to: increase market access substantially, to reduce gradually the many forms of export subsidies with the final goal of eliminating this practice entirely, and to promote significant reductions in trade-distorting domestic support.[17] In the same paragraph it was foreseen that special and differential treatment (SDT) for developing countries would be an integral part of the negotiations and would be incorporated into the schedules of concessions. Non-commercial concerns expressed by the members would also be addressed.

During 2000 and 2001, more than one hundred proposals submitted in the realm of the agriculture negotiations highlighted the palpable differences that existed among member countries. For example, the EU's initial proposal called for the adoption of a linear tariff reduction formula as used during the Uruguay Round, with just a few mechanisms to manage tariff-quotas. The US had an aggressive position in relation to market access, but very defensive interests when it came to domestic support and tariff reductions for what are considered to be 'sensitive'

---

[14] It is true that there are many differences between developing and least-developed countries, but agriculture allowed for the construction of a common position on the current multilateral negotiations.

[15] Permanent Mission of Brazil in Geneva 2002a, 4. The three pillars of the agriculture negotiations seek to increase market access, reduce the levels of domestic support and eliminate export subsidies.

[16] For example, see Permanent Mission of Brazil in Geneva 2002b.

[17] WTO 2001.

products (e.g. sugar, orange juice, tobacco and others). In other words, at the outset of the Doha Round, the two biggest players did not have a joint position on farm trade. However, on 13 July 2003 prior to the Cancún ministerial conference, the EU and US presented a joint proposal on agriculture that substantially lowered the level of ambition expressed by the Doha mandate. This joint proposal preserved the export subsidies programmes and defended European interests on market access as much as the US's interests concerning domestic support.

Brazil believed that an ambitious understanding between the EU and US was necessary to unblock the agriculture negotiations and thereby continue with the Doha process.[18] For many developing countries, including Brazil, the DDA could only progress once there was satisfactory agreement on agriculture. In sum, if the understanding between the EU and US could help the purposes of the Doha mandate without lowering the round's level of ambition, it was simply an agreement between major players, which did not necessarily take into consideration the positions of the other WTO members.

The EU-US proposal was not well received by Brazil and countries such as Argentina, China, India and South Africa. Brazil therefore led an initiative to formulate a joint alternative that would reflect the DMD's central objectives in the agriculture negotiations. On 20 August 2003, these developing countries submitted their own proposal which they believed better reflected Doha's original landmark. This initiative, known as the G20[19] proposal, enjoyed widespread support among developing countries as well as the Cairns group.

However, when then-President of the WTO General Council, Ambassador Carlos Perez Del Castillo, presented the revised version of the Cancún ministerial declaration on 25 August 2003, it became apparent that he had reproduced the EU-US agriculture document, ignoring completely the G20 proposal. The chapter related to NAMA also took up entirely the proposals of developed countries. This caused an immediate negative reaction. Brazil and the other members of the G20 therefore circulated their proposal as an official document at Cancún.

---

[18] In the meeting at which the Joint EU/US document was presented, Brazil stated that: 'Brazil welcomes the joint document EC-USA on agriculture. It is important that the two majors have come together on a proposal. Their concurrence is a necessary – but not sufficient – condition for progress in our negotiations' (Permanent Mission of Brazil in Geneva 2003a).

[19] The name 'G20' derived its name from both a proposal presented on 20 August 2003 and from support from twenty developing countries. The original G20 formation in August 2003 was: Argentina, Bolivia, Brazil, Chile, China, Colombia, Costa Rica, Ecuador, Guatemala, India, Mexico, Paraguay, Peru, Philippines, South Africa, Thailand and Uruguay.

The Cancún ministerial conference was the first moment of great impasse in the Doha Round. This resulted from the fact that the Castillo proposal, which drew from the EU-US document, reflected only the interests of the two biggest players, without allowing for the other members' interests to be accommodated. But there was also a new and extremely positive dimension to the endgame at Cancún. At Brazil's initiative, this involved the formation of a coalition of like-minded Southern countries (including Argentina, China, India and South Africa) and sufficient political power to counterbalance the relationship between developed and developing countries.

The G20 proposal sought to preserve the level of ambition enjoined by Doha's original mandate. This new bargaining coalition managed to successfully aggregate countries at relatively lower levels of development in a real conciliatory effort with developed countries. It could be said that the G20 found a way to clearly express the objectives of participating countries and demonstrate ways to accommodate other interests present in the multilateral trading system. In short, it was a strong, yet constructive position.

Reflecting on the Cancún Ministerial Conference, then-Brazilian Ambassador to the WTO Felipe de Seixas Corrêa suggested that:

> 1) while we would prefer to bring from Cancún a good agreement in agriculture, it was better to come back with no results than with a bad text; 2) we strengthened significantly our negotiating role through the creation and coordination of G20; 3) we showed that our bond to 'developing countries' is solid and operational; 4) we assured the prominence of agriculture as a central theme in the round; and 5) we got broad recognition from the world public opinion and from NGO's as to the fairness of our positions. At the same time, we exposed very clearly how fragile is the position of subsidizing countries.[20]

Following the Cancún Ministerial Conference, Brazil's negotiating position was strengthened by its continued capacity to lead the G20 and by establishing a constructive dialogue with the developed countries, particularly the EU, US and Japan. Brazil's efforts to advance the process of the Doha negotiations by coordinating the G20 and maintaining an understanding with the developed country majors contributed to the adoption of the July 2004 Framework, which set a basic structure for the agriculture negotiations and NAMA. The approval by the WTO General Council of the so-called July Framework Package was a decisive step to overcome the first great impasse of the Doha Round. The Framework

---

[20] Permanent Mission of Brazil in Geneva 2003b, 3.

Package incorporated effective measures related to SDT and emphasised the need for trade to complement development. In general, the following guidelines were established for the three pillars of the farm trade negotiations, namely domestic support, export competition and market access:

Domestic support: an ambitious reduction of cotton and other trade-distorting subsidies (including subsidy caps) was proposed. This included the proposal to create a new 'blue box' to accommodate the US's agricultural policy established by the 2002 Farm Bill (especially counter-cyclical payments) and the EU's Common Agricultural Policy, from 2003 and 2004.

Export competition: it was agreed that on a date to be decided, export subsidies would be eliminated. Further disciplines were established for export credit regulation, distorting practices used by state commercial enterprises and the abuse of food aid programmes.

Market access: a stated goal was to reduce the highest tariffs, with adjustments for specific sensitive products (e.g. market access through import quotas and smaller tariff cuts). However, the text on market access is rather vague and would therefore impose difficulties on future negotiations.

The July 2004 Framework reaffirmed paragraph 16 of the Doha mandate related to the NAMA negotiations. Attention was given to developing a non-linear formula to reduce tariffs, applied on a line-by-line basis. According to the document, the formula would have as its main objective the reduction or elimination of tariffs and *a priori*, would not exclude any line.[21] According to the Framework, non-consolidated tariffs should have a reduction of [2] times the tariff of the most favoured nation (MFN) applied tariff, with 2001 as a base year.[22] Besides, negotiators should also make an effort to convert all non-*ad valorem* tariffs into equivalent *ad valorem* tariffs, through a methodology to be determined. As to nomenclature, the document proposed that negotiations should initially use the Harmonised System of 1996 (SH1996) or the Harmonised System of 2002 (SH2002)[23], but the final result should be based on SH2002. In addition, it reiterated the mandate's position on

---

[21] In order to respect the principle of less-than-full-reciprocity, paragraph 8 of the July 2004 Framework Annex B covers possible flexibilities for the implementation of tariff reductions by developing countries and LDCs.

[22] For the calculus, importation data from the 1999/2001 period is used.

[23] The World Customs Organisation amends the Harmonised System every 5 years. The negotiations for these changes involve different reasons, the revision of SH publications, negotiations in the WTO realm, national legislative procedures, translations and conflict interests. For more information access: http://www.wcoomd.org/ie/En/Topics_Issues/topics_issues.html

non-agricultural environment goods, which sets the guidelines for the negotiation on sectorial initiatives[24], and points to the elimination of low duties by developed countries and others. The document also recognises the efforts on unilateral tariff reduction by developing countries. Finally, it should be noted that Brazil's active position in the WTO's dispute settlement process – particularly in the case of sugar (DS 266)[25] and cotton (DS 267)[26] – was part of Brazil's larger diplomatic strategy to guarantee that the goals of the Doha mandate would be effectively reached.[27]

3   THE DOHA ROUND MODALITIES AND JULY 2008

It was hoped that with the conclusion of the July 2004 Framework it would be possible to conclude the Doha Round in time to counter the

---

[24] In the sectoral initiatives, there are discussions on tariffs and NTBs. There is a need to determine a minimum number of participants for each sector, so that there can be a discussion made by a so-called 'critical mass'. The sectoral initiatives are: automobiles, bicycles and parts, shoes, electronics, sports equipment, medical and pharmaceutical equipment, precious stones and jewelry, raw materials, fishing and fishing products, wood products, IT products, forest and chemical products. Brazil's position is to not participate in sectorial initatives.

[25] DS266 European Communities – Export Subsidies on Sugar. Complainants: Australia, Brazil and Thailand. Respondent: European Communities. Third Parties: Australia; Barbados; Belize; Canada; China; Colombia; Cuba; Fiji; Guyana; India; Jamaica; Kenya; Madagascar; Malawi; Mauritius; New Zealand; Paraguay; St. Kitts and Nevis; Swaziland; Tanzania; Thailand; Trinidad and Tobago; United States; Côte d'Ivoire. Establishment of Panel: 29 August 2003. Adoption: 19 May 2005. Measure at issue: EC measures relating to subsidisation of the sugar industry (Common Organisation for Sugar - CMO): two categories of production quotas – 'A sugar' and 'B sugar' – were established under the CMO. Sugar produced in excess of A and B quota level is called 'C sugar', which is not eligible for domestic price support or direct export subsidies and must be exported. The Panel concluded that the EU was in fact exceeding the levels allowed to subsidised sugar export since 1995 and the ACP sugar and C sugar were receiving subsidies, proving the incoherence of those measures in regard of the Agricultural Agreement arrangements.

[26] DS267 United States – Upland Cotton. Complainant: Brazil. Respondent: United States. Third Parties: Argentina; Australia; Benin; Canada; Chad; China; Chinese Taipei; European Communities; India; New Zealand; Pakistan; Paraguay; Venezuela; Japan; Thailand. Establishment of Panel: 18 March 2003. Adoption: 21 March 2005. Article 21.5 Panel Report circulated: 18 December 2007. Article 21.5 Appellate Body Report circulated: 2 June 2008.Measure at issue: US agricultural 'domestic support' measures, export credit guarantees and other measures alleged to be export and domestic content subsidies. The Panel recommended that the programmes related to prohibited subsidies which were causing damage to Brazil would be suspended until 1 July 2005. The US appealed the decision to the Appellate Body. The Appellate Body report supported the Panel conclusions in the Enabling Clause; serious damage caused to Brazil; as well as the export credits programmes. Despite the fact that US had informed its intention to adopt the Dispute Settlement Body decisions, the recommendations about the prohibited and actionable ('amber light') subsidies were not applied.

[27] See Padua Lima and Rosenberg 2008.

probable prorogation, until the first semester of 2007, of Trade Promotion Authority (TPA) given by the US Congress to the Executive. Due to the peculiarities of the American internal process and the crucial role that the US plays in the multilateral trading system, it was imperative that the negotiations be finalised while TPA was still valid. However, as is well-known, this objective was not reached.

The Geneva talks that preceded the 2005 Hong Kong Ministerial Conference had aimed to conclude the modalities in Agriculture and NAMA in order to advance negotiations in other areas at the next ministerial conference. However, due to the deadlock already at Cancún, this was an extremely difficult objective to reach. During the preparatory period for the Hong Kong Ministerial Conference, Brazil tried to keep the cohesion of the G20 and to develop the group's proposal in a way for the modalities in agriculture to reflect the level of ambition in the original mandate, and to balance the three pillars of negotiation. The country also suggested that the G20 become a forum for discussing other themes from the DDA.

By the time the Hong Kong Ministerial Conference had finished (even with modest advances), Brazil agreed with the position taken by WTO Director-General Pascal Lamy that members should coordinate their movements in order to reach a successful Doha conclusion. While the suspension *sine die* of the Doha Round in July 2006 represented the second moment of great impasse in the DDA, it did not freeze the efforts for its conclusion. Therefore, draft texts on Agriculture and NAMA modalities were elaborated based on documents presented in July and August 2007 and revised in May and July of 2008, representing the efforts of member countries to conclude the Doha Round. Once again, Brazil has played a very active part in this process, whether as the coordinator of the G20 activities or as a spokesperson for the developing countries together with the G4. The last twelve months of 2008 can be considered to be the most intensive and productive phase in the Doha Round since it began in 2001 and since the agriculture negotiations began in March 2000.

In a general sense, the Brazilian position in the negotiation process was that the texts on modalities in agriculture and NAMA should clearly and completely include the contributions from developing countries and should also reflect a balance between the advances made in agriculture and concessions in NAMA, so that the horizontal negotiation process is able to begin. It was hoped that in this way it would be possible to overcome and unblock the negotiations suspended since July 2006. The table below synthesises positions taken by the EU, US, and different coalitions on agriculture in the Doha negotiations, particularly their evolution from the launch of the DDA to the deadlock at Cancun.

Table 1. Farm Trade Interests: 2001-2003

Negotiation	Group	Members	Profile and objectives
Initial position 2001	**Cairns Group**	*Argentina, Australia, Bolivia, Brazil, Canada, Chile, Colombia, Guatemala, Hungary, Indonesia, Malaysia, New Zealand, Paraguay, Philippines, South Africa, Thailand, Uruguay*	Major exporters of agricultural goods. Search for market access and the elimination/reduction of trade-distorting domestic support and export subsidies.
	US	*US*	Offensive in regards to market access. Defensive in export subsidies and domestic support issues. Offensive in the liberalisation of industrial goods.
	Europe	*EU-25*	Defensive in issues of domestic support, export subsidies and market access. Offensive in liberalisation of industrial goods.
	Special Treatment plaintiffs	*LDCs and other developing countries*	Aligned to developed countries, due to its position as vulnerable and poor countries that demand privileges to protect exported commodities.
Cancún 2003	**US-EU**	*US + EU-25*	Joint proposal that strongly reduces Doha Mandate's ambitions on agriculture. Defensive in agriculture and offensive in NAMA.
	G20	*Argentina, Bolivia, Brazil, Chile, China, Colombia, Costa Rica, Ecuador, Guatemala, India, Mexico, Paraguay, Peru, Philippines, South Africa, Thailand, Uruguay*	Proposal that tries to preserve the objectives from the Doha Mandate – which would be a significant advance in the liberalisation of agricultural trade – and at the same time accommodating the interests of developed countries.
	G10	*Bulgaria, Chinese Taipei, Iceland, Israel, Korea, Japan, Liechtenstein, Mauritius, Norway, Switzerland*	In general, support of EU-US platforms. Interest in issues that are not specifically related to trade.

Negotiation	Group	Members	Profile and objectives
	G33 + G90	*Antigua/Barbuda, Botswana, Cuba, Dominican Republic, Haiti, Honduras, Indonesia, Jamaica, Kenya, Mongolia, Nicaragua, Nigeria, Pakistan, Panama, Peru, Philippines, Suriname, Tanzania, Trinidad and Tobago, Turkey, Uganda, Venezuela, Zambia and other LDCs*	General support for G20 but with concerns regarding sensitive products and preferential treatment

Source: Jank 2005, 32.

From 21-26 July 2008, a mini-ministerial meeting with a Trade Negotiations Committee (TNC) session took place in Geneva with the goal of reaching agreement on the agriculture and NAMA modalities. It is believed that this is the essential step to unblock the Doha Round and get to a new negotiation phase, closer to its conclusion. However, according to the Brazilian position, there were still many obstacles to reaching this objective. While high food prices during the first half of 2008 provided an incentive for reducing trade-distorting subsidies, the resistance from developed countries to advance significantly in their positions was still solid. Brazil and the G20 felt that it was essential to reduce domestic support measures and to introduce product specific disciplines to limit the concentration of subsidies in some determined products. Due to the difficulties encountered in the agricultural negotiations, the possibility of advancing NAMA was also compromised. Brazil has emphasised that there should be a balance between agricultural and NAMA modalities so that it will be possible to accommodate the interests of developed and developing countries. However, in Geneva the US did not reduce substantially the upper limit for domestic support – the lower limit of US$13 billion represents more than two times the current spending – and the EU did not expand market access for sensitive products. There was thus no reason for Brazil, India, South Africa and other developing countries to agree to a rapid reduction of industrial tariff limits. In the end, the July 2008 mini-ministerial did not reach an agreement, mainly due to disagreement over the Special Safeguard Mechanism. The impasse remains. However, the onset of the global economic crisis in late 2008 has raised the stakes for urgently concluding the WTO's DDA.

4   IMPACT OF THE FINANCIAL CRISIS ON BRAZIL

The first signs of the US financial crisis were visible by the end of 2006. However, it was only in the second half of 2008 that the Brazilian economy was affected by the deterioration in global financial conditions following the bankruptcy of the fourth largest investment bank in the US, Lehman Brothers. Until then, most economic indicators for the Brazilian economy were very positive. Until September 2008, not even a decline in the high prices of the country's commodity exports had affected the economy's performance as a whole. The consequences of the international panic that followed the bankruptcy of Lehman Brothers were at first minimised by the Brazilian authorities, who were extremely confident[28] about the dynamism of the domestic market and the integrity of the domestic financial system. However, the dramatic restriction of credit in the international market, the sharp plunge of the Brazilian stock market and a sudden change to the recent appreciation of the Brazilian currency buried the optimistic expectations of both the government and private sector that Brazil could possibly emerge unscathed from the worst economic crisis since 1930. The acute deterioration of credit conditions in Brazil, especially with regard to exports, the devaluation of the currency (which negatively impacted on big companies involved in operations with currency derivatives) and a sharp decline in the stock value of Brazilian companies forced the Brazilian authorities to take a series of emergency actions. These included several measures to expand the economy's liquidity by: reducing reserve requirements; promoting dollar auctions; creating special credit lines for the productive sector in general and more particularly for exporters; postponing the payment of taxes; and expanding the resources available for public banks, amongst others.[29]

In October 2008, the Ministry of Economy decided to call the first emergency meeting of the financial G20, which was then led by Brazil.[30] The Brazilian authorities believed that given the repercussions and gravity of the crisis, as well as the interdependency of most economies, only coordinated measures could lead to an adequate solution of the serious international situation. In the words of Foreign Minister Celso

---

[28] In a speech on 4 October 2008, President Lula stated that: 'The crisis is a tsunami for USA, and if it reaches Brazil, it will only be an insignificant wave'. This quote became notorious and was widely publicised by the press.

[29] Especially for the National Bank for the Economic and Social Development (BNDES), *Banco do Brasil* and *Caixa Econômica Federal*.

[30] The financial G20 is composed of the Finance Ministers and Central Bank Governors from the following countries or authorities: Argentina, Australia, Brazil, Canada, China, EU, France, Germany, India, Indonesia, Italy, Japan, Mexico, Russia, Saudi Arabia, South Africa, South Korea, Turkey, the United Kingdom and the US.

Amorim: 'This crisis points out the need to coordinate with other developing economies, as for example, the so-called BRICS. We have a huge trade flow with these countries, and it is growing, but we cannot be vulnerable to the credit difficulties that might come from rich countries' problem'.[31]

The Brazilian monetary authorities for long resisted reducing interest rates, which serve as a reference for the Brazilian economy.[32] Only in January 2009, following the free-fall of economic activity during the last three months of 2008[33], did they initiate the process of carefully reducing interest rates.[34] The first six months of 2009 have seen continued negative economic headlines globally and in Brazil. With regard to international trade, the drastic reduction of exports and the plunge in the price of commodities, combined with the severe restriction on credit, directly affected the Brazilian economy. It is extremely worrying that as a consequence of the international crisis, the threat of protectionism is becoming more concrete.

Up to this point, the Brazilian government had resisted relatively well the inevitable pressures to increase protection for domestic producers or react to protectionist measures adopted by Brazil's trading partners. In particular, the non-automatic licenses imposed by Argentina on many products exported by Brazil and the 'Buy America' clause of the US fiscal programme sparked a strong reaction from Brazilian productive sectors. It is worth mentioning that in January 2009, following the first negative result for Brazil's trade balance in almost eight years[35], the Department of Foreign Trade from the Ministry of Development, Industry and International Trade (DECEX/MDIC) sought to impose a previous importing license on more than 60 per cent of Brazilian imports (around 3000 items). However, the strong reaction from importing sectors[36] that

---

[31] *Folha de São Paulo*, 8 October 2008.

[32] SELIC is the basic interest rate for the Brazilian economy.

[33] During the last three months of 2008, Brazilian gross domestic product (GDP) declined 3.6 per cent compared to the three months before that. However, the solid performance the economy during the preceding quarters still allowed the country to record a growth rate of 5.1 per cent for 2008. The dismal performance of the economy towards the end of 2008 was still a major shock for the government and private sector.

[34] Even with the reduction of the nominal value of the SELIC interest rate from 13.75 per cent to 11.25 per cent in the first months of 2009, Brazil still has the highest real interest rate in the world.

[35] In January 2009, Brazil's trade balance recorded a negative result of US$518-million, the first negative result since March 2001. Furthermore, since November 2000 the country did not register a monthly deficit greater than US$500-million, as was the case in January 2009 (see www.mdic.gov.br).

[36] The main sectors affected by the imposition of previous licenses were the flour and wheat industry, plastic, rubber, iron and steel, cast iron works, copper and aluminum, capital stock, electric machinery and equipment, textiles, transport material (auto-parts), automobiles and tractors, optical appliances and surgical instruments.

would be directly affected by the imposition of these licenses led to quick annulment of the controversial measure.

A recent study by the World Bank[37] on protectionist measures adopted by the G20[38] following the November 2008 summit includes a reduction of the Tax on Industrialised Products (IPI) on the sale of new vehicles (automobiles and trucks), which was established by the Brazilian government in December 2008 and valid for three renewable months.[39] While the reduction of the IPI could, in fact, be qualified as a fiscal incentive, it is very modest when compared to the vast stimulus provided by developed countries, particularly the US. The World Bank study recognises that it is impossible for developing countries to match the vast incentives given by developed countries (a point South Africa has reiterated too, as Brendan Vickers notes in Chapter 7). Given the clarifications above, it appears that Brazil's position at international meetings in opposing protectionist measures reflects the country's practical behaviour thus far.

Nonetheless, several factors suggest that Brazil may present a faster recovery compared to other big developing and developed countries. First, the Brazilian economy has a more modest grade of openness when compared to other developing economies[40], especially China. Ironically, the non-adoption of the Asian model of growth based on exports (previously pointed out as one of the main reasons for the poor performance of the Brazilian economy in the past), is now one of the reasons for believing that Brazil's recovery might happen faster. Second, the regulation of the Brazilian financial system, formerly considered excessive, has guaranteed the greater integrity of this sector when compared to more advanced countries. Last but not least is the irony of ironies: the extremely restrictive Brazilian monetary policy, inherited from the difficult process of internal price stabilisation and one of the major obstacles for better performance in past years, still offers space for maneuver. In a scenario where most developed countries have already exhausted the possibility of reducing interest rates (which is now operating at nominal rates close to zero and negative real rates), Brazil still has a positive interest rate that floats above 6 per cent per year. With a degree of sarcasm, it is possible to say

---

[37] World Bank 2009.

[38] At the G20 summit in Washington, DC in November 2009, the G20 agreed to suspend, for a minimum period of twelve months, the adoption of any new trade barrier as way to stimulate foreign trade.

[39] The reduction of the IPI on new automobiles and trucks was extended for another three months on 30 March 2009, with the condition that companies will not reduce their levels of employment during this period. At the same time, there was also a reduction of IPI on some items used by the civil construction sector.

[40] China's grade of openness is 63 per cent, Russia's 48 per cent, India's, 32 per cent and Brazil's around 21 per cent of the GDP.

that Brazil's advantages in confronting the present global crisis are its recognised internal handicaps; its resistance to embracing the globalisation process; and its restless insistence on keeping the multilateral trading system as the overriding sphere for trade negotiation. The possibility of economic recovery in a shorter period of time than many other economies, coupled with the fact that Brazil has consolidated its position as a key player in international negotiations related to trade, energy, the environment and the reconstruction of global governance rules, suggest that the country's leading global role will be enhanced during this difficult moment for the international economy.

5   CONCLUSION

Brazil is a competitive exporter of many goods that are highly protected in world markets. For this reason, the country's participation in international trade is still modest. The main products exported by Brazil are: soy, meat, orange juice, textiles, foot wear and iron products. The nature of Brazil's insertion into the global economy means that it must effectively deploy its trade negotiating capacity and trade defense instruments to ensure greater market access for its exporters, particularly in developed countries. This suggests that the priority that Brazil ascribes to the multilateral trading system represented by the WTO – as well as Brazilian activism in the rules-based system – must be maintained in the future. Evidently, Brazil still believes in the possibility of concluding the Doha Round, without a significant loss in the original level of ambition.

However, the Doha mandate put the US and the other developed countries in a very sensitive and defensive position. The year 2003 will be marked for the way that the US started to manage the negotiation of regional trade agreements in response to the difficulties encountered in the DDA. The new trade negotiation strategy of the Bush administration consisted of concentrating efforts in advancing commercial discussions and stimulating initiatives on multiple fronts of trade negotiations (see Geoffrey Allen Pigman's discussion of US-Brazilian relations in Chapter 3). According to Bergsten[41], the US went back to the strategy of so-called 'competitive liberalization'[42], even if its objectives were very different

---

[41] Bergsten 1996.

[42] The concept of 'competitive liberalisation' (developed by the United States Trade Representative), was used to qualify the process of competition between multilateral and preferential agreements. The agility in obtaining preferential agreements, according to this idea, expresses the ability of certain countries in recognising and taking advantage of the opportunities that result from bilateral agreements proposed by the US and, in that sense, the new American trade policy would induce countries that are more inclined to protectionism to accept the rules of free trade.

from the Uruguay Round.[43] It can be argued that this strategy reinforced Washington's defensive position in the Doha Round: on the one hand, the US promoted preferential commercial negotiations, and on the other hand, it favored the application of North American normative models inside of these free trade agreements.

The current financial crisis in the US (with a significant impact on domestic employment and income) has generated growing discomfort vis-à-vis globalisation and consequently trade liberalisation. In a certain way, the measures adopted thus far by the new US Administration of President Barack Obama appear to reflect protectionist yearnings within American society. The new government will have to continue to deal with both the disappointment generated by the current financial crisis (with repercussions in the realm of trade policy), as well as the erosion of the US's international credibility during the Bush years.

Considering that the necessary revision of foreign policy by the new American government with the objective of reconstructing USA's international leadership and the exhaustion of the competitive liberalisation strategy conducted by the Bush administration, it is possible to think that a constructive position by USA to conclude the Doha Round would strongly collaborate to this major goal of restoring credibility and leadership. However, it is a difficult but essential standing: to avoid the erroneously easiest road of protectionism and to strengthen the multilateral system of trade.

Finally, Brazilian government's critical position on free trade agreements in the north-American model, as well as the persistence in keeping essential issues for the country's interests in the realm of the multilateral negotiations, will probably show itself to be the most correct option, especially due to the very serious international financial crisis.

---

[43] It should be noted that until the Uruguay Round (1986-1994), the US was not only considered the creator of the multilateral trade system but also the absolute leader of this trade regime, having signed only one preferential agreement (with Israel). It could be argued that the difficulties in obtaining the necessary consensus to conclude this round of multilateral negotiation produced the strategy known as 'competitive liberalisation', according to which the countries that are more prone to free trade would create pressure on the most resistant ones in the direction of greater trade liberalisation through the execution of preferential agreements. In this sense, the search for preferential agreements at that time was seen by the American government as a proper way to pressure for the unblocking of trade negotiations at the multilateral realm, considered as a priority.

REFERENCES

Baldwin, Richard and Simon Evenett. 2009. *The collapse of global trade, murky protectionism, and the crisis: Recommendations for the G20.* London: A VoxEU.org publication, Centre for Economic Policy Research.

Bergsten, C. Fred. 1996. Competitive Liberalization and Global Free Trade: A Vision for the Early 21st Century. Working Paper 96-15. Washington, DC: Institute for International Economics.

Bergsten, C. Fred. 2008. World Trade in Risk. Policy Brief. Washington, DC: Peterson Institute of International Economics, May.

Bresser Pereira, Luiz Carlos. 1991. *A crise da América Latina Consenso de Washington ou crise fiscal. Pesquisa e Planejamento Econômico* 21(1):3-23.

Furtado, Celso. 2007. *Formação Econômica do Brasil-* 34ª ed. São Paulo: Companhia das Letras.

Gasques J.G., E. T. Bastos, M. P. R. Bacchi and J.C.P.R Conceição. 2004. Condicionantes da produtividade da agropecuária Brasileira. *Revista de Política Agrícola* 13(3):73-90.

Hufbauer, Gary Clyde and Ben Goodrich. 2003. More Pain, More Gain: Politics and Economics of Eliminating Tariffs. International Economics Policy Brief PB03-8.

Jank, Marcos Sawaya and Mário de Queiroz Monteiro Jales. 2004. On Product, Box, and Blame-Shifting: Negotiating Frameworks for Agriculture in the WTO Doha Round. Paper presented at the second IDB-CEPII Conference on 'The Economic Implications of the Doha Development Agenda for Latin America and the Caribbean', São Paulo, 14 May.

Jank, Marcos Sawaya. 2005. Agricultura. In *O Brasil e os Grandes Temas do Comércio Internacional,* edited by Vera Thorstensen and Marcos Sawaya Jank. São Paulo: Aduaneiras.

Padua Lima, Maria L. M., Allexandro Mori Coelho, Allexandro Mori, Samir Cury and Sergio Goldbaum. 2007. *Brazil: Impacts of the proposals for tariff reductions in non-agricultural goods (NAMA).* Rio de Janeiro: Revista Brasileira de Comércio Exterior.

Padua Lima, Maria L. M. and Barbara Rosenberg (eds.). 2008. *O Brasil e o contencioso na OMC.* SP: Editora Saraiva.

Permanent Mission of Brazil in Geneva. 2002a. *Carta de Genebra* 1(1), January.

Permanent Mission of Brazil in Geneva. 2002b. *Carta de Genebra* 1(2), March.

Permanent Mission of Brazil in Geneva. 2003a. *Carta de Genebra* 2(6), September.

Permanent Mission of Brazil in Geneva. 2003b. *Carta de Genebra* 2(7), October.

Tavares, Maria da Conceição. 1972. *Da substituição de importações ao capitalismo financeiro.* Rio de Janeiro: Zahar.

Thorstensen, Vera. 1999. *OMC – Organização Mundial do Comércio: As Regras do Comércio Internacional e a Rodada do Milênio.* São Paulo: Aduaneiras.

Thorstensen, Vera and Marcos Sawaya Jank. 2005. *O Brasil e os Grandes Temas do Comércio Internacional.* São Paulo: Editora Aduaneiras.

World Bank. 2009. *Trade Protection: Incipient but Worrisome Trends.* Washington, DC: World Bank.

WTO. 2000. Proposal by the Cairns Group to the Committee on Agriculture Special Session. 10 November, G/AG/NG/W/54.

WTO. 2001. Doha Ministerial Declaration. 20 November, WT/MIN(01)/Dec/1.

AMIT SHOVON RAY AND SABYASACHI SAHA

5. SHIFTING COORDINATES OF INDIA'S STANCE IN THE WTO: UNDERSTANDING THE DOMESTIC AND INTERNATIONAL ECONOMIC DRIVERS

India remained a virtually closed economy for nearly four decades after its independence in 1947. Its inward-looking development strategy was significantly inspired by the Soviet model of development. Trade received very little attention in the foundation of India's post-colonial development strategy. The notion of *self-reliance* played a major role in defining the *norm* of development in India. The aspiration was perhaps to mimic the development trajectories of the 'advanced' west, although very much within the framework of import-substitution and self-reliance. It was perhaps important to the Indian policymakers to signal to the rest of the world that India could do whatever the advanced nations can. Accordingly, a diversified industrial production base was meticulously planned out for India, ranging from simple consumer items to sophisticated capital goods and heavy machinery. This drive towards self-reliance also prompted India to engage in highly complex and resource-intensive activities like space research or nuclear technology. The notion of natural comparative advantage took a back seat in this planning process.[1]

Notwithstanding India's closed economy policy stance, India has been one of the initial signatories to the General Agreement on Tariffs and Trade (GATT) 1947, which was formed following the Second World War. GATT was as an effort on the part of the developed world faced with mixed fortunes at the end of the war, to discipline themselves in trade in goods and to limit the spread of proactive protectionist policies by individual national governments. India in-principle was supposed to have accepted the mandate, but it remained firm on its trade and development policies aimed at self-reliance and import-substitution.

The flipside of this protectionist trade policy regime soon revealed itself in the form of inefficiencies of various kinds. For one thing, there was no incentive to keep pace with the fast changing global technology frontier in many of the manufacturing sectors, which resulted in Indian

---

[1] Ray 2006.

A. Narlikar, B. Vickers (eds.), Leadership and Change in the Multilateral Trading System, 97–120.
© 2009 Republic of Letters Publishing. All rights reserved.

industry becoming technologically backward and inefficient with respect to global standards of costs and quality. From the mid 1980s, a technological view of development started gaining momentum in India's development policy. It was increasingly realised that being able to produce everything could not be the end-all goal. It is very important to be able to do things 'efficiently' as well. That may require opening up the doors to latest technological development on the global frontier, quite a departure from its earlier protectionist policy regime. This, in a sense, marked the beginning of India's policy of liberalisation.[2]

But initially (during the latter half of the 1980s), this process was mostly limited to liberalising particular aspects of the control system both in the spheres of manufacturing and trade, without any major change affecting the system itself in any fundamental way. These attempts of liberalisation have, however, been arguably piecemeal and somewhat ad-hoc without a comprehensive programme of reforms that some of the other inward-looking economies had already adopted (including China from 1978).

It was the year 1991 that marked a radical departure from the past when, faced with an exceptionally severe balance of payments crisis, India launched a massive economic reforms package consisting of short-term stabilisation measures along with a longer-term programme of comprehensive structural reforms. These reforms were much wider and deeper than earlier piecemeal attempts, and which ushered in a complete paradigmatic shift in policymaking that now emphasised not only liberalisation of government controls, a larger role for the private sector as the engine of growth, freer operation of market and competitive forces in order to boost efficiency, but greater integration with the world economy through free and unrestricted trade flows.

Interestingly, the Uruguay Round of the GATT negotiations began in 1986, precisely when India's development policymaking process was at a watershed. By the time India launched its massive economic reforms package in 1991, marking a paradigm shift in its policy, the Uruguay Round negotiations were well under way, paving the path towards Marrakesh in 1994 and the establishment of the World Trade Organisation (WTO). India's attitude towards the WTO may be best understood against this perspective of the changing mental frame of the Indian policymakers from the mid 1980s onwards, both reinforcing each other.

It is hardly surprising that India remained a *cautious* and somewhat *passive* player during the initial years of the Uruguay Round negotiations, given its long legacy of inward-looking development strategy

---

[2] Ray 2006.

and protectionist trade policy regime. With the liberalisation of its trade regime from 1991, India could perhaps slowly perceive an alignment of its policy interests with the core philosophy of the WTO. Free trade and greater engagement with the world economy was therefore no more a taboo among Indian policymakers. However, this is not to suggest that the 1991-reforms made India euphoric about the prospects of WTO and its consequences for India. It is natural that the Indian intelligentsia remained rather sceptical about potential vulnerabilities of the nation from the sudden exposure to the world economy. It was only in the area of manufacturing that India's unilateral trade liberalisation was carried out during the early1990s. Therefore during the Uruguay Round, India was clearly reluctant to move beyond trade in manufactured goods at the WTO.

The post-Marrakesh period is primarily identified with negotiations at three ministerial conferences, namely Singapore (1996), Geneva (1998) and Seattle (1999). This phase saw multiple instances of loss of mutual confidence among negotiating partners, in spite of the Marrakesh agreement signed by all members that led to the establishment of the WTO with sector specific commitments to liberalise trade regimes. Developed countries tried to use the Singapore (1996) platform to broaden the agenda of WTO to areas popularly known as the Singapore Issues, namely investment, competition policy, transparency in government procurement and trade facilitation. They also wanted to introduce core labour issues in the negotiations. Developing countries including India objected to such designs, arguing that the Singapore Issues were essentially non-trade issues and for negotiating labour standards, the International Labour Organisation (ILO) should be the right platform and not the WTO. Geneva (1998) was an intermediate phase where members were keener on facilitating the process of negotiations by working on issues pertaining to agriculture and services, already mandated. Instead of whipping up the Singapore Issues, the Geneva ministerial only endorsed the earlier mandate of continuing the *work programmes* on these issues. But Seattle (1999) proved to be yet another failed attempt by the developed world to promote an expansionary agenda within the WTO, incorporating labour standards and issues of coherence in global economic architecture (the Singapore Issues). For the present analysis, it is worth noting that even towards the end of the Uruguay Round (Seattle in 1999), the US, EC and Japan remained stubborn on anti-dumping and agricultural subsidies.[3]

All this prompted India to take a hard line on not endorsing a new round at Doha in 2001, arguing that commitments of the Uruguay Round

---

[3] http://www.indianembassy.org/Policy/WTO/overview.html

has not been fulfilled (especially on the part of the developed countries as mandated in Article 20 of the Agreement on Agriculture and hence it is pointless to initiate a new *round* of negotiating agenda. Perhaps India was also being wary of the various *dispute settlement* cases arising out of its Marrakesh commitments throughout the latter half of the 1990s.[4] This is hardly surprising, given India's lack of capacity to tackle these cases, especially against developed nations that were much better equipped with legal manpower and expertise in these matters.

In the end, India reluctantly agreed to launch the Doha Development Agenda (DDA) in 2001. India was quite happy with the outcome of the Doha Ministerial Conference because of its success on three issues: several concessions on implementation issues, weakening of the Agreement on Trade-related Aspects of Intellectual Property Rights (TRIPS) to accommodate access to medicine and public health concerns of developing countries, and most significantly keeping the Singapore Issues at bay.[5] In fact, it was post-Doha that India emerged as a leading and key negotiating partner at the WTO and assumed the role of a pro-active player in the whole process. There was a clear shift from its earlier position of cautious, or at best passive, participation.

1   INDIA'S SHIFTING COORDINATES: SECTORAL PERSPECTIVES

To understand the shifting coordinates of India's stance at the WTO, more specifically, let us briefly examine its position with respect to agriculture, IPR and services. These also happen to be some of the most important areas of India's engagement with the WTO.

Agriculture

Before the Uruguay, agriculture essentially remained outside the purview of the GATT.[6] GATT in a way allowed export subsidies on agricultural primary products and most certainly allowed import restrictions under certain conditions. Farm lobby politics in developed countries ensured high levels of domestic support for their agricultural sector, completely distorting agricultural trade. The Uruguay Round of multilateral trade deliberations thus rightly started approaching issues beyond import restrictions to bring down the prevailing scale of distortions in trade in agricultural products, primarily in the form of massive farm subsidies

---

[4] Panagariya 2002b.
[5] Panagariya 2002a.
[6] Panagariya 2005.

offered by developed countries. The Agreement on Agriculture, which came into force on 1 January 1995, intended to set the ground for a fair and market oriented agricultural trading system with reform programmes comprising of specific commitments to reduce farm support, export subsidies and to promote market access within a stipulated time frame.[7]

For India, agriculture is a major area of concern, as it supports the livelihood of 65-70 per cent of India's population of 1.02 billion. Any multilateral negotiation on agricultural market access and farm subsidies is bound to have its implications for Indian agriculture and its vast population dependent on it. In an attempt to protect this vulnerability and to ensure food security, India continued with a protectionist trade policy in agriculture. Agricultural trade was never quite favourably considered, even to the extent of imposing export taxes on certain food crops. Moreover, India continued to pursue its commitment to provide various input subsides to agriculture, concomitant with its policy objectives of food security, rural development, rural employment and crop diversification.

Therefore, India's stance on agriculture at the WTO has always been somewhat defensive. It has maintained its demand for flexibilities to carry out with its measures of support for agriculture and rural development and therefore be exempt from any reduction commitments on these counts.[8] According to the initial submissions made by India at the WTO, it is seen that product specific support in India is negative while total amount of non-product specific support is well below the *de minimis* level.[9] This amounted to negative aggregate measure of support (AMS) for India, implying that Indian agriculture is net taxed. On the tariff front, although India's bound rates have been quite high, the applied rates for major items, such as rice, wheat, pulses and sugar, made them at par with world prices. Indian agricultural exports did not receive any form of direct export subsidies, although selected areas like horticulture and floriculture received some support in the form of export profit tax exemptions.[10]

Against this backdrop, we may look at India's stance on agriculture at Doha. Regarding market access, India demanded that developed countries must bring down their bound tariff rates, and suggested the creation of a separate safeguard mechanism, along the lines of the Special Agricultural Safeguard (SSG), for food security in developing countries. In fact, India continued to emphasise on food security as a prime *non-trade concern* and wanted that any measures adopted for its poverty alleviation

---

[7] Panagariya 2005.
[8] Mattoo and Subramanian 2003.
[9] Pal 2005.
[10] Mattoo and Subramanian 2003.

programme, food security and other social objectives, be exempt from any reduction commitments, while it demanded that developed countries should cut back their domestic farm support below the *de minimis* levels.[11]

Given that agriculture was recognised to be at the heart of the DDA,[12] the Doha Ministerial Declaration flagged off the Doha Round with promises of substantial improvements in agricultural market access and reductions in trade distorting domestic support in agriculture, while paying *equal* attention to developing country concerns:

> We agree that special and differential treatment for developing countries shall be an integral part of all elements of the negotiations and shall be embodied in the schedules of concessions and commitments and as appropriate in the rules and disciplines to be negotiated, so as to be operationally effective and to enable developing countries to effectively take account of their development needs, including food security and rural development. We take note of the non-trade concerns reflected in the negotiating proposals submitted by Members and confirm that non-trade concerns will be taken into account in the negotiations as provided for in the Agreement on Agriculture for special and differential treatment to be made an integral part of agricultural negotiations and for including non-trade concerns in the negotiating agenda.[13]

Post-Doha and in the lead up to Cancún, the EU failed to keep up to its Doha commitments to come up with a meaningful proposal for cutting down their enormous volumes of farm subsidies. Furthermore, the US Farm Bill 2002, meant to roll out additional support to their domestic agricultural sector, was a big blow to the progress made at Doha. Just a few weeks ahead of Cancún, the two main accused in the distortion of global trade in agriculture, the EU and the US, struck an alliance to come up with a joint text on agriculture (explored by Maria Lima in her chapter, Chapter 4). The developing country lobby was in no position to accept the EU-US mandate for Cancún negotiations. Led by Brazil, China, India and South Africa, the developing countries forged a broad-based alliance prior to Cancún, which took shape in the formation of the Group of 20 (G20), to ensure a level playing field in agriculture trade and fulfilment of developmental objectives of the Doha Round. Cancún failed because of strong opposition of the chair's text (the Derbez Draft) by the G20, the African, Caribbean and Pacific (ACP) group and the

---

[11] Chakraborty 2004.
[12] Ismail 2007.
[13] WTO 2001.

LDC group. India strongly objected to the Derbez Draft on the basis of its concerns pertaining to the issue of domestic farm support as well as the draft's intention to initiate negotiations on Singapore Issues without explicit consensus.[14]

India as a part of the G20 continued its attempt to reach an agreement through informal negotiations with the US, the EU and other members in order to break the stalemate. But it was at the initiative of the US that an agriculture negotiating group comprising of the US, EU, Australia, India and Brazil was formed in the third week of March, 2004 (which already had several meetings earlier) and came up with a the July 2004 Draft. This draft emphasised the elimination of export subsidies, reduction in farm support, promises of substantial market access and lower reduction commitments (SDT) for developing countries.[15]

There was minimal progress in Hong Kong beyond the July 2004 framework, the most significant being the hesitant offer by the EU to eliminate export subsidies by 2013 (see Manfred Elsig's discussion of EU trade policy in Chapter 2). India was successful in getting conditional flexibilities in determining the products (under special products) which need to be safeguarded to ensure food security, rural development and the livelihood of poor farmers and under Special Safeguard Mechanism (SSM) to use both price and quantity instruments in curbing import surges.[16] Developing countries agreed to make concessions in non-agricultural market access (NAMA), but linked it to market access negotiations in agriculture, so that possibilities that developed countries making more in roads into the developing country markets with developing countries still facing high levels of protection and distortions in global markets for products of export interest to them can be minimised.

But post-Hong Kong, it turned out that the US became more cautious and inflexible on the issue of farm support, while the EU continued to appear somewhat flexible on market access. *The three controversial issues of agricultural market access, agricultural domestic support and market access for industrial tariffs (NAMA) posed a serious threat to the ongoing negotiations. The EU had to improve its offer on agricultural market access, the US its offer on agricultural domestic support and the G20 its offer on NAMA.*

To take forward the negotiations at this juncture, the G6 (a small group of major stakeholders in the above three issues: EU, US, Australia, Japan, India and Brazil) started having meetings to sort out the differences. The G6 ministers, in spite of repeated meetings, failed to make any real

---

[14] Ismail 2007.
[15] Ismail 2007.
[16] Oxfam 2005.

progress on the core issue of agriculture. This resulted in the suspension of the Doha Round in July 2006 at Geneva. Later this G6 shrunk to the so-called G4 with US, EU, Brazil and India. The G4 ministers negotiated in Delhi, Brussels and Potsdam during 2007 to invigorate the Round. But talks collapsed in Potsdam on 21 June 2007. Unlike in earlier occasions when EU was the most uncompromising party, it was now the US that adopted an extremely inflexible stance.[17]

Intellectual property rights (IPRs)

India's position on making IPR a standard for the global trading system has seen a sea change. India's *shifting* stance on IPR at the GATT/WTO spanning over entire period of the Uruguay and the Doha Rounds (1986 till date) has drawn a lot of attention in contemporary analysis. India initially had a strong opposition to include IPRs within the ambit of trade negotiations. But over time this defensive approach became more moderate and finally turned somewhat aggressive with respect to specific dimensions.

At the Uruguay Round, developed nations (the US, in particular), under pressure from their pharmaceutical corporate lobby, proposed to introduce a uniformly strong IPR regime on all nations as part of a multilateral trading agreement through the TRIPS agreement.[18] This was in spite of the fact that a strong IPR goes against the core philosophy of the WTO's principle of promoting competition and free trade.[19] Moreover, there is now a large body of theoretical and empirical literature, firmly establishing that IPR regime must be endogenously determined within the economy, depending on the technological learning and capability levels of the country in question. Exogenous imposition of a strong IPR regime may severely hinder the process of technological catch up. Ironically, there is historical evidence to suggest that the developed world has had the flexibility to adopt an appropriate IPR regime during their process of development and technological learning. Countries like Switzerland, Germany, Japan and Italy did not adopt a strong product for a long time.[20]

India, beginning in the 1970s and well into the 1980s, was going through a phase of 'know-why' oriented technological learning. It was building up process development capabilities through reverse engineering – both infringing process for off-patent items and non-infringing processes

---

[17] Ismail 2007.

[18] They wanted to enjoy their patent monopolies across countries by enforcing uniform IPR protection globally through the WTO.

[19] Machlup (1958) discusses how the free trade movement of the nineteenth century strongly opposed patents.

[20] Ray and Bhaduri 2008.

for patented ones. This was possible because of its 1970 patent act which allowed only process (and not product patents) on chemical substances.[21] Switching over to strong product patent regime at that point would have put a pre-mature halt to this technological capability building process. The Indian pharmaceutical industry lobby, which was experiencing a phenomenal growth and development based on its process development capabilities (often referred to as the *process revolution*), was extremely apprehensive about the TRIPS agreement. India's strong opposition to TRIPS in the initial years of the Uruguay Round appears to be natural and justified.

A clear shift in India's attitude was visible post-1989. Many believe that this sudden change of stance was a result of trade threats from the US (Super 301), which Geoffrey Allen Pigman explores in Chapter 3. Perhaps, it was a merely strategic move for India to adopt this changing stance towards TRIPS in 1989, as a tool for extracting concessions in other aspects of WTO negotiations.

But during the 1990s, the domestic business interests also got sharply divided. The associations dominated by multinational corporations came out openly in support of the TRIPS. Some major domestic players, especially in pharmaceuticals, felt that the technological levels they had reached by then warranted a stronger patent regime for their long run business interests. But a large segment of the domestic industry, still at a nascent stage of technological catch up, continued to pose opposition.[22]

Having signed the TRIPS agreement in 1994, India was mandated to change its patent regime by 2005. The domestic pressure was now enormous. Concerns were expressed about the potential increase in drug prices and its adverse effects on access to medicine and public health in India. While the pressure from the industrial lobby was getting weaker and milder compared to what it was in the 1980s, the opposition from the civil society lobby against TRIPS was gaining momentum. This did have an influence on India's position on IPR yet again.

At Doha, India along with other developing countries notably Brazil and South Africa (constituting the IBSA group), pushed for an explicit acknowledgement of the primacy of the member countries' rights to protect public health and promote access to affordable medicines. This was achieved in the form of a Declaration on TRIPS and Public Health at Doha that came as major victory for the developing world and an important feather in IBSA's cap at WTO negotiations. The declaration recognises members' 'right to grant compulsory licenses and the freedom to determine the grounds upon which such licenses are granted'. Moreover

---

[21] Ray 2005.
[22] Ramanna 2002.

it grants each member the 'right to determine what constitutes a national emergency or other circumstances of extreme urgency' in implementing TRIPS.

Two other IPR related issues were raised by India at Doha. First, it wanted to extend protection under 'geographical indication' (GI) beyond wine and spirits, to other products. The entire episode of the artificial development of rice variety similar to the Indian *Basmati* rice by the US agro-company Ricetec was under scanner. Second, it demanded restrictions on misappropriation of biological and genetic resources and traditional knowledge (TK).[23]

India's position on TRIPS has remained unchanged post-Doha up to Hong Kong. Presently it has focused on three prime concerns: technology transfer, biodiversity and geographical indications. India is of the view that LDCs face serious difficulties in procuring new technologies which could be overcome by suitable safeguards in the domestic IPR laws of LDCs and thereby check the sole rent seeking objectives of the developed country firms in many cases. The other aspect of north-south technology transfer is the growing tendency of intra-firm transfer of technology backed by market seeking motives that relies more on intellectual property protection. This has prompted India to take up the case of technology transfer at the WTO, so that adequate arrangements can be made to ensure such transfers cater to developmental and environmental needs also.

In patenting of organic inventions in terms of micro-organisms and microbiological processes, India proposed harmonisation of TRIPS Agreement with the UN Convention on Biological Diversity (CBD) and suggested that TRIPS should conform to CBD rather than the other way round. The fault line between the two approaches i.e. CBD and TRIPS, is that CBD considers intellectual property protection as a means to achieving the end of sustainable development, while Agreement on TRIPS considers IPRs as an end in itself. India along with Brazil is at loggerheads with developed countries like the US and Japan in pushing for appropriate amendments in the TRIPS Agreement, to make disclosure of the origin of biological material and traditional knowledge mandatory during filing of patent applications. It should be noted that under present provisions a simple GI protection *per se* does not help preventing 'bio-piracy' since it can only protect the product but not the genetic uniqueness and the traditional knowledge associated with it.

---

[23] Panagariya 2002a.

Services

Although trade in services is not essentially a new phenomenon, its explicit recognition as an important component of trade flows is rather recent. Travel, transport and tourism services have always been traded, accounting for significant foreign exchange transactions for many countries. However, a major bulk of services has traditionally been regarded as 'non-tradable'. This perception has undergone a sea change especially with the initiation of the General Agreement on Trade in Services (GATS) under the WTO, with a wide range of services now being actively 'traded' worldwide through new organisational and modal channels. Indeed it was during the Uruguay Round that this new area (services) was brought under the purview of trade negotiations and the outcome was the GATS Agreement that came into force along with the WTO in 1995. GATS classify the provision of services into four modes, namely, cross-border supply (mode 1), consumption abroad (mode 2), commercial presence (mode 3) and movement of natural persons (mode 4). It mandated liberalisation of service trade, but adopted a 'bottom-up' approach, giving the members full flexibility to undertake trade liberalisation in services as per their own priorities and pace, under the provision of 'specific commitments'.

Similar to the case of IPR, India, in the initial years of the Uruguay Round, strongly opposed any proposal for the inclusion of services in the WTO agreement. Indeed during the 1980s, the contribution of services to India's GDP remained quite modest (35-40 per cent). Clearly, it was difficult for Indian policymakers to foresee India's service led growth that the country is experiencing currently.

The upturn of India's services sector began only in the mid-1990s and it has expanded very rapidly in the last decade and a half. Between 1994 and 2004, the services sector grew at the rate of 7.9 per cent, much higher than the growth rates of other sectors as well as that of total GDP (3 per cent for agriculture and allied, 5.3 per cent for manufacturing and 5.9 per cent for total GDP). The share of the services sector in India's GDP increased from 29 per cent in the 1980s to 41 per cent in the 1990s and to 50 per cent in this decade. The expansion of the services sector has been accompanied with a rising trade in services for India. India's share in world services exports almost doubled between 1998-1999 and 2004-2005 (from 0.99 per cent to 1.8 per cent). Nearly 50 per cent of India's exports of services are software services.[24]

Mode 3 (commercial presence) has been the most important mode, accounting for 57 per cent of India's services trade. The inflow of

---

[24] Banga (2006)

foreign direct investment (FDI) in services is mostly concentrated in the telecommunications and the financial services sectors. There is also a rising trend in outward FDI in services from India. In fact, services account for 30 per cent of total Indian outward FDI, which is primarily concentrated in information technology (IT) and information technology enabled services (ITES).

India's mode 1 (cross border supply) trade in services, accounting for 28 per cent of India's total services trade, is also dominated by IT and ITES. India's competitive advantage in off-shoring is attributed to its growing pool of highly skilled, low cost workers. The growth in service industry particularly in the high-end software and business services has been immensely facilitated by on-site delivery in many cases in addition to offshore provisioning. Mode 2 (consumption abroad) is gaining importance, especially in areas of health education and tourism. It accounts of 14 per cent of India's total trade in services. Finally, mode 4 (movement of natural persons) remains an insignificant fraction (1 per cent) of India's total services trade, primarily due to restrictions and regulations on movement of natural persons imposed by member nations. This is one area where trade liberalisation has been resisted the most. Against this backdrop, it is easy to understand how India, from the mid-1990s, slowly started shifting away from its rigid opposition to services trade and finally by the mid-2000s adopted an aggressive pro-services trade liberalisation posture.

Post-1995, negotiations continued on four major areas of services – financial services, telecom, maritime transport and GATS mode 4. Agreements on the first two were reached in 1997. India complied without much hesitation and the consequences are evident in terms of a paradigm shift especially in telecom in India, also to some extent in banking. Negotiations on maritime transport were suspended and not much progress was made in the negotiations on mode 4. India remained, by and large, conservative during the post-Uruguay Round negotiations in services, particularly in making commitments in sectors like energy, distribution, environment, education and professional services. In mode 4, India did not undertake any commitments, like most other members.[25]

Services negotiations entered a new era under the GATS 2000 framework that became an integral part of the DDA since November 2001. This framework, resulting from proposals made by India and other developing countries, recognised the need for appropriate flexibilities to developing countries and the importance of bilateral *request-offer* approach

---

[25] Das 2006.

as the main method of negotiations. This approach of *bilateral request-offer* does not lead to a direct outcome in terms of arriving at any bilateral understanding between two countries or groups, rather it involves a process of repeated offers, negotiation, and reorientation before it is finally accepted as a GATS schedule.

Under this approach, India received requests for full commitments under modes 1, 2, and 3 stressing on the removal of mode 3 restrictions. On the other hand India submitted requests to more than 60 countries, including some major developed countries like US, EU, Japan, Australia, Canada and New Zealand and developing countries like China, Mexico, Brazil, Malaysia and Indonesia mostly in architectural services, audio-visual services, computer and related services, tourism and travel related services, health and maritime transport services across all modes with significant focus on mode 4 and stressed subsequent dismantling of the existing levels of *domestic regulation* in the trading countries.

Although in the Conditional Initial Offer of January 2004, India was regarded as conservative, in its Revised Offer the very next year, August 2005, India's stance became one of the most ambitious in liberalising services trade. India was practically offensive in all four modes with improved horizontal commitments and minimal restrictions under market access or national treatment (NT).

Given that the services negotiation under bilateral request-offer approach lacked momentum, at Hong Kong (2005), at the behest of developed countries, a new methodology of *plurilateral request-offer* was suggested in a manner that could put pressure on LDCs. According to this method, a group of members may place a collective request, on a specific sector or mode, directly to a target country, which in turn is obliged to *consider* it while submitting its revised offers.[26] India was seen as colluding with developed countries in pushing this agenda. Not surprisingly, India, by December 2005 had realised its potential gain from services trade liberalisation and took an aggressive stance in this regard, even at the cost of annoying and dissociating with some of its long standing developing country allies. India was accused of digressing from more serious issues of agriculture and NAMA at Hong Kong, to run after its perceived immediate benefits arising out of services trade liberalisation.

---

[26] As noted by Das (2006), the insertion of the word 'consider' in the final text was an improvement over the original version, which obliged members to enter into negotiations rather than merely considering doing so.

2   THE POLITICAL ECONOMY OF INDIA'S SHIFTING COORDINATES

In the previous section, we have discussed how India adopted its stance on these three issues (agriculture, IPR and services) at the WTO at different points in time. Based on these evidences, we now attempt to analyse the underlying political economy forces that have shaped India's stance at the WTO. We may offer *two hypotheses* to begin with – one suggesting that India's stance has been consistently domestic interest driven, while the other indicates towards international economic diplomacy as the important driver.

Domestic compulsions

To illustrate how domestic compulsions have shaped India's negotiating stance at the WTO, we review instances from amongst all three issues discussed above. We must remember that domestic compulsions may arise out of a complex interplay of conflicting interests of different constituencies and their ability to influence the decision-making process, leveraged by the democratic fabric as well as the changing economic profile of the nation.[27] Hence one may not expect domestic compulsions, as perceived by the government, to remain static over time even on the same negotiating issue.

India's approach towards the TRIPS Agreement may be cited to exemplify the importance of this changing nature of domestic compulsions in shaping the stance. India's vehement opposition to TRIPS pre-1989 is perfectly understood in the light of the interests of its pharmaceutical industry, still at a nascent stage of technological maturity, which required a weak patent regime to prosper and develop. Eventually, during the 1990s, the industry got divided with one segment, perhaps the more powerful one, beginning to support TRIPS in their *own* business interest. When India signed the TRIPS Agreement in 1994, it did not face much opposition from the industry lobby therefore. However, now there was stiff opposition from the civil society lobby against TRIPS on grounds of public health and access to medicine. India's democratic polity ensured that these civil society outcries get reflected in its stance at the WTO.[28] This was reflected in Doha and the resultant Declaration on TRIPS and Public Health. One may also argue that apart from the civil society lobby,

---

[27] See Zahrnt (2008) for a candid discussion of the influences exerted by various domestic constituents in shaping the negotiating positions adopted by member states.

[28] This might appear to be in line with Zahrnt's (2008) conclusion that non-economic interests lobbied by influential civil society organisations exert greater influence on the negotiating positions of member states than pure trade/ economic interests of the nations.

the Indian pharmaceutical industry with competitive strength in the global generic market had a clear business interest in this Doha declaration on public health.[29] Subsequently, India's persistent initiative for the extension of GIs and mandatory disclosure of the origin of biological materials and traditional knowledge also reflects its domestic interest driven stance, given its rich biodiversity and traditional knowledge resources.

In agriculture, India's stance has not undergone much change. Its demand for flexibilities and SDT to take care of developmental concerns, including food security, livelihood and rural development, is a result of a strong agricultural lobby in India's domestic politics as well as its declared policy priority towards the poor and the vulnerable. Indeed, it has been noted that India's preoccupation with developmental concerns perhaps indicates its greater alignment with the Group of 33 (G33) on agricultural negotiations, rather than with G20 which aimed to achieve a more ambitious outcome in liberalising agricultural trade by reducing farm subsidies and trade restrictions in the US and the EU.[30] But this is not to suggest that there were any major divergence of interests of the two groups. Both were fighting against the US/EU coalition in agricultural negotiation.

Services negotiations perhaps illustrate the most noticeable shift in India's stance at the WTO, entirely driven by domestic imperatives. From being a strong opponent of GATS during the Uruguay Round, India became one of the most aggressive proponents of services trade liberalisation in the Doha Round, especially at the Hong Kong Ministerial Conference in 2005. While Indian policymakers failed to foresee in the 1980s, the importance and the enormous potential of the services sector in India's economic prosperity, by 2005 it was evident that India's emergence in the world economy was largely driven by its services sector boom. It was, therefore, in India's interest now to push for liberalisation of trade in services, especially through modes 1, 2 and 4. Of course, India's aggressive stance on mode 4 reflects its inclination to please its vast constituency of the upwardly mobile educated middle class, who have been the prime beneficiary of India's service sector boom and have been on board *India Incorporated* taking off into the world economy.

In spite of the apparent eagerness to liberalise trade in services, certain areas pertaining to mode 3 have always been cautiously guarded in India, because of their traditional role in generating mass employment through direct and indirect linkages (as in retail trade) or else for being the principally trusted channel (like government provision) for services like education and health (even in specialised forms) and most certainly

---

[29] This point was brought to our notice during discussions with Saradindu Bhaduri.
[30] Ismail 2007.

fulfilling the needs of a large segment of its population. Possible benefits, if any, due to foreign presence in these services are perceived to be outweighed by possible welfare losses in terms of equity, universality and employment. This has perhaps deterred unconditional opening up of these sectors to foreign players by India.

International economic diplomacy

The way in which WTO negotiations are carried out, one gets the impression that it is more of striking 'deals' among conflicting members rather than engaging in debates on matters of principles. Members, driven by their narrow domestic imperatives, strive to strike a balance between its gains and losses from striking a deal and arrive at an agreement that optimises their payoff subject to the constraints of unequal bargaining power. The role of economic diplomacy in this respect cannot be denied. Let us take a look the extent to which this factor has shaped India's stance at the WTO, again with reference to the three issues of TRIPS, agriculture and services.

India's sudden turn around on TRIPS way back in 1989 has often been linked to economic threats from the US. India perhaps changed its course of action by softening on TRIPS to receive concessions on other aspects of trade liberalisation as well as its domestic economic needs. This is a clear case of economic diplomacy at work in determining India's WTO stance.

India went to Doha with a negative attitude towards initiating a new round of negotiations. But it gave in and signed the Doha Declaration on the last day. One may again notice the role of international economic diplomacy in this shifting position. India did make a long list of submissions to push for developmental concerns in various aspects of WTO negotiations, TRIPS and public health and agriculture being the most prominent among these. While agreeing to a new round, India could succeed in extracting clear mandates on many of these developmental concerns being explicitly mentioned in the declaration. This was indeed seen as a major victory for India at Doha, the reversal of its stance on a new round notwithstanding.

Finally, at the Hong Kong Ministerial Conference, India was seen to align with the US and the EU in pushing for an ambitious services agenda. It was even accused of being a party to the initial version of the infamous Annex C of the Hong Kong Ministerial Declaration. At this point, India's economic diplomacy prompted it to align with long standing adversaries at the WTO (for immediate gains from trade in services), even at the cost of dissociating itself from its developing country allies and digressing from its development agenda.

Summary of drivers

On balance, we conclude that the primacy of domestic drivers in shaping India's stance at the WTO, especially on specific issues, is clearly evident. Indeed, in many cases, India has *reversed* its position with its changing economic structures and parameters that completely altered its domestic imperatives. This is most clearly visible in case of services and also to an extent in case of TRIPS.

Nevertheless, the role of economic diplomacy cannot be ignored either. India has also been a part of this negotiating game based on striking deals and balancing priorities through economic diplomacy. Interestingly, even the character of its economic diplomacy has changed over time as it achieved a heightened profile at the WTO. For instance, India succumbing to the US pressure on TRIPS in 1989 reflects a very different diplomatic profile compared to India's more assertive post Hong Kong stance as part of the G4. This brings us to the concluding section of the chapter, which critically explores India's heightened profile and its potential leadership role at the WTO, especially at this critical juncture of global financial crisis and economic slowdown.

3   THE GLOBAL CRISIS AND THE FUTURE OF THE DDA: THE ROLE FOR INDIA

The global financial crisis, originating in the US in 2007 and culminating in a major financial meltdown in September 2008, has severely hit the global financial architecture and has taken a toll on the real economies across the world. There is a serious apprehension that the global economy is on the brink of a major recession. While advanced economies have already been badly hit by this financial crisis, both in their financial and real sectors, the emerging economies are also not being spared, thanks to the complete integration of the global financial, investment and trading systems. The impact of the global crisis on India has been somewhat cushioned in the financial sector, since India has maintained stringent regulatory norms for its financial markets especially with respect to international financial flows. However, India has not been able to escape the adverse impact of the global recession on its real economy, with a major slowdown of its economic growth and export performance.[31] The outlook for the next year or two looks even bleaker.

It is against this background that we would like to address the question of how far India, with its heightened profile at the WTO, can succeed in playing a constructive leadership role to salvage the Doha

---

[31] See, for instance, a recent study by Kumar et al (2009).

Round. Before we answer this loaded question, it is necessary to understand the genesis of India's heightened profile at the WTO gained over all these years. India at the beginning of the Uruguay Round was a nearly closed economy and a negligible player in the world economy (and world trade) and it is of little surprise that India never received much importance and attention during the initial phase of the multilateral trade negotiations. However, the decades to follow witnessed a phenomenal transformation of the Indian economy, resulting in India's emergence as a major player in the world economy, with the fourth largest gross domestic product (GDP) (measured in purchasing power parity), experiencing growth rates of 7-9 per cent for consecutive years, and trade-GDP ratio of more than 35 per cent. As a result, India now hogs the limelight of global economic attention along with China and a few other emerging economies.[32] Given the dynamics of mutual interdependence in the global economy, the prosperity of the world becomes critically linked to the parameters of economic policies and performance of the key players. India's emergence as a major economic player in the world has, therefore, definitely contributed to its heightened profile at the WTO.

India's increasing attention from the world on WTO negotiations can perhaps be traced back to Singapore (1996), where India posed a stiff opposition to the inclusion of the so-called Singapore Issues. Again in Seattle (1999), India played an active role in scuttling the issue of labour standards, championing the cause of developing countries. Later in Doha (2001), India received a lot of criticism and negative publicity, especially from the western media for its stand on resisting a new round.[33] While India was being branded as having a negative attitude towards negotiations in the sense of adopting a position of what *should not* be included rather than a positive stand on what *could* conceivably be included for its own interests, the publicity brought India to the limelight and conveyed a signal that India could potentially block the progress of multilateral negotiations and India's withdrawal from the negotiating table might prove costly.

Indeed, India's claimed victory on counts of developmental concerns being acceded to at Doha, gave it a renewed confidence to adopt a more pro-active and enthusiastic posture at the WTO negotiations. Later in the run up to Cancún, the formation of G20 to resist the US-EU agenda on agriculture, India again played a leading role along with its allies

---

[32] Even at this juncture of global financial crisis, the Indian financial sector has remained much more insulated and resilient, compared to many other emerging economies, thanks to the stringent controls in its financial sector.

[33] Panagariya 2002a.

Brazil, South Africa and China and this further contributed to India's importance at the WTO.

Finally, when the Doha round was suspended at Geneva (2006), India was considered to be among the select key members, which could salvage the round. Along with the US, the EU and Brazil, India became a part of the high profile G4 to take forward the round and break the stalemate. There could, of course, be several interpretations for India's inclusion in this group. But, there is a strong perception that the US and the EU, which enjoyed the maximum bargaining power and could easily drive the WTO agenda/negotiations in the early days, were now losing ground. Especially post-Doha, with developmental concerns being explicitly recognised, the US-EU coalition found it increasingly difficult to ignore the developing country positions, which were vehemently put forward by countries like India (among others) with global support from civil society lobbies. Under the circumstances, the only sensible step was to co-opt some of these countries into a closed group to seek out solutions. India, being a large emerging economy with a large poor population (giving it legitimacy to fight for developmental concerns) and already acknowledged as an important negotiator at the WTO, was a natural choice. In addition, India's aggressive pro-liberalisation stance on services at Hong Kong perhaps convinced the developed countries that there could be potential overlap of their interest with that of India's.

Against the backdrop of this heightened profile, the immediate question that comes to one's mind is how far India could use its profile to give a mature and constructive leadership to the developing world without having to stall the progress made in the multilateral trade negotiations made so far. There is clearly a large overlap between India's domestic interests and the larger interests of the developing world. India's developmental concerns at the WTO, especially with respect to food security, livelihood and public health have, therefore, nicely championed the cause of the developing world, although much of it India has adopted for its own domestic priorities. Likewise, India's focus on traditional knowledge and bio-piracy reflects its own interests which also coincide with the interests of many developing countries.[34] Nevertheless, there is evidence to suggest that India's stance at the WTO has not always been driven by narrow domestic priorities. For instance, India's concern for technology transfer (to cater to environmental and developmental needs) and preservation of biodiversity as part of its TRIPS negotiating agenda during the Doha Round is a clear reflection of its global concern for

---

[34] Note that more than 80 per cent of the biodiversity hotspots are located in the developing world. www.biodiversityhotspots.org.

sustainable development, as expected from a mature player in the world economy.

But, as in any other democracy, much of India's negotiating stance at the WTO has naturally focussed on domestic drivers and that too largely determined by political-economy forces based on the relative strengths and influence of various interest lobbies within the framework of democratic polity. No wonder, we see India at Hong Kong, trying to push for services with over–enthusiasm. Perhaps India could have been a little more cautious and particular in signalling its equally enthusiastic posture on its long standing developmental concerns that it had championed so far. This could have prevented developing countries from accusing India of aligning with developed nations to make headway in specific sectors of interest, and the possible doubts that it might have created among developing nations about India's sincerity in championing the cause of development at the WTO. Later, of course, we do find India back on track its clear developmental focus at the G6 and G4 meetings post-Hong Kong. India's candid statement in the latest Economic Survey vindicates this point:

> While safeguarding the interests of India's low income and resource poor agricultural producers (which cannot be traded off against any gains elsewhere in the negotiations) remains paramount for India, making real gains in services negotiations where it is a demander is no less important. In the case of industrial tariffs, India's growth and development concerns need to be addressed where India has taken a stand along with NAMA-11 coalition. These concerns are reflected in India's position on different WTO issues for negotiations.[35]

On balance, there is absolutely no reason to believe that India will be sold out to the US-EU pressure. But in case, India sees that its own economic interest lies in aligning with this group, it would perhaps adopt a balanced approach towards its negotiating stance without compromising on its firm commitment to global developmental issues.

However, nothing seemed to have changed over the two years since 2006, when on the ninth day of July 2008 negotiations, WTO Director-General Pascal Lamy announced that the talks were again on the verge of collapse. However, on the tenth day it was seemingly agreed to preserve the issues settled in nine days of talk among ministers and the Doha Round should agreeably continue. India was part of the newly-formed G7, alongside Australia, Brazil, China, the EU, Japan, and the US. It was this group of seven countries that would now decide the fate of the Doha Round. The SSM for developing countries perhaps remained

---

[35] Government of India 2008.

the major bone of contention in reaching an agreement. It may be worth noting that in July 2008, members had little idea of the imminent calamity that was about to hit the world economy in the form of the global financial meltdown and how it would affect multilateral trade negotiations in the near future. Indeed, the global financial crisis, triggering fears of an unprecedented global recession, can pose to be a very serious impediment to the progress in the Doha Round of WTO negotiations. It is under such state of global affairs that the Doha Round is now caught in between the apprehensions of a total collapse after years of negotiations and deliberations, on one hand, and getting to act as the most relevant and competent institution to co-ordinate efforts to foster an environment of 'trust' to deter the snarls of crisis, on the other.

There are already indications of a significant slowing down of global trade over the last few months. Protectionist forces have started surfacing and will perhaps get stronger as the recession gets worse.[36] Many countries have been devising policy interventions that effectively boil down to the suppression of free trade and investment flows, without necessarily subverting the WTO commitments. The 'Buy America' clause under the US fiscal stimulus package is a notable example of an aggressive protectionist move by the US government. Allegedly, even India has adopted a protectionist stance by banning the import of all Chinese toys in January 2009 for six months and raising tariffs on a couple of selected products like iron and steel and soybean oil. However, the ban was merely a response to an apprehension of dumping of toys by China in the Indian market due to the global slowdown and was promptly relaxed in March 2009. The tariff hikes in specific commodities were meant to restore the tariff rates to the pre-March 2008 levels, when India reduced it considerably on these items to combat domestic inflation. We therefore do not perceive India's policy response to the slowdown to be aggressively protectionist in any way.

Policymakers in many countries are now pre-occupied with their immediate concern to revive their domestic economies by bringing their own houses in order through domestic economic policies and reforms, over their attention towards multilateral trade negotiations and to make concessions for creating a free and fair global trading and economic system through the WTO. The interest and the urgency with which the Doha Round was being pursued by the international community might therefore get dampened in the face of this unforeseen global economic crisis.

What should be in India's interest at this juncture? While there is no doubt that India must also focus on this domestic countercyclical

---

[36] Baldwin and Evenett 2009.

macro policy interventions as well as structural reforms to boost its competitiveness, we believe that it is in India's interest to see a logical conclusion of the Doha Round. The progress made so far by India and its allies in setting the rules of the WTO game to accommodate the developmental concerns and interests of the emerging nations cannot be sacrificed at this point. India must, at all costs, strive to strike the final deal in the larger interest of the round. The pending issues, if any, may be mandated for negotiations during the next round of negotiations that could perhaps take off only after the world economy recovers from the present shock.

We conclude our chapter with a general observation about India's engagement with the world. It is worth noting that India's ideational influence on the world, in its immediate post-independence period (1950s), far exceeded its material capability at that juncture. India was proactive in generating new ideas of world order that attracted the world's attention.[37] Even at this present juncture in the new millennium, India is drawing a lot of attention from the world, but much of it is primarily attributable to economic parameters. Diplomacy nowadays is used as tool for exploring possibilities of trade and economic cooperation. It is, therefore, understandable that India's foreign policy has become economics driven with specific business interests playing a major role in defining the coordinates. India is busy forging *strategic* alliances, primarily on the basis of its *economic needs and priorities*. However, what is needed at this hour is to reflect more on the perspectives of diplomacy and international political economy.

India must appreciate that there is no other global forum where it commands as much more clout and importance as it does in the WTO. Alongside the unsolved issues pertaining to agriculture and NAMA, under these changed circumstances India may have to take up positions against developed countries' attempts to render the process of trade negotiations meaningless by turning protectionist after all these years of preaching the virtues of free trade. Indeed, India *can* now aim at a grand foreign policy design to promote a fair and equitable world order. India's heightened profile at the WTO at this juncture provides a clear opportunity for the country to capitalise on the platform of WTO negotiations as a major *foreign policy instrument* to play a competent leadership role for the developing world.

---

[37] This point was brought to our notice during discussions with Siddharth Mallavarapu.

REFERENCES

Baldwin, Richard and Simon Evenett. 2009. Introduction and recommendations for the G20. In *The collapse of global trade, murky protectionism, and the crisis: Recommendations for the G20,* edited by Richard Baldwin and Simon Evenett. London: A VoxEU.org publication, Centre for Economic Policy Research.

Banga, R. 2006. Statistical Overview of India's Trade in Services. In *Trade in Services & India. Prospects and Strategies,* edited by Rupa Chanda. New Delhi: CENTAD Wiley India (Pvt.) Ltd.

Chakraborty, D. 2004. Recent Negotiation Trends on Agriculture under WTO. RGCIS Working Paper 47, September.

Das, Kasturi. 2006. GATS Negotiations and India: Evolution and State of Play. Working Paper 7. New Delhi: Centre for Trade and Development.

Government of India. 2008. *Economic Survey 2007-2008.* New Delhi: Ministry of Finance, Government of India.

Ismail, Faizel. 2007. *Mainstreaming Development in the WTO. Developing Countries in the Doha Round.* Jaipur and Geneva: CUTS International and Friedrich Ebert Stiftung.

Kumar, Rajiv et al. 2009. Indian Economic Outlook: 2008-09 and 2009-10. Working Paper 234. New Delhi: Indian Council for Research on International Economic Relations.

Machlup, F. 1958. *An Economic Review of the Patent System.* Study of the Sub-committee on Patents, Trademarks and Copyrights of the Committee on the Judiciary, United States Senate. Washington DC: US Government Printing Press.

Mattoo, Aaditya and Arvind Subramanian. 2003. India and the Multilateral Trading System Post-Doha: Defensive or Proactive? In *India and the WTO,* edited by Aaditya Mattoo and Robert M. Stern. Washington, DC: World Bank and Oxford University Press.

Oxfam. 2005. What Happened in Hong Kong? Initial Analysis of the WTO Ministerial. Oxfam Briefing Paper 85, December.

Pal, Parthapratim. 2005. Current WTO Negotiations on Domestic Subsidies in Agriculture: Implications for India. Working Paper 177. New Delhi: Indian Council for Research on International Economic Relations.

Panagariya, Arvind. 2002a. India at Doha: Retrospect and Prospect. *Economic and Political Weekly* 37(4): 279-284, 26 January.

Panagariya, Arvind. 2002b. Developing Countries at Doha: A Political Economy Analysis. *World Economy* 25(9):1205-33, September.

Panagariya, Arvind. 2005. Liberalizing Agriculture. *Foreign Affairs,* December, pp. 56-66.

Ramanna, Anitha. 2002. India's Patent Policy and Negotiations in TRIPS: Future options for India and other Developing Countries. Paper presented in the *National Conference on TRIPS - Next Agenda for Developing*

Countries, Shyamprasad Institute for Social Service, Hyderabad, 11-12 October.

Ray, Amit S. 2005. The Indian Pharmaceutical Industry at Crossroads: Implications for India's Health Care. In *Maladies, Preventives and Curatives: Debates in Public Health in India*, edited by Amiya Bagchi and Krishna Soman. New Delhi: Tulika Books.

Ray, Amit S. 2006. India's Economic Reforms: Opportunities, Challenges and Political Economy Perspectives. In *Is there an Economic Orthodoxy? Growth and Reform in Africa, Asia and Latin America*, edited by Lyal White. Johannesburg: South African Institute of International Affairs.

Ray, Amit S. and Saradindu Bhaduri. 2008. Co-evolution of IPR Policy and Technological Learning in Developing Countries: A Game-theoretic Model. Paper for *Globelics 6th International Conference, Mexico City*, September 2008.

Zahrnt, Valentin. 2008. Domestic Constituents and the Formulations of WTO Negotiating Positions: What the Delegates Say. *World Trade Review* 7(2): 393-421.

GREGORY CHIN

6. REFORMING THE WTO: CHINA, THE DOHA ROUND AND BEYOND

China's decision to side with India at the July 2008 World Trade Organisation (WTO) Doha meetings and reject the United States (US) offer signalled an important watershed in its global politics: it sent the message, intended or otherwise, that China was transitioning from being a low key, somewhat aloof actor in the Doha talks to a more active, even assertive role. Pressured repeatedly by the developed country majors to exert its growing influence over the developing countries to conclude the Doha Development Agenda (DDA), China instead supported India, to press the US and the European Union (EU) to compromise. Some in Washington saw Beijing's actions as signalling that China had woken from its slumber, was '[n]ow aggressively challenging the system', and causing a collapse of the Doha Round.[1] Beijing saw its actions as necessary to bring a balancing of interests among all the participants.

International Relations scholars theorising from the realist tradition remind that even if India and China were negotiating from their national interests, they were still negotiating within the confines of the international trade regime. Rather than perceiving their lack of acquiescence to the US offer as spelling the end of the world trading regime, their willingness to negotiate from within the WTO could be seen as affirmation of the international regime.[2] A number of observers suggest that an enhanced role for developing countries in the negotiations should not be equated with the collapse of the Doha Round or the global trade regime, but rather as part of its evolution, even maturation.[3]

This chapter is based on interviews and discussions with Chinese economic and trade officials, and their foreign counterparts from September 2000 to April 2007. I thank the Chinese officials and other government officials for their comments, and acknowledge the support of the Social Sciences and Humanities Research Council of Canada.

[1] Bergsten 2008a.

[2] I thank Jeffrey Legro for this point.

[3] Author's notes on remarks by Harsha Varhana Singh, Deputy Secretary General of the WTO at a Centre for International Governance Innovation (CIGI) trade experts' meeting, Waterloo, August 2008. See also Grammling 2008, 1-3.

The emergence of the so-called 'BRICs' (i.e. Brazil, Russia, India, and China) is changing the configuration of power in the WTO and the global trading system. It is reflected, economically, in the increasingly favourable balance of trade and balance of payments that Brazil, India and China enjoy. It is starting to be reflected, politically, in the shift of systemic influence from the 'traditional' Quad powers in the Uruguay Round (i.e. US, EU, Japan and Canada) to an emerging bloc of powers in the Doha Round around the US, EU, Brazil, and India. China has been added (somewhat belatedly) to this new informal 'steering committee'. It can be argued that the multilateral trading system has become more inclusive as a consequence. At the same time, there is no refuting that decision-making in the international regime has become more complicated and drawn-out. The experience of the Doha Round shows that the WTO membership faces a complex institutional challenge of balancing inclusiveness and effectiveness as a negotiating forum.

This chapter examines China's evolving role inside the WTO after formally joining in December 2001. The prevailing view, at least until the failed talks in summer 2008, was that China had taken a low-key, somewhat aloof approach to the DDA, giving rhetorical support to developing country members, and emphasising its role as a bridge-builder between North and South, while actually taking negotiating positions that were motivated by national self-interest. The most systematic research on China's behaviour after joining the WTO has suggested that China has, on balance, acted as a status quo power, taking a constructive yet low profile approach to the Doha talks, and mainly in a learning mode inside the WTO.[4] In joining the Group of 20 (G20) coalition of developing countries, but leaving it to Brazil and India to take leadership roles, China is said to have acted like a Great Power that is exercising restraint on its newfound international power capabilities and keeping options open, whether siding with the traditional trading powers or the Southern coalitions. Since summer 2008, the tone of international commentary has become more critical, portraying China, together with India, as *the* main factors causing the collapse of the Doha Round.[5]

The paradox of the China case, if one accepts the conventional wisdom, is that China has seemingly gone, overnight, from a low profile actor whose role as a political change agent did not match its growing weight in the world trade system into a robust international actor that is now taking aggressive actions to impair the multilateral trading system. This chapter suggests that the above understandings of China's roles suffer from two problems. First, both of the portrayals – China as low-key

---

[4] Pearson 2006, 242-271; Liang 2007, 125-149; Zhao 2007, 535-558.
[5] Bergsten 2008a.

detached actor in the Doha Round or active disabler – tend to draw their conclusions by measuring the quality of China's engagement in relation to its degree of 'cooperation' with the traditional rule-makers, specifically the extent to which Beijing is helping to press the G20 coalition into accepting the terms set out by the developed country majors.[6] This alludes to the need in scholarship to distinguish between China's actual behaviour in international governance versus diplomatic tussles over China's international image. Second, much of the limited research on China's behaviour inside the WTO focuses excessively on China's role in the Doha Round trade talks, and underestimates the significance of the more concerted efforts that Beijing has put into reforming the rules and operational procedures and mechanisms of the ruling bodies of the WTO. The most significant 'Southern leadership' roles that China has taken have not been in the Doha negotiations *per se*, but in championing incremental reforms to the rules, operating procedures, standards and ruling bodies of the WTO. These changes, it can be suggested, are more lasting in terms of institutional governance of the global economy.

This chapter has two purposes: first, to dissect through the diplomatic rhetoric, and distinguish between the diplomatic tussle over the construction of China's international image and its actual role in the multilateral trading regime; second, to analyse the reform proposals that Beijing has championed both in the Doha Round negotiations, as well as for the ruling bodies of the WTO. In so doing, China actually emerges as one of the most active developing countries among the WTO members, both when it was branded as a 'low key, aloof' actor, and more recently, as active 'system disabler'. Furthermore, it is strong exaggeration to classify China's reforms proposals as 'aggressively challenging' the global trading system – even if its reformist behaviour does lean toward cautious revision of the international trade regime.

1   INTERNATIONAL IMAGING: CHINA IN THE DOHA ROUND

A more accurate grasp of how China has acted inside the WTO starts with cutting through the diplomatic verbiage on all sides, which has heavily framed the conventional understanding of China's behaviour

---

[6] Andrew Hurrell and Daniel Drezner have each identified an analytical bias or shortcoming in the institutionalist literature on international organisation, a tendency to ignore 'noncooperation' or assume away fundamental differences in state preferences or cultural outlook and social organisation that may block or complicate international cooperative action. See Hurell 2005, 35-36; Drezner 2007, 23-24.

inside the global trading regime, and examining the details of China's concrete interventions.

Phase I: The Honeymoon Period

Chinese trade officials have been battling an international image problem since China acceded to the WTO – initially, the impression that China was a somewhat detached, if not disinterested actor, in the Doha round of trade talks to, more recently, China (and India) as the main blockers of progress. Chinese officials and commentators inadvertently reinforced this image when, for example, one Chinese WTO official offered up that China's interests were '[d]ifferent from both the developed and developing country members of the WTO', and '[b]elonging to no trade group'[7]. Or when the Standing Councillor of the China Society for World Trade Organisation Studies remarked that China has a 'unique status' that is 'different from its peers among developing countries'; unlike other developing counties, 'China is not totally reliant on agriculture for its economic growth and export revenue, and therefore has taken a smaller role in agricultural negotiations of the Doha Round'.[8] Although the point was made to emphasise that China could serve as a bridge and communicator between the developing and developed worlds, the emphasis on China's supposed 'uniqueness' could be read as justification for China's 'stand-offish', somewhat aloof behaviour.

Central figures in the construction of China's image in the Doha Round have been the chief trade representatives of the EU and US, senior WTO officials, and prominent policy analysts and commentators in leading international think tanks. Beijing has not helped its own cause by how it responded to calls for China to take a more active role in the Doha Round. In the initial period after entry in the WTO, Chinese authorities would respond by emphasising that their hands were full with implementing China's accession commitments, and that they would need to focus on building China's domestic institutional capacity to fulfil its membership obligations. Some Chinese commentators added that no one national actor could overcome the impasse, and that collective efforts were needed – thus seemingly absolving Beijing of the international spotlight.[9] Beijing also responded by suggesting that, as a newcomer, it was most appropriate for China to be a 'bridge' between the have and have-not members of the WTO (a role South Africa has also sought to script, as

---

[7] Statements made by a WTO analyst from China's commerce ministry in an op-ed piece in the *Asian Wall Journal*, and subsequently retracted (Pearson 2006, 255).
[8] Remarks by Zhou Shijian are cited in Wang and Wen 2006.
[9] Ibid.

Brendan Vickers writes in his chapter, Chapter 7). While this positioning gave Beijing some temporary breathing time, there have been longer-term consequences for China's international image.

One of the most prominent international commentators on China's behaviour in the WTO and a key spokesperson in constructing China's image in the DDA has been Peter Mandelson, as EU Trade Commissioner, who publicly urged China to play a more proactive role in resolving the deadlocks. Contrary to the previous concerns that China would be a destructive force that would paralyse the WTO from within, after its accession, the diplomatic pressure shifted to pressing China to play a more active role in the Doha Round. Mandelson painted China as somewhat distant and detached, and not appropriately active in the Doha Round:

> Europeans need to have a clearer sense that China is assuming the responsibilities that accompany its new power within the global community. As we all learn in life, the greater our power the greater our responsibility. Europeans are now looking to China to play a greater role in the international community in many areas... In my own area of work, trade, I too am calling on China to demonstrate responsibility and leadership. In trade policy the greatest single challenge before us is to bring to a successful conclusion the ongoing Doha Development Agenda negotiations.[10]

Mandelson further lectured:

> I am aware that many in China feel that the country paid a high price in 2001 to get into the WTO... So although I recognise the particular status of China as a 'recently acceded' WTO member, we are looking to you to contribute again... I am looking to China, as the greatest, most powerful and most rapidly advancing developing economy, to show leadership in the run up to our Ministerial meeting in Hong Kong in December this year (2005)... you can contribute more than may at first sight appear necessary or reasonable. I should add that this is often the price for leadership.[11]

He called China a 'commercial superpower' that will:

> ...rock the global trading system, but it need not break it. Effective governance of free and fair global trade could not work with the mainland on the outside. Now that China has a stake in the system, it can turn its formidable influence to securing it for the future.

---

[10] Mandelson 2005a.
[11] Ibid.

China, as the world's most advanced developing country, had a
crucial leadership role to play in the Doha round.

Exercising such leadership, according to Mandelson, required China to do
some '[h]eavy lifting to help get other developing countries to the table
before the Hong Kong meeting in December'.[12] However, the lack of
major breakthroughs at the Hong Kong Ministerial Conference in
December 2005 and afterwards left Mandelson and others frustrated.[13]
Policy analysts, such as Aurore Wanlin of the Centre for European
Reform, have contributed to the imagery, arguing that China's role in the
Doha Round is not proportionate to its global economic weight, yet more
needed than ever: 'What makes the Doha round different from previous
rounds was that it is no longer enough for the US and EU to agree to a
deal and expect the rest of the members to fall in line'.[14] This Doha
'Development' Round, according to Wanlin, requires leadership from
leading emerging economies, such as Brazil, India and China, to forge
greater coherence among the developing countries on the various
negotiation issues. China should be more engaged in the talks, rather than
being content to benefit from what the EU and US gain through
negotiations.

China's low-key approach to the Doha Round from 2001 to 2006
should not be surprising if one examined the trade flows in this period. In
this phase, China enjoyed historically unprecedented increases in its trade,
despite the fact that the Doha Round was deadlocked. Without taking a
more robust approach to the trade talks, the volume of China's trade with
all regions of the world was growing at exponential rates. Bilateral trade
volumes grew hand in hand with increasing direct investment into China,
and new flows of Chinese investment to the Global South. China's trade
with its Asian neighbours grew rapidly in the aftermath of its WTO
accession. Total trade between China and ASEAN increased from US$38
billion in 2001 to over US$78.2 billion in 2003, to US$105.88 billion by
2004 and US$202 billion in 2007.[15] China, in this period, surpassed the
US as Japan's largest trading partner[16], and became the most important

---

[12] Mandelson 2005b. Beijing's offer to host a mini-ministerial meeting in July 2005, in
advance of the Hong Kong Ministerial Conference, was seen by Mandelson as a 'very
positive sign'.

[13] Mandelson 2006.

[14] Wanlin 2005.

[15] Official Chinese statistics from the Customs General Administration of China. See:
http://www.customs.gov.cn/tongjishujv/index.asp; "China, ASEAN become fourth largest
trade partners", *Chinaview* February 29, 2008, http://www.chinadaily.com.cn/china/2008-
02/29/content_6497860.htm.

[16] See also UNCTAD 2004, iv.

trading partner to South Korea.[17] The growing dependence in East Asia on Chinese demand for sustained economic growth has meant increasing influence for Beijing within the region. A United Nations report cited China as a '[m]ajor engine of growth for most of the economies of the region. China's imports accelerated more than its exports, with a large proportion coming from the rest of Asia'.[18] China's sustained, high-speed economic growth was being translated into international influence inside the region.[19]

In the same period China's trade with its number one and two export markets, the US and EU, also saw major gains. In 2003, China overtook Japan as America's third-largest trading partner; by 2006, it passed Mexico to become the second-largest (by 2008, it surpassed Canada to become the number one trading partner). In 2006, bilateral US-China trade totalled US$343 billion, with a staggering US$232 billion trade surplus for China (see Geoffrey Allen Pigman's chapter in this volume, Chapter 3). The EU's bilateral trade deficit with China followed a similar pattern as the US. In 2006, the EU's trade with China was worth more than €255 billion, with a deficit for the EU of €128 billion, and it was projected to reach €170 billion in 2007. China was the EU's biggest source of merchandise imports (valued at €191 billion for 2006), as exports grew at 15-20 per cent. China was the EU's fastest growing trade partner.

China also expanded its trade relations beyond its established partners, building new ties with Africa and Latin America/the Caribbean. China's annual trade with Africa grew rapidly, from US$10.6 billion in 2000 to US$60 billion in 2006, and was projected to reach US$100 billion by 2010. China became the third-largest trading partner to Africa, trailing only the US and France. Its trade with Latin America and the Caribbean also expanded rapidly, increasing more than seven-fold from 2000 to 2006. What is noteworthy is how the new trade flows, from 2000 to 2006 allowed China to position itself as a key nexus in the world economy, running trade deficits with developing countries in ASEAN, Latin America and Africa, and strong trade surpluses with the developed world (except Japan and South Korea).

The favourable balance of trade which China enjoyed in the aftermath of its WTO accession was most obvious in the massive foreign

---

[17] One Chinese report estimated that 3 to 4 million jobs in South Korea were related to trade in China. Source: "Han dui zhongguo jingji yilaidu zheng 3.6bei 400wan renkou zhongguo shenghuo" [South Korea's economic dependence on China increases 3.6 fold, 4 million people depend on China for living], *Renmin ribao* [People's Daily], January 8, 2005.

[18] UNCTAD 2004, iv.

[19] Chin and Stubbs 2008.

exchange reserves it was amassing. In February 2006, China's FOREX holdings surpassed those of Japan, rising to US$850.1 billion, and in early 2007 its holdings broke the US$1-trillion mark. As Geoffrey Allen Pigman also notes in his chapter (see Chapter 3), during this period China became the primary source of funding for the massive US current account deficit. China accumulated huge dollar asset holdings in order to maintain the stability of its own currency (arguably propping up an overvalued dollar) and kept inflation and interest rates low in the US. China's US dollar asset holdings have enabled Chinese authorities to resist American efforts to pressure China into a large-scale appreciation of the *renminbi* (RMB), aimed at 'correcting' the trade imbalance along the lines that Japan accepted in the 1985 to 1987 period.[20] In addition to exerting such defensive power, or power as autonomy, Beijing has translated its foreign currency reserves into international creditor influence by providing new official and non-official lending to the developing world.

With the above trade data in mind, it is little wonder that Beijing lacked the motivation to adjust its approach to the Doha Round.[21] In fact, Chinese authorities had every reason to maintain their low-key and selective approach to the world multilateral trade talks.[22] Stephen Roach, the chief economist for Morgan Stanley, drew similar conclusions about the lack of significance of the Doha Round in general. He argued that: '[t]he global trade dynamic matters much more than a high profile media event staged around a breakthrough in multilateral negotiations. Despite repeatedly stiff resistance to the Doha agenda for nearly five-years, there can be no mistaking the powerful gains in world trade that have occurred over the same period. Global trade volumes… rose by 6.6 per cent per annum over the 2002-05 period'.[23] China was consistently on the winning side of this growth in world trade and arguably *the* largest benefactor. The data helps explain why Beijing took a low-key approach during the early stages of the Doha Round.

Phase II: Intensifying Criticism

The appointment of a new US Trade Representative (USTR) Susan Schwab under the second Bush administration, combined with another set of failed high-level talks in July 2006 served to bring renewed pressure

---

[20] Chin and Helleiner 2008, 87-102.

[21] Discussion with Canadian trade officials (Beijing, January 2005 and August 2006).

[22] Arthur Stein has explained that if states perceive an international organisation to be in need of reform, their interest in multilateralism must be sufficiently great to exceed the expected costs of reform; otherwise, unilateralism or ad hoc multilateralism will be the result (see Stein 1990).

[23] Roach 2006.

on Beijing. In August 2006, Schwab met with her Chinese counterparts and directly pressed Beijing 'to step up and play an active role' in bringing a successful conclusion to the Doha Round.[24] She specifically referred to China needing to play a greater leadership role in pressing the G20 group of developing countries and the 'G33 camp', which was seeking protection for its subsistence farmers.

Schwab encouraged Beijing to see China's interests as different from other countries in the G20 and the Group of 33 (G33) trade coalitions, stating:

> In both groups, other countries – with trade interests decidedly different from China's – are playing the leading roles. Is it really in China's best interest, I asked Minister Bo yesterday, to have these other countries appearing to speak for China? To influence the outcome of negotiations in ways that do not necessarily reflect China's strength and needs?

She continued:

> Goods trade as a share of GDP for India, increased from 13% in 1990 to 25% in 2004. For China, it increased to almost 60% over the same period. Surely, now is the time for China to play a great role – commensurate with its status as the third largest trading nation in the world.

According to Schwab, China needed to 'lead by example', by further opening its own markets and spur domestic consumption and growth; minimise loopholes that counter tariff cuts; and reassure foreign markets of reciprocal opening, including Southern markets.

The USTR also pressed Beijing to take a more proactive approach to the Doha Round, since: 'As an export powerhouse, China should be clear about its stake in a multilateral round that maximizes market opening and trade facilitation'. Schwab added a more coercive message: '[a] failed Doha Round could foster greater protectionism around the world. There are dozens of bills in the U.S. Congress proposed by members who want us to "get tough" or "stand up to China"'. There is growing concern inside the US over American jobs, but that: 'Responsible actions and leadership by China can help allay those concerns'. The US chief trade representative also cast doubt on Beijing's self-identification as a 'developing country', stating:

> I would note that this is an instance where traditional labels – 'developing country' and 'recently acceded member' – simply don't

---

[24] Schwab 2006, 2.

work for China. China has legitimate development concerns, but it is also a manufacturing giant, as big and competitive in many sectors as any developed country in the world. Rather than expend time debating whether or how China fits into these categories, we should work practically and pragmatically to find a way forward.

Similar to the EU Trade Commissioner, America's chief trade representative painted Beijing as hedging its interests and passively uncooperative in the Doha Round. Schwab summed up this image as follows: 'When China wants to make things happen in the Doha Round, it can be both influential and constructive. But it is also clear that at present, China is still assessing its role in the WTO and in the Round'.[25]

With each set of failed ministerial conferences and mini-ministerial gatherings, the senior executive of the WTO also put a spotlight on Beijing to play a greater role, and issued statements that reinforced the image of China as a partial participant in the trade talks. At well publicised 'mediating meetings' in Beijing in September 2006, WTO Director-General Pascal Lamy urged Chinese leaders to play a greater role in revitalising the DDA talks. Lamy urged China to '[p]lay a positive and constructive role in rekindling the Doha Round, and pushing forward the talks to reach an agreement'.[26] He asked Beijing to strengthen its efforts and play a greater global leadership role for the trade negotiations.[27] The implicit message was that China could be doing more to resolve the embattled trade round.

A number of think-tank commentators added their voices to the imaging of China as partially supportive, partially cooperative and somewhat paradoxical. Jeffrey Schott of the Institute for International Economics described China as a 'constructive but low-key participant in the Doha Round':

China has played a useful role in advancing the negotiating process through its membership in the G-20 coalition of developing countries. That said, China's low profile in the WTO talks is not befitting its status as one of the world's largest economies and trading nations. It has not offered additional reforms beyond the extensive commitments undertaken in its 2001 protocols of accession, and

[25] Ibid, 7.

[26] 'China Calls for Reviving Doha Talks, Urges Developed Nations to Make Concessions', *Xinhua*, 6 September 2006 (online: http://english,people.com.cn).

[27] 'Pascal Lamy in China to Revive Doha Round', *Xinhua* (posted on *WebIndia News*, online), 17 June 2007; Wang and Wen 2006.

deserves blame – along with other major trading nations – for the current impasse in the talks.[28]

He added: 'China has an important stake in a well-functioning multilateral trading system – that's why…it needs to take a more active leadership role in reviving the Doha Round'.[29]

The above images of China in the Doha Round were not completely without base – especially for the period up to the US subprime crisis in summer 2008, and the onset of the global financial crisis. It had become clear that regardless of external pressure from the US, EU and WTO representatives, Chinese authorities were reluctant to enrol themselves in pressuring India and Brazil, the G20, the G33 or the Group of 77 (G77) – in public – to accept the US and EU counter-offers in the agricultural negotiations or other issue-areas. Beijing demonstrated some willingness to engage in behind-the-scenes brokering, as seen at the Hong Kong meetings when Chinese trade officials tried to encourage African and Indian representatives to give more consideration to the American and European counter-offers. However, they would only go so far in pressing their Southern counterparts. Since WTO accession, Chinese authorities have been far from eager to take on 'collaborative leadership' together with the established members of the WTO. In public, they made sure to remain steadfast in their rhetorical support to developing countries and avoided siding against the G20, even when Chinese national economic interests were at stake.

After another set of failed WTO talks in July 2007, and in the lead up to the July 2008 high-level talks, American and European authorities toughened their negotiating positions with respect to China.[30] As they watched as the country's trade surplus rose 73 per cent in May from a year earlier to US$22.45 billion, lawmakers in the US (and Europe) accused China of unfairly supporting exporters by maintaining an undervalued currency. In the first week of June 2008, four US senators introduced legislation that would allow American companies to petition for steeper anti-dumping duties to counter the benefit of any undervalued currencies in China or other countries. Meanwhile, EU Trade Commissioner Peter Mandelson warned China against ignoring violations of WTO rules.[31] New French President Nicolas Sarkozy added his voice

---

[28] Jeffrey Schott's statements are quoted in Wang and Wen 2006.

[29] Ibid.

[30] Simon Kennedy and Mark Drejam, 'Beggar-Thy-Neighbour Protectionism Loom after Doha Trade Talks', *Bloomberg*, 18 June 2008.

[31] The WTO reported that products from China were targeted in 36 of the 103 investigations into whether goods were being dumped in the last six months of 2006.

to the mix calling unrestricted free trade a 'policy of naïveté' and vowed that he would 'fight to defend' French interests in the trade talks.

The July 2008 mini-ministerial gathering in Geneva again failed to reach a conclusion to the DDA, as the negotiations stalled over disagreement between the US, and India and China on the specifics of the Special Safeguard Mechanism (SSM). It was now the third time in a row that a major high-level meeting broke down, after July 2006 and July 2007. But this time was not the 'same procedure' as in the previous summers. Ministers from about 40 countries had met in a 9-day and night negotiating marathon, but failed to reach agreement on modalities in agriculture and non-agricultural market access (NAMA), the major sticking areas for concluding the Doha Round. The collapse of the talks this time was a major setback for the Doha Round, a political debacle in the eyes of the WTO caretakers, and huge frustration for all involved. One commentator notes that: '[t]he meeting made clear that developing countries, such as India, China and Brazil, had emerged as coequal powers, irrevocably changing the negotiation dynamics. They showed that no deal would be possible against their development interests'.[32]

Emerging from a Group of 7 (G7) strategy meeting the day before the talks formally ended in open hostility, Schwab bluntly told reporters: 'We are very much concerned about the direction that a couple of countries are taking [implicitly referring to India and China]. We had on Friday night a real path forward to a successful Doha round'. She said there had been a delicate balance in the text and six of the seven countries had embraced the outcome. If one thread is pulled, she said, the deal would unravel. But one country was not party to the agreement and now a second country is backtracking on commitments it made, and there is a real risk as that country is advocating selectively reopening the package. She added that the US will continue to bring the negotiation back to a form where we can have a successful outcome. Indian Commerce Minister Kamal Nath emerged a half-hour after Schwab. He said that when the package was initially presented, it was made clear that India had not agreed to it, and emphasised that the SSM is an issue for 90 countries, since it is a safeguard to protect the poorest of the poor. The statements from Schwab and Nath foreshadowed the very open contestation that would come the next day, which ended the talks.

WTO Director-General (DG) Pascal Lamy, who had put a lot of personal investment into this meeting, stated: 'There is no use beating about the bush. This meeting has collapsed'. Peter Sutherland, a former DG of the organisation warned: 'I don't want to be apocalyptic about the

---

[32] Grammling 2008, 1.

world trading system, but it is in danger, no doubt about that'.[33] A succession of comments linked China and India to the failed talks. Chinese trade officials countered by chastising American and other officials for engaging in finger-pointing. The usually diplomatic Chinese WTO Ambassador Sun Zhenyu told the informal Trade Negotiations Committee (TNC) meeting: 'We have tried very hard to contribute to the success of the round. It is surprising that at this time, the US started this finger pointing. I am surprised because they are now talking about cotton, sugar, rice of China as if we are not going to make any more efforts there'.[34] China's top trade representative, Commerce Minister Chen Deming, emphasised that: 'WTO members should make collective efforts to ensure a successful conclusion of the Doha Round trade negotiations'.[35] Minister Chen told a meeting of WTO Ambassadors in Geneva (July 2008) that: 'We should work together with a concerted mind, collective wisdom and maximum courage so as to pave a solid ground for the successful conclusion of the negotiations'.

Noting the unfavourable international reaction to Schwab's remarks, the USTR moderated its official statement on the talks. However, Fred Bergsten, one of the more prominent voices in US think-tank circles, went public with a highly critical rendering of China's role in the Doha Round in the journal *Foreign Affairs*, referring to Beijing's '[k]ey role in torpedoing the Doha Round of the global trade negotiations in July [2008]'.[36] Bergsten notes:

China's actions over the past few years have challenged some of the most fundamental norms and rules of the existing global order... As the world's second largest economy (and its second-largest exporter), China bears a great deal of responsibility for preserving the global trading system. In the past, China never played an active role in the Doha talks, but *it is now aggressively challenging the system*. At the WTO ministerial meeting in Geneva in late July, China joined the organization's inner steering committee for the first time. It seemed that China might be willing to help promote a fruitful outcome. But China, far from supporting liberalization, used its newfound clout to join India in seeking new protection beyond the red lines of most of the other participants, including many developing countries.[37]

---

[33] Simon Kennedy and Mark Drejam, 'Beggar-Thy-Neighbour Protectionism Loom after Doha Trade Talks', *Bloomberg*, 18 June 2008.
[34] 'Trade: US Attack on China, India Sours the Mood at WTO Talks', *Third World Network*, 29 July 2008.
[35] 'China Calls for Collective Effort to Conclude Doha Round', *Xinhua*, 22 July 2008.
[36] Bergsten 2008a.
[37] Ibid. (emphasis added).

He added: 'China's refusal to accept a significant share of systemic responsibility for the global economy also bodes ill for other upcoming international negotiations – particularly on climate change... the China-India alliance that emerged in Geneva could fundamentally alter the politics of global economic negotiations'.[38] In Bergsten's account, it is as if China has turned overnight from a disinterested and somewhat aloof actor inside the WTO into an active disruptor of the global trading regime.

Bergsten's criticism continued in a follow-up article: 'China has been playing at best a passive and at worst a disruptive role'; Beijing holds a preference for 'low quality, politically motivated bilateral and regional trade arrangements rather than economically meaningful (and demanding) multilateral trade liberalization through the WTO'.[39] He described China as refusing to contribute positively to the Doha Round; this has all but ensured the failure of the talks. In sum: 'Despite its growing economic clout, China continues to act like a small country with little impact on the global system at large and therefore little responsibility for it. This behaviour threatens to undermine the existing international economic architecture'. Bergsten was not only echoing the frustrations of the USTR – minus the diplomatic veil – but also reinforcing a negative image of China's role in the Doha Round.

2   REMAKING CHINA'S IMAGE

By early 2007, Chinese trade officials could see that the inherent macroeconomic biases in the US-China relationship were setting up the two countries for incessant trade conflict, and that the US-China trade dynamic was becoming a lightening rod in the Doha Round. America, with its massive trade deficit, was feeling more exposed than ever. Washington was facing a US$200 billion bilateral imbalance with China in 2005, which accounted for 25 per cent of America's record US$800 billion trade deficit of that year, Washington fell into the blame game. The result was over 20 pieces of China-oriented trade legislation introduced in the US Congress within a short period.

Rising protectionism in the US and Europe made Chinese authorities take notice, and they began to rethink their Doha strategy. Having paid little heed to the pressure from foreign trade representatives to take a greater role in pressing the developing countries in the DDA, this confluence of changing world economic conditions and more trenchant criticism of China's role in the Doha Round forced Beijing to react.

---

[38] Ibid.
[39] Bergsten 2008b, 57-70.

Similar to how Chinese foreign policy strategists had in the recent past awoken to China's international image and recognised the need to remake China's image on a range of issues (from human rights to its security relations with regional neighbours threatened by China's rise)[40], the Chinese government started to grasp the potential damage that could be caused from the criticism levelled at Beijing from summer 2008 onwards. That China's trade performance was starting to feel the effects of the increasing protectionism further compounded the sense that change in Beijing's Doha strategy was needed.

In the course of dealing with international human rights pressure and the 'China threat' perception, Beijing had become much more sophisticated in replying to international criticism.[41] Chinese trade diplomats had learned that blunt, defensive and angry denials directed at 'foreign' commentators would not transform the impression of China held by the foreign audience. And that empirical refutation was also not enough. Chinese trade officials had realised the need to strengthen their diplomatic management of China's international image even though Beijing saw the criticism as groundless. They convinced Chinese leaders that China could no longer afford to deflect the pressure and criticism from the US and EU; that they needed to make more of their opportunities to reassure the international community about how much effort China was putting into the Doha Round. The Party and government leadership had come to better appreciate the power of these images, especially in a multilateral setting, and agreed to sanction its leading trade officials to take it upon themselves to 'improve the world's understanding of China's intentions' through enhancing information dissemination to the public. Rather than maintain a low profile, Chinese trade officials formulated a strategy for disclosing more information in order to 'let the world better understand' China's motives and intentions. Chinese officials re-moulded China's image in the Doha Round and increased their diplomatic efforts to convince others of 'China's intentions', and persuade audiences to see Chinese actions in the desired manner.

Since summer 2008, Chinese trade officials have focused on doing a better job of branding China, to shift the international image away from the negative images. A marked shift was initiated in Beijing's language in late 2008, as it began offering more reassuring statements, such as the following from Commerce Minister Chen Deming:

China attaches great importance to the Doha Round because its success will contribute to even fairer and more rational rules for international trade over the next decade or two. It will also create a more stable

---

[40] Rabinovitch 2008, 40.
[41] Ibid.

international environment essential for all members, which will help especially the large number of developing members to develop their economies. As a developing member and a recently acceded member as well, China has fulfilled its obligations and exerted its utmost efforts to push the round toward a successful conclusion.[42]

To counter the impression that China was providing only partial support to the Doha Round, Chinese authorities noted that since the start of DDA, 'China has submitted over 100 proposals on various negotiation items', either independently or jointly with other members, and has played an 'active role' ever since the start of the DDA negotiations.[43]

As the global financial crisis worsened, Chinese trade officials have increasingly emphasised China's role as a bridge-builder between the developing and developed countries, especially to ensure a 'development-friendly' multilateral trading system. Commerce Minister Chen Deming noted at the WTO informal ministerial meetings in July 2008 in Geneva that China has played a constructive bridging role during the G7 (WTO) consultations: 'At a critical moment when the negotiations were at the verge of breakdown, China urged other members to *bridge* their differences. Meanwhile, China worked with other members, sparing no effort to reach agreement on modalities for agriculture and non-agricultural market access'.[44]

3   SETTING THE RECORD STRAIGHT

Does the bridge-building metaphor adequately capture the role that China played inside the WTO, from its entry in late 2000 to July 2008? It is suggested here that this was only part of the story. While China has not tried to take a strong leadership role inside the Doha Round, it would also be inaccurate to call it a passive actor.

Reforming WTO rules and ruling bodies[45]

In a study of country participation in WTO activities undertaken by Hakan Nordstrom that examines data on written submissions which member countries have undertaken both individually and with others, in

---

[42] Chen Deming, 'China's Top Trade Official: Don't Abandon the Doha Round', *Business Week*, 15 September 2008 (online: http://www.businessweek.com/globalbiz/content/sep2008/gb20080915_757484.htm)

[43] Ibid.

[44] Ibid. (emphasis added)

[45] Much of the empirical information in this section is drawn from: Pearson 2006; Luan 2003, 1097-1116.

2003 alone, China emerges as the most active developing country and the third most active WTO member.[46] This data includes submissions to both the ruling bodies of the WTO as well as the Doha Round. The data revealed that China has been particularly active in the Rules Committee, with eighteen submissions.[47] While trade rounds garner most of the media attention on the WTO, China has instead focused on advancing reforms at a less high-profile, but ultimately more fundamental level. Beijing will have a deep and lasting effect on the international regime and the architecture of global governance (by influencing the interpretation and development of the rules of the global trading regime, and its ruling bodies and mechanisms).

The bridge metaphor captures only a part of China's role inside the WTO. It has been more than a broker among competing interests between like-minded groups, or facilitator of other countries' interests in the Doha negotiations. Beijing has also promoted a number of reformist measures on the rules and procedural mechanisms of the global trade regime. These reforms are in the interest of China, newly-acceded members and developing countries. The bridge metaphor does not capture how Beijing has subtly but assertively defended and advanced such interests. It has, however, done so, constructively, from within the WTO, rather than threatening the international regime from the outside, or from a position of radical rejection. In this regard, China has not acted as a *radically* revisionist power. Below, we describe how Beijing has championed *moderate* revision of the international regime.

In the time period since becoming a WTO member, and prior to its stand with India in summer 2008, China supported two 'development-minded' governance reform initiatives within the WTO. Rather than identifying with the traditional trading powers, as some analysts had assumed, China gave its support to procedural reforms which aimed to moderate the influence of the developed countries over the WTO's Secretariat and committee chairs. These committees have a strong hand in agenda setting for the international organisation as a whole. In the language of international political economy, China was supporting developing country efforts to moderate the 'structural power' of the developed countries over the international trade regime – their ability to set the agenda.[48] Pearson has noted that, at the onset of the Doha Round, China joined a large group of developing countries in January 2002 to

---

[46] China's total of 65 written submissions was significantly below the EU (120 submissions) and the US (116), but more than India, the second most active developing country.
[47] Ten of these submissions related to subsidies and countervailing duties.
[48] Strange 1988, 24-29.

demand that the chairmanship of the Trade Negotiations Committee (TNC) for the Doha Round be rotated among member ambassadors rather than be appointed by the Director-General of the WTO.[49] The proposal was not adopted in the short term, but China indicated that it would only be conceding for this trade round.

China also joined a group of developing countries to advocate for restrictions on the discretionary authority of the chairs of the six TNC subcommittees in determining which alternative positions are included for consideration in draft proposals.[50] The developing countries wanted to prevent compromise texts that did not reflect their interests and to open up the deliberation process in determining the language in the text (Faizel Ismail further critiques the role of the NAMA chair in Chapter 9). Although China was seen by many observers as following the initiatives of others in these two instances, there are other reports that China was actually quite active in influencing these initiatives. Nonetheless Pearson surmised in China's early years in the WTO that Beijing's support for WTO reforms were to gain easy, no-cost tactical wins, 'rather than a serious gambit to alter the power structure' of the international organisation.[51]

Beijing has, however, proposed reforms at the level of reforming the ruling bodies of the WTO – where most of the organisation's work actually occurs. China's gradual reform impact can be seen in the area of the WTO's Dispute Settlement Mechanism (DSM). Beijing has learned how to use the WTO's DSM to protect itself, in essence, using the WTO's own levers to become protectionist, but in a WTO-compliant manner.[52] It has learned to do this by closely examining the DSM process. As of 2006, China had participated on an unprecedented 55 cases as a third party. Chinese officials suggest that this shows their commitment to learn the rules of the dispute-settlement game. Being a third party also means that China can make written submissions to the adjudication panel, and review the submissions made by the parties in dispute. It has enabled China to gain experience while investing minimal resources (symbolic and material), and information that is useful for ensuring smooth integration into the system of rules. It also allows China to draw important tactical and strategic lessons (with an eye to future

---

[49] Pearson 2006, 253. This reform proposal was pushed by a broad coalition of developing countries, including most African countries, many countries in the Caribbean and Central America, and Pakistan, and was opposed by the Quad countries (US, EU, Canada, and Japan), Southeast Asian countries, and India. See also: Kanth 2002 and *Inside US-China Trade*, 25 January 2002.

[50] Pearson 2006, 253.

[51] Ibid.

[52] Kennedy 2005, 407-432.

disputes) in a no-risk learning process. Participation in dispute cases as third party also allows China to increase its influence. Ji and Jiang explain that China, by frequently airing its opinion in WTO cases, can register its view and position on the disputes to other members, thus expanding its influence inside the global trade regime.[53]

Beijing has also tried to influence the development of the rules by advancing reforms of the DSM. Within the Doha Round Working Group, China has raised the problem of delays in DSM panel proceedings, and technical and administrative difficulties that developing countries face. China tabled *Specific Amendments to the Dispute Settlement Understanding – Drafting Inputs from China*.[54] This proposed called for 'restraint' in cases from developed countries against developing country members, and offered specific measures through which developing country members could gain protection in cases brought against them by developed countries.[55]

The Chinese reform proposal would mean placing limits on the number of cases that individual developed country members could bring to Geneva in any single year. Beijing proposed that: '[d]eveloped country members shall not bring more than two cases to the WTO Dispute Settlement Body against a particular developing country members in one calendar year'.[56] The proposal did not call for similar constraints on developing countries. The second proposal was for a developed country member to pay to the developing country member's litigation costs if a developed country brings a case against a developing country.[57] This proposal indirectly highlights the inherent disadvantages the developing countries have experienced with the legalistic turn in international organisation; and the legal-cultural and normative advantages that the traditional trading powers have enjoyed as the rule-makers. It also highlights the legal and administrative capacity-building costs that developing countries have to undertake when they become members of the global trading regime. The Chinese proposals essentially call for Northern burden sharing on the South's legal and normative adjustment costs.

The DSM reform proposals position China as an active and constructive new member, working inside the international institution. The spirit of the reform proposals are in keeping with Beijing's foreign policy of self-identification with the developing world. The Chinese proposals aim

---

[53] Ji and Jiang 2005, 4. Cited in Gu et al 2008, 284.
[54] WTO 2003, 1-3. Cited in Gu, Humphrey and Messner 2008, 283.
[55] Gu, Humphrey and Messner 2008, 283.
[56] WTO 2003, 2.
[57] WTO 2003, 2.

at restraining the Northern country members from using the DSM to
'harass' Southern members, who lack human and financial resources for
lengthy litigation.[58] Beijing's approach could also be motivated by Chinese
political-cultural traditions, specifically the combination of 'right' (*yi* –
which refer to just, impartial and rational legal provisions), and 'tact'
(*mou*) for settling disputes.[59] The normative implication for the WTO
would be adding 'goodwill' and 'trust' to the normative mix for the
settlement of disputes in the global trading regime.

China's DSM reform activities are motivated by a desire to
protect and advance its own interests, while also advancing institutional
reforms that it views as shared by other developing countries. With the
DSM reforms, China could be working to build new consensus in the
global trading regime, initially around operational and procedural
standards on dispute settlement, before taking on deeper 'dissensus'
issues such as the substantive values of the regime itself (e.g. the WTO's
current definition of 'transparency'). Beijing is building on the activism
of the G20 developing country coalition and the call for the global trading
regime to be reformed to better reflect the needs of developing countries.
In the reform agenda discussed above, we see examples of China's
potential to promote procedural shifts that could result in gradual but
cumulatively fundamental changes in the organisational character and
systemic culture of the global trade regime. Suffice it is to say at this
point that the notion of China as a low profile actor is misleading. It
ignores cultural differences in negotiating style as well the fact that China
has directed most of its reform attention at procedural reforms in the
operational norms, rules and ruling bodies of the WTO regime – rather
than the Doha trade talks.

China's role in the G20 coalition

Recent appraisals of China's performance in the WTO appear to support
the image of an active China. Robert Lawrence of the Peterson Institute
of International Economics suggests that China has been 'active in the
Doha Round negotiations'.[60] He notes that China has been actively
engaged in the NAMA discussions on formulas that should be employed
for tariff reduction. Although it would be in China's national interests to
see as much liberalisation as possible (since it would benefit
economically from lower barriers to its agricultural exports to developing
countries), in agriculture it has joined the G20 to push for reductions in

---

[58] Luan 2003.
[59] Ibid.
[60] Lawrence 2008, 151.

subsidies and protections in developed countries. China has also backed G20 and G33 demands for flexibility for developing countries to assist poor farmers. In the services area, China is interested in seeing greater liberalisation for movement of natural persons (mode-four liberalisation), which would increase opportunities for Chinese workers to work abroad. Beijing has shown particular concern for the rules and more disciplined procedures for gauging dumping. Lawrence concludes that although China has not tried to play as strong a leadership role as Brazil, it has 'by no means been passive'.[61]

China's relations with the G20 coalition reveal important insight into how China's approach to the Doha Round can be characterised as a selective approach to intervening in G20 issues, together with consistent rhetorical support for South-South cooperation. A number of scholars have remarked that although China has participated in the G20 (together with Brazil, India and South Africa, as discussed in this volume), it has not been a proactive member. In a number of instances, China has allowed itself to be called a 'leader' on issues championed by the G20 coalition, and allowed its standing to be leveraged by the G20 to lend additional credibility on a particular issue. However, China's role in this coalition has been seen as mainly lending support – rather than to lead or give sustained force – to advancing the group's agendas.[62] Chinese trade officials have admitted that it is not in China's best interest to align itself too closely with this coalition of developing countries.[63] China, unlike many other developing countries, has been a major beneficiary of economic globalisation. China has already made significant concessions – what one analyst called terms 'so onerous they violate fundamental WTO principles'[64] – to gain entry into the WTO. Rather than sharing the desire of many developing countries to delay full external economic liberalisation, China actually shares an interest with the US and EU in seeing greater access to developing country markets.

Beijing has avoided pushing too hard on G20 issues and alienating the developed countries. At the same time, it has its own domestic agricultural sector to protect.[65] China has had to manage the contradictions between its interests as an international buyer and as a seller in its bilateral trade relations with the major developing economies (e.g. Brazil and India), as well as the least-developed countries. China, like any major

---

[61] Ibid, 152.
[62] Pearson 2006, 255.
[63] Liang 2007, 133-135.
[64] Lardy 2002.
[65] Lampton 2008, 94; Pearson 2006, 251-255.

trading power, gains and looses friends when exercising its power as a buyer and seller. Chinese officials have questioned whether it is possible to find enduring complementary interests that can form the basis for sustained alliances with the other developing countries. Here, there are big questions. Chinese trade officials have noted the fractious nature of this developing country group, remarking that because of divergent interests, the G20 'cannot be led'.[66]

However, at a crucial moment in the Doha Round, Beijing did side with the countries hurt by agricultural import barriers in the developed countries, and started to take a greater leadership role, even if not pushing its own agenda among the G20. China's position as a major agricultural producer and buyer gives it potential normative power, if Beijing decided to promote the interests of the developing countries that are struggling because of the disadvantages of agricultural protectionism of the wealthy countries. The differences within the G20 notwithstanding, Beijing responded to the call to take a more active role in the Doha Round. This response was stirred not mainly by high-level pressure from the US, EU and the WTO itself, or rising trade protectionism, but by the growing concern expressed by the G77. At a G77 plus China ministerial meeting in Ghana in April 2008, the G77 called attention to the impasse of the Doha Round and raised their concern about the spreading of the subprime financial and credit crises.[67] The G77 was '[p]articularly concerned that the Doha Round negotiations so far have not met the expectations of developing countries', and emphasised that '[a]ll WTO members should uphold and reiterate their commitment for the WTO to promote an open, equitable, rule-based, predictable and non-discriminatory and development-friendly multilateral trading system'.[68] The G77 declared that the Doha Round should bring about improvement in multilateral rules that address and remove existing asymmetries, enhance the fairness and equity of the multilateral trading system, and eliminate all forms of export subsidies.

How are we to understand the Chinese government's consistent self-identification with the developing world and then its decision to stand with India and the other 90 countries that wanted the SSM reassurances in summer 2008? Margaret Pearson, reflecting on the first-two years of China's WTO membership, reported that 'these [China's South-South cooperation] efforts are said by those close to the process to

---

[66] Pearson 2006, 254.

[67] 'G77 Plus China Ministerial meeting Highlights Doha Round Talk', *Xinhua* (online), 21 April 2008.

[68] These concerns were listed in the ministerial declaration of the meeting.

have been a deliberate tactic to lay a foundation for future negotiating leverage'.[69] She found that: 'Ultimately, China has not been a forceful advocate of the development agenda. Rather, its "developmental" positions have been closely linked to its own economic interests'. The understanding is that Beijing's self-identification with the developing world is motivated mainly by national economic gain, rather than authentic altruistic identification with the global South.

A different understanding is offered here, which sees the Chinese government's self-identification with the developing world as motivated partly by national interests and also by enduring ideological legacies of the Maoist period, namely 'Third Worldist' foreign policy self-identification. More specifically, the continuing influence of Deng Xiaoping's insistence in the early post-Mao period that China must align and identify itself as part of the Third World; that as a 'socialist nation', China must never seek hegemonic leadership or 'bully others' – that 'it shares a common destiny with all Third World countries and that it will remain one of them even when it becomes prosperous and powerful,'[70] China's self-identification with the G20 rather than the established trading powers is similar to Beijing's discomfort with realigning itself with the G7/8, the so-called 'club of rich nations', despite the fact that the established powers now seem serious about establishing more structured relations with China, even if not ready to enlarge its membership to include China.[71] Despite becoming the world's factory and being a *de facto* Great Power, it has served Beijing's strategic interests and ideological needs to put concerted attention and resources into reaffirming China's self-identification with the global South.[72] This desire to self-identify with the South helps to explain why China, despite its more narrow national economic interests, has participated in the G20 coalition. Its decision to side with India in July 2008 shows that it has done so, even when this has required sacrificing a measure of China's national interests, to support the cause of this developing country coalition.

4   CONCLUSION

The discussion has shown that China has shifted from a fairly low key, selective, somewhat aloof though generally supportive approach to the Doha Round in the period since joining the WTO in December 2001, to taking a firmer stand on the side of the G20 by summer 2008. At the same time – and under-emphasised in the literature – is the fact that China has

---

[69] Pearson 2006, 252.
[70] Deng 1987, 46.
[71] Cooper 2008, 1-18.
[72] Chin 2008, 83-114.

been quite active in the international trading regime in terms of advancing concrete proposals for reforming the rules, operational norms and ruling bodies of the WTO. Beijing has advanced reform proposals and taken positions that place it on side with the general interests of developing countries and has even, in some cases such as the agricultural negotiations, willingly supported G20 bargaining positions that may not serve its immediate interests. It has shown some willingness to sacrifice for the 'greater good' of the Southern coalitions.

There is, however, nothing like a global financial and economic crisis to clarify strategic priorities. This chapter has shown that during the first-five years after China acceded to the WTO, Beijing did not respond to pressure from either the US or EU to take a more active role in urging developing countries to concede on their demands in order to conclude the DDA. The Chinese government's somewhat arms-length 'non-cooperation' with the traditional trading powers should not, however, be confused with seeing China as a passive actor inside the WTO. What is difficult to determine is whether Beijing will continue to support the G20, including backing India or Brazil against the developed country majors, as pressure builds from all sides for the WTO membership to conclude the current trade round.

The expansion of the global financial crisis into a broader economic crisis starting in summer 2008 has led to a fall in world trade and China has seen a major drop in its exports. Beijing has been in close communication with its trade-dependent East Asian neighbours, trying to develop a collective regional response. Chinese authorities have also communicated closely with major emerging economy partners – including India, Brazil and Russia – on how best to respond. China has kept close contact with its other allies in the global South, who are also very concerned about rising protectionism and falling commodity prices. In all cases, there is a desire to push the G7, particularly the US and EU, to restart the trade talks. The basic objective is to draw on the multilateral trading regime to try to contain rising trade protectionism in the major consumer markets of the world economy. The leading emerging economies have been unanimous in emphasising that there will be no sustained global economic recovery until the economic situation in the US and EU improves.

Amid the worsening global crisis, China has responded in ways that the former USTR Susan Schwab was hoping: '[t]hat China will carry out a clear-eyed assessment of the costs and benefits of a successful Doha Round, and conclude that it is in China's long-term self-interest to play an active role in ensuring the Round's ultimate success'.[73] This chapter has suggested that Beijing was actually doing this all along. However,

---

[73] Schwab 2006, 2.

until recently, it was not in China's national interests, as understood by the Party leadership, to burn up its political capital pressing the G20 or G33 coalitions to concede on previous offers from the US and EU. However, this was prior to the deepening of the global economic crisis. Global conditions have changed since summer 2008 and Beijing – together with India, Brazil and many developing countries – now see the possibility of continued declines in consumption in their key export markets and rising of trade barriers. This could result in a fundamental shift in China's approach to the Doha Round.

In playing a 'bridging' role, Beijing has mainly sided heretofore with the developing world in the Doha negotiations and in advancing organisational reforms. Yet at some crucial moments, it has tilted toward the developed countries, using its influence to direct the South toward the industrialised world. One such moment was when Beijing used the Shanghai APEC meetings in 2001 to build support to launch the Doha Round, convincing reluctant Southeast Asian nations of the utility of the round. More recently, the decision by Beijing and Washington in spring 2009 to re-commence with a 'high-level' US-China Strategic and Economic Dialogue suggests that it is likely there will be more instances in the future when these two governments will attempt to coordinate their approaches on the major strategic issues that directly affect each of them, usually matters that are also of global importance.

Despite the strong likelihood of continued economic tension between China and the US into the future[74], it is also likely that Beijing will work more closely with the US to resolve some difficult negotiation issues in the DDA, even if only behind closed doors.[75] However, in so doing, China's leaders will try to strike a balance between their Great Power relations, and their role in advancing and mediating the interests of developing country coalitions.

---

[74] Kirshner 2008, 238-259.
[75] Department of State 2009.

REFERENCES

Bergsten, C. Fred. 2008a. China and the Collapse of Doha. *Foreign Affairs*, 27 August (online: http://www.foreignaffairs.com/articles/64917/c-fred-bergsten/china- and-the-collapse-of-doha).

Bergsten, C. Fred. 2008b. A Partnership of Equals: How Washington Should Respond to China's Economic Challenge. *Foreign Affairs* 87(4):57-70, July-August.

Chin, Gregory and Eric Helleiner. 2008. China as a Creditor: A Rising Financial Power? *Journal of International Affairs* 62(1):87-102.

Chin, Gregory. 2008. China's Evolving G8 Engagement: Complex Interests and Multiple Identity in Global Governance Reform. In *Emerging Powers in Global Governance: Lesson from the Heiligendamm Process*, edited by Andrew F. Cooper and Agata Antkiewicz. Waterloo: Wilfred Laurier University Press.

Chin, Gregory and Richard Stubbs. 2008. Economic Diplomacy and Feedback Effects in the China-ASEAN FTA: Explaining 'Giving Six, Taking Four'. Paper presented at the Annual Meeting of the International Studies Association, March, San Francisco, Calif.

Cooper, Andrew F. 2008. The Heiligendamm Process: Structural Reordering and Diplomatic Agency. In *Emerging Powers in Global Governance: Lesson from the Heiligendamm Process*, edited by Andrew F. Cooper and Agata Antkiewicz. Waterloo: Wilfred Laurier University Press.

Deng, Xiaoping. 1984. Safeguard World Peace and Ensure Domestic Development. In *Fundamental Issues in Present-Day China*, edited by Deng Xiaoping. Beijing: Foreign Languages Press.

Department of State. 2009. Remarks by Hilary Rodham Clinton. *Toward a Deeper and Broader Relationship with China*. 21 February (online: http//www.state.gov/ secretary/rm/2009a/02/119432.htm).

Drezner, Daniel. 2007. *All Politics is Global: Explaining International Regulatory Regimes*. Princeton: Princeton University Press.

Grammling, Steffen. 2008. Major Setback for WTO's Doha Round: 'Mini-Ministerial' Failed and Future Looks Dim – A Chance for Reclaiming Its 'Development Dimension'? *Dialogue on Globalization Fact Sheet*, Friedrich-Ebert Stiftung, Geneva Office (August), pp. 1-6.

Hurell, Andrew. 2005. Power, Institutions, and the Production of Inequality. In *Power in Global Governance*, edited by Michael Barnett and Raymond Duvall. Cambridge: Cambridge University Press.

Ji, Wulian and Jiang Ling. 2005. *WTO Dispute Settlement Rules and China's Practice* [Chinese]. Beijing: Peking University Press.

Gu, Jing, John Humphrey and Dirk Messner. 2008. Global Governance and Developing Countries: The Implications of the Rise of China. *World Development* 36(2):274-292.

Kennedy, Scott. 2005. China's Porous Protectionism: The Changing Political Economy of Trade Policy. *Political Science Quarterly* 120(3):407-432.

Kirshner, Jonathan. 2008. The Consequences of China's Economic Rise for Sino-U.S. Relations: Rivalry, Political Conflict, and (Not) War. In *China's Ascent: Power, Security, and the Future of International Politics*, edited by Robert S. Ross and Zhu Feng. Ithaca, NY: Cornell University Press.

Lampton, David M. 2008. *Three Face of Chinese Power: Might, Money, and Minds.* Berkeley: University of California Press.

Lardy, Nicholas. 2002. *Integrating China into the Global Economy.* Washington, DC: Brookings Institution Press.

Lawrence, Robert Z. 2008. China and the Multilateral Trading System. In *China, Asia, and the New World Economy*, edited by Barry Eichengreen, Charles Wyplosz and Yung Chul Park. Oxford: Oxford University Press.

Liang, Wei. 2007. China: Globalization and the Emergence of a New Status Quo Power? *Asian Perspective* 31(4):125-149.

Luan, Xinjie. 2003. Dispute Settlement Mechanism Reforms in China's Proposal: Taking 'Right' as a Keystone. *Journal of World Trade* 37(6): 1097-1116.

Mandelson, Peter. 2005a. The EU and China: Partnership and Responsibility in the Global Economy. Speech by Peter Mandelson at the University of International Business and Economics, Beijing, 24 February.

Mandelson, Peter. 2005b. China: Global Trade's Make-Or-Break Player. *South China Morning Post*, 26 February.

Mandelson, Peter. 2006. Europe has to accept fierce competition: China has to ensure it is fair competition. Strasbourg, European Union.

Pearson, Margaret M. 2006. China in Geneva: Lessons from China's Early Years in the World Trade Organization. In *New Directions in the Study of China's Foreign Policy*, edited by Alastair Iain Johnston and Robert S. Ross. Stanford: Stanford University Press, pp. 242-271.

Rabinovitch, Simon. 2008. The Rise of an Image-Conscious China. *China Security* 4(3):33-47.

Schwab, Susan. 2006. Remarks by US Trade Representative Susan C. Schwab, American Chamber of Commerce-US China Business Council Event Luncheon, Kerry Center Ballroom, Beijing, 29 August.

Stein, Arthur A. 1990. *Why Nations Cooperate: Circumstance and Choice in International Relations.* Ithaca, NY: Cornell University Press.

Strange, Susan. 1988. *States and Markets.* New York: Basil Blackwell.

UNCTAD. 2004. *Trade and Development Report, 2004: Overview.* New York & Geneva: UNCTAD.

Wang, Yanjuan and Chen Wen. 2006. 'China and Doha'. *Beijing Review*, 14 December.

Wanlin, Aurore. 2005. The Doha Round: What Hope for Hong Kong? Centre for European Reform, *Briefing Note*, December 2: 1-5.

Zhao, Yuhong. 2007. Overcoming 'Green Barriers': China's First Five Years into the WTO. *Journal of World Trade*, 41(3):535-558.

BRENDAN VICKERS

7. 'RECLAIMING DEVELOPMENT' IN MULTILATERAL TRADE:

South Africa and the Doha Development Agenda

In truth the history of trade relations is largely one of inequality between peoples. [1]

Alec Erwin, former South African Minister of Trade and Industry.

Let's not go into a multilateral disarmament process and come out unilaterally disarmed. [2]

Rob Davies, South African Minister of Trade and Industry.

South Africa has in recent years played an increasingly active and assertive role in advancing the trade and development objectives of the Doha Development Agenda (DDA) in the World Trade Organisation (WTO). As a typical middle-income developing economy, South Africa is not ranked among the established or emerging 'big beasts'[3] of global trade, such as Brazil, China and India. The country's regional credentials as the largest, most industrialised and diversified economy on the African continent have also not secured Pretoria a seat at the High Table of the Doha negotiations, represented by the Group of 7 (G7) that emerged at Geneva in July 2008. Nonetheless, over the past fifteen years since the establishment of the WTO in 1995, South Africa has cultivated a credible reputation for its principled commitment to strengthening multilateralism, reforming global trade governance, and redressing the more pernicious effects of globalisation, particularly Africa's marginalisation in the world economy.

Like the bulk of the WTO's membership, South Africa's role in multilateral trade has been shaped by the confluence of domestic politics and foreign policy considerations. With an economy that relies heavily

---

[1] Erwin 2003.
[2] *Engineering News* 8 April 2009.
[3] Sally 2008, 112.

A. Narlikar, B. Vickers (eds.), Leadership and Change in the Multilateral Trading System, 149–180.

on global trade and investment inflows, South Africa has a strong interest in maintaining an open, orderly and development-friendly multilateral trading regime. But the country also confronts pressing socioeconomic pathologies that are typical of most developing nations. These include persistently high levels of structural unemployment, grinding poverty, and widening inequality. These domestic challenges, coupled with growing liberalisation scepticism following ambitious trade policy reform during the 1990s and more recent 'de-industrialisation' concerns, have led to a more inward-looking trade policy.[4] Today, industrial policy and other domestic-level considerations designed to strengthen and diversify the country's productive capabilities, rather than outward competitiveness reforms, provide the guiding lodestar for Pretoria's Doha diplomacy. In particular, this extends to the non-agricultural market access (NAMA) and services negotiations, where South Africa opposes ambitious liberalisation proposals, while defending the country's domestic and regional policy space to promote industrial development.

On the foreign policy front, the establishment of the WTO shortly after South Africa's own democratic transformation has provided a strategic global platform for the country to publicly project and build its post-apartheid identity as a responsible global citizen that plays by the rules of the game. Pretoria's active internationalism in multilateral trade and other global fora has promoted a reformist agenda premised on fairer trade for developing countries, more balanced global trade governance and inclusive and transparent global rule-making. With this principled attachment to multilateralism and a collaborative world order, South Africa's system-supporting role in the WTO has been widely regarded as quintessential middle-power-ship.[5]

This chapter explores South Africa's heightened activism and leadership agency in the Doha Round, both as a system-supporter in the WTO and a change-agent for greater equity in global trade. The chapter seeks to redress two gaps in the literature on South Africa's role in multilateral trade. First, beginning at Cancún in 2003 and particularly since the Hong Kong Ministerial Conference two years later, in 2005, South Africa's strategic positioning in the DDA has shifted to more closely align with the bargaining coalitions and normative claims of the majority developing world in the WTO. It appears that South Africa's Doha diplomacy is no longer simply predicated on the cautious and integrative 'middle power' agencies of facilitation, mediation and compromise positions between the industrialised and developing worlds, as happened at

---

[4] Davies 2009b.
[5] Nel Taylor and van der Westhuizen 2001; Taylor 2001; Lee 2006.

Seattle in 1999 and Doha in 2001.[6] Instead, an incipient 'developmental state' paradigm – coupled with greater distributive or value-claiming bargaining[7] – and an alternative norm of development to neoclassical free trade economics appears to drive South Africa's multilateral trade diplomacy, particularly in NAMA and services.

The second contribution to the literature suggests that this emerging phase of Pretoria's multilateral trade diplomacy is informed by a more progressive, if still broadly conformist politics of trade. Given South Africa's support for launching the omnibus DDA (contrary to the blocking strategy of the Africa Group), Lee makes a fair argument that by the endgame at Cancún in 2003: 'On all the key issues within the Doha negotiations, South Africa has advocated and supported neoliberal principles'.[8] The latter included agriculture, goods trade and services. However, with an increasingly inward-looking trade policy and a more interrogatory posture on the trade-growth paradigm, it is no longer the case that: *'No other Southern country has so comprehensively conformed to the orthodoxy'.*[9]

Since the time of Hong Kong in 2005, South Africa has led a concerted effort to 'reclaim' and reassert the development content of the Doha Round. The country has sought to shift the debate and focus of the negotiations from their mercantilist preoccupations, back to the heady spirit, letter and mandate of the 2001 Doha Ministerial Declaration (DMD). The corollary to this soft power[10] strategy is Pretoria's call for a fundamental paradigm shift in the negotiations, since it is deeply embedded historical or structural – and not simply *technical* – discontents that have precipitated the recurrent deadlock.[11] From Pretoria's understanding (a perspective it has sought to advance), the stasis in the WTO stems from an inexorable tension between the South's legitimate developmental concerns on the one hand, and the narrow commercial demands of developed country interest groups that benefit from the status quo and hence resist reform on the other.[12]

This chapter explores South Africa's role in the WTO and seeks to understand the strategic rationale and purpose of Pretoria's more recent change-agency activism in the Doha Round. Given the instrumental role that domestic-level compulsions have played in shaping South Africa's bargaining position in the DDA, the first part of the chapter

---

[6] See Keet 2004.
[7] Odell 2000.
[8] Lee 2006, 63.
[9] Lee 2006, 63 (emphasis added).
[10] Nye 2004.
[11] See Wilkinson 2006.
[12] Davies 2009a.

analyses the domestic drivers of the country's multilateral trade diplomacy and the two-level games of trade policy reform. The chapter then turns to explore South Africa's role in the WTO since the launch of the Doha negotiations in 2001. The chapter concludes by placing South Africa's multilateral trade diplomacy into a wider political economy perspective and suggests how this may evolve in the future, given the impact of the global financial crisis and the inauguration in May 2009 of a more progressive Zuma administration (including an apparent 'leftward' tilt in key economic ministries).

1   THE DOMESTIC DRIVERS OF SOUTH AFRICA'S TRADE DIPLOMACY

In 1994 when the African National Congress (ANC) came to power – with the Congress of South African Trade Unions (COSATU) and the South African Communist Party (SACP) as its governing partners – the new leadership inherited an economy in stagnation and crisis. Notwithstanding episodic trade policy reforms since the 1970s[13], the government confronted the challenge of building a modern, vibrant and outward-oriented economy that is internationally competitive, while also addressing the massive backlogs in access to social and economic services. The completion of the Uruguay Round (1986-1994) just two weeks prior to South Africa's historic democratic elections in April 1994 provided a ready springboard to reform the country's tariff regime and restructure local industries after decades of unabashed protectionism.[14] Indeed, with an evident ambition to promote domestic competitiveness and overcome past economic isolation, South Africa used the Uruguay Round to 'lock-in' *developed country* commitments.[15] This implied faster and deeper liberalisation of agriculture, goods trade, and services markets

---

[13] See Bell 1997.

[14] Fine and Rustomjee 1997.

[15] South Africa was one of the founding members of the General Agreement on Tariffs and Trade (GATT) in 1948. During the 1960s, when the GATT allowed differentiation between developed and developing countries to permit the latter to receive more gentle treatment, South Africa did not consider changing its status. According to Hirsch (2006:109): 'Its white rulers believed they lived like wealthy western European or American societies, and would have seen developing country status as an insult'. In 1993 towards the end of the Uruguay Round, South Africa sought to change its status to 'developing country', but this was opposed by the United States (US), EU and Japan, who insisted that South Africa would be entitled to more lenient treatment similar to the economies in transition.

than comparable countries in the South.[16] The transitional government did, however, secure key derogations for some of the country's sensitive sectors.[17] This 'historical injustice' of South Africa's misclassification in the Uruguay Round has in recent years emerged as Pretoria's main *cri de coeur* in the DDA, specifically for the NAMA negotiations where the government has stridently opposed ambitious Northern liberalisation demands. Since South Africa's negotiating position in NAMA is partly framed by an appeal to norms of fairness and equity for the country, it is useful to briefly consider the genesis of this historical incongruity.

Perturbed by the possibility of greater redistributive and statist policies under a post-apartheid regime, the outgoing white government forged a neo-corporatist compact with business and labour (the latter informally including the liberation movement) to astutely 'lock-in' their successor to a major trade policy reform programme. Notwithstanding South Africa's present lobbying for additional flexibilities in the Doha negotiations, importantly, the ANC had tacitly accepted these externally-imposed terms for the country's global economic reintegration. 'By and large', writes Hirsch, 'the trade policy community in South Africa could accept the retention of "developed country" status as far as the Uruguay Round was concerned'.[18] Four reasons appear to explain the avowedly progressive ANC's 'unholy pact' with free trade. First, the transition to democracy resulted in the ANC and COSATU prioritising the interests of working class, low-income and unemployed consumers, with import liberalisation then uncritically viewed as welfare-enhancing.[19] Second, the ANC informally participated in the National Economic Forum (NEF), which was established to consensually re-negotiate South Africa's 1990 GATT offer, resubmitted to Geneva in 1993. Third, ANC stalwart Professor Kader Asmal chaperoned South African Trade, Industry and Finance Minister Derek Keys to the Marrakesh Ministerial Conference that concluded the Uruguay Round, signalling the future government's acceptance of the trade deal – even if they did not fully appreciate its ramifications. Finally, the ANC's own well-documented conversion to orthodox macroeconomic policies in the early 1990s played

---

[16] South Africa's services commitments in the Uruguay Round were on par with the US, EU and Japan. This sector of the economy is relatively open, notwithstanding restrictions in transport and telecommunications.

[17] Through the good offices of then-ANC President Nelson Mandela, the US granted South Africa additional flexibilities for the clothing and textiles and automotive sectors to shield these industries from early competition.

[18] Hirsch 2005, 110.

[19] Bell 1997.

an instrumental role in building normative consensus for greater import liberalisation.[20]

During Trevor Manuel's brief spell as South Africa's first post-apartheid trade minister, trade policy considerations held a special place in policymaking, reflecting the outward economic philosophy of the new elite.[21] As could arguably be expected of a newly-democratised polity[22], the government embarked on broad-based tariff reform, underpinned by prodigious unilateral liberalisation that cut nominal protection ahead of the country's set WTO schedule. In the absence of a comprehensive industrial strategy or flanking measures, even big business protested: 'We don't need ministers to be holier-than-GATT'.[23] Manuel's departure for the Finance Ministry and the appointment of Alec Erwin as his successor in 1996 coincided with South Africa's first post-apartheid financial crisis. In the wake of this turmoil, the government jettisoned its earlier Reconstruction and Development Programme, adopting the fiscally-conservative Growth, Employment and Redistribution (GEAR) macroeconomic strategy. The latter quickly consolidated South Africa's emerging credentials as an Afro-neoliberal 'competition state' in a globalising world economy.[24] With strong emphasis on export-led growth (especially non-gold manufactured goods), investor confidence, fiscal discipline and global competitiveness as the orthodox vectors for promoting growth and development, GEAR was broadly complementary to the WTO's normative prescriptions.

By the turn of the millennium, GEAR had however missed most of its targets outside of the macroeconomic realm. Unemployment and poverty had grown, while the supply-side measures that flanked accelerated tariff reform were insufficient to support sectoral and spatial restructuring. The domestic climate of ideas soon shifted away from the market fundamentalism of GEAR and towards a greater state-led developmental idiom. Since 2001, sector-based industrial policy has been back in vogue, albeit with mixed results. The adoption first of microeconomic reforms targeting the economy's high cost structure, followed by more robust state-led interventions designed to 'fast-track industrial development'[25] implied that: 'From an austere outward-looking state, the South African state slipped into Keynesian mode'.[26] The notion of a South African

---

[20] Marais 1998; Taylor 2001.

[21] Bell 1997.

[22] On the relationship between democratisation and trade openness, see Milner and Kubota 2005.

[23] Comment attributed to Leslie Boyd, chairman of the Anglo-American Industrial Corporation.

[24] Cerny 2000; Taylor and Nel 2002.

[25] Mpahlwa 2006.

[26] Hirsch 2005, 259.

democratic developmental state that balances both equity and efficiency through greater coordination and planning provided fertile ground for a post-GEAR economic paradigm during the second Mbeki administration.

In 2006, the government launched a new growth strategy called the Accelerated and Shared Growth Initiative for South Africa (ASGISA), which aims to accelerate growth to 6 per cent and halve unemployment by 2014. Advised by a team of international economists linked to Harvard University, ASGISA broadly combines a government 'big push' strategy in public investment with public policies designed to unlock domestic 'binding constraints' to growth.[27] Although South Africa's weak export performance[28] is widely regarded as a key constraint for attaining these growth objectives, ASGISA accords trade policy little direct emphasis beyond competitiveness concerns linked to exchange rate volatility and the high current account deficit.[29] By contrast, a National Industrial Policy Framework (NIPF) and an accompanying action plan outlining policy interventions and targets were adopted in 2007 as pillars of this newly-articulated statist paradigm. Drawing on an interventionist reading of the (contested) East Asian growth model, the NIPF proposes to use financial incentives and strategically sequenced tariff reforms to engage in creative 'cost-discovery' processes, drive industrial development and promote export diversification. This marks the onset of the era of activist industrial policy, which stands in stark contrast to South Africa's earlier position during the heyday of GEAR, when policymakers largely heeded the 'government failure' arguments that characterised the World Bank's interpretation of the East Asian miracle.[30]

While the government accepts the liberal precept that it must make tariff reductions within Doha's broader reciprocity dynamic, these must be framed by NIPF's injunction that: 'Our fundamental approach is that tariff policy should be decided primarily on a sector-by-sector basis dictated by the needs and imperatives of sector strategies'.[31] In similar vein, the resolution on economic transformation adopted at the ANC's policy conference in Polokwane in 2007 calls for more hawkish stands

---

[27] Gelb 2007.

[28] South African exports have underperformed the world average and that of other middle-income and resource-based countries (Alves and Kaplan 2004; Haussman and Klinger 2006).

[29] Since 2002, South Africa has experienced unprecedented current account deficits, rising to 7.4 per cent of GDP in 2008. This has raised concerns over macroeconomic stability. Draper and Freytag (2008) offer an alternative perspective by arguing that the deficit could point to the strength of the economy and may be sustainable. South Africa may even be at the beginning of a 'beneficial debt cycle', whereby debt enables the country to increase employment and growth.

[30] See World Bank 1993.

[31] Department of Trade and Industry 2007a.

on goods trade and services: 'In general, industrial policy should lead our overall approach to sector development, whilst trade policy should play a supporting role and be sensitive to employment outcomes'.[32] The inauguration of President Jacob Zuma and his new administration in May 2009 is likely to consolidate and up-scale this industrial policy doctrine. This may portend even greater distributive bargaining in the WTO to deliver a fair, equitable and balanced Doha agreement. Before turning to South Africa's leadership agency in the WTO, the next section briefly explores the industrial policy ideas and interests – i.e. politics – that have palpably underpinned the country's heightened agency in multilateral trade.

2   THE TWO LEVEL GAMES OF TRADE POLICY REFORM IN THE WTO

While there was no quixotic East Asian economic miracle, the South African government has in recent years adjusted its policy radar in the direction of the 'late-industrialisers'[33] in order to draw industrial policy expertise and guidance for the country:

> The lesson of economic history is that those very few developing countries that have succeeded in breaking out of their colonially defined place in the global division of labour as producers and exporters of cheap primary products and importers of higher value added products all had one thing in common: industrial policies that were led by an active Developmental State.[34]

Policymakers have since the early 1990s always had a soft spot for the manufacturing sector, given its growth-pulling effects, creating employment and reducing poverty. This appears to follow the injunction that: 'The development of a strong manufacturing sector has been at the core of all successful catch-up experiences over the past 250 years, which suggests that achieving a lasting productivity-based increase in manufacturing is indispensable for a sustained rise in income levels and, ultimately, the eradication of poverty'.[35] For this reason, the stated objective of the NIPF is to build a diversified, value-adding manufacturing economy that creates low-skilled jobs for export.[36] The NIPF accordingly identifies four lead sectors (or sunrise industries) for public support: capital goods and transport equipment industries linked to the country's R787 billion

---

[32] ANC 2007.
[33] See Amsden 2001.
[34] Davies 2007.
[35] UNCTAD 2006, 150.
[36] Department of Trade and Industry 2007a-b.

infrastructure development programme; motor vehicles and component manufacturing; chemical sectors focusing on plastics fabrication and pharmaceutical products; and forestry, pulp and paper, and furniture industries. These are in addition to the existing ASGISA priority sectors of business process outsourcing, biofuels and tourism.

While its motives are salutary, the NIPF represents a renewed gamble on manufacturing for export, since local and exogenous conditions make replicating the East Asian model highly improbable, particularly in a world economy disciplined by WTO rules. Other factors include, inter alia: South Africa's historical reliance on mining and a minerals-energy complex (MEC)[37]; commodity-led real exchange rate volatility, including symptoms of so-called 'Dutch disease'; a high domestic cost structure that impacts on producers; lower productivity growth than Asia; and distance from major markets. Although the NIPF has a strong production bias, it is salutary that policymakers also emphasise the knowledge and services economy, particularly given their competitiveness linkages vis-à-vis agriculture and manufacturing. Not only are services increasingly tradable globally, but this sector dominates the modern South African economy, contributing more than 70 per cent of gross domestic product (GDP) and employment. Some economists even estimate that the employment multipliers of combined private services may exceed the pull of manufacturing.[38]

Within the country's domestic growth equation, the relative role of trade policy and the impact of liberalisation on the structure of trade, employment and output remain contested. Two broad schools of thought have recently animated domestic debates on the future direction of trade policy reform (and hence trade negotiations). On the left is an avowed interventionist camp led by the ANC as the ruling party, its tripartite governing partners COSATU and the SACP, some industry lobby groups and progressive civil society formations (such as the eclectic Trade Strategy Group, which prior to the Hong Kong Ministerial Conference played a key role in shaping the government's perspective on NAMA). This flank of the debate has advocated for a comprehensive industrial policy that promotes more sector-driven and labour-absorbing economic activities, particularly light manufacturing for export.[39] From COSATU's perspective, the 'harsh winds of competition'[40] unleashed by over-hasty liberalisation in the 1990s has led to massive attrition of manufacturing jobs and industrial capacity. Strategic tariff policy, local production and

---

[37] Fine and Rustomjee 1997.
[38] Tregenna 2007.
[39] COSATU 2006.
[40] Seboni 2005.

procurement, a competitive and 'growth-friendly' exchange rate and proposals for some 'import replacement sectors'[41] are all deemed to be legitimate industrial policy tools to govern the South African market and discipline financial capital.

The opposite pole of the debate is populated by more sceptical perspectives on the state's capabilities to optimally 'pick winners' in the face of imperfect information and strong rent-seeking interests in key sectors of the economy.[42] Represented by more mainstream think-tanks, such as the South African Institute of International Affairs (SAIIA) and the Free Market Foundation, the financial press and big business, this neoclassical perspective places a stronger premium on trade policy and the economy-wide benefits of unilateral liberalisation, regulatory reform and sector-neutral support that targets economic and social infrastructure. Proponents argue that the country's current tariff structure is inefficient, regressive in its impact on income distribution and preservationist rather than strategic. Additional liberalisation could therefore be a complementary strategy to the NIPF's export diversification drive, since trade liberalisation in the 1990s actually boosted the country's exports by reducing input costs and the relative profitability of domestic sales.[43] While acknowledging that less-skilled workers in labour-intensive industries, especially women, have borne the brunt of previous reform exercises (which has amplified the country's inequality levels)[44], economists calculate that the net effect on employment demand in the 1990s was neutral. Employment generated through export growth – still low, reflecting a capital/skills bias in the economy's structural transformation – closely matched employment lost through import penetration.[45] The conclusion to be drawn is that additional trade liberalisation is unlikely to generate pro-poor growth or address prevailing inequalities, particularly given the country's serious dearth of skills.

Like most developing countries in the WTO, the South African government thus confronts the conundrum of balancing the welfare advantages of low uniform tariffs with the industrial policy tool of

---

[41] ANC 2007.

[42] Draper and Alves 2007; IMF 2007; OECD 2008;

[43] Edwards and Lawrence 2006.

[44] Thurlow 2006.

[45] Lawrence and Stern 2006; Thurlow 2006. Within the manufacturing sector, Edwards and Dunne (2006) find that net trade raised employment within resource-based industries (e.g. iron and steel, food and beverages) and chemical industries (e.g. basic chemicals, plastics and rubber, etc); and reduced employment in labour-intensive sectors (e.g. clothing, textiles, footwear) and metal products sectors (e.g. machinery, vehicles, metal products).

flexible and differentiated tariffs.[46] In recent years, this has publicly pitted the Department of Trade and Industry (DTI) as the custodian of sectoral industrial policy – and an increasingly autonomous trade policy actor – against the powerful National Treasury, which was led by Trevor Manuel from 1996 to 2009. Manuel took an economy-wide perspective and called for more competitiveness-enhancing unilateral liberalisation, rather than relying on the protracted and politicised Doha Round to deliver an outcome. Rebuffing Manuel in the financial press, then Trade and Industry Minister Mandisi Mpahlwa provided an alternative epistemic perspective: 'Proposals for unilateral trade liberalisation, outside of a coherent industrial and trade policy, represent a fundamental misreading of the South African and international empirical evidence'.[47] Mpahlwa cautioned against exaggerating the correlation between tariffs and export competitiveness, and warned that unilateral tariff reductions would reduce South Africa's bargaining leverage in bilateral and multilateral trade negotiations. In particular, this would affect the potential scope for horizontal trade-offs in the DDA between agriculture, NAMA and services.

In order to better appreciate the strategic rationale and purpose of South Africa's heightened agency in the WTO's DDA negotiations, especially NAMA, it is important to appreciate the logic that underpins South Africa's industrial policy process. With the launch of the NIPF, then Deputy Trade and Industry Minister Rob Davies declared: 'We are not signalling our intention to increase tariffs, but we must claim the space to use tariff policy'.[48] Preserving this policy flexibility is a major concern for South Africa in the Doha Round and will continue to precipitate deadlock unless these concerns are sufficiently accommodated. Policy space is deemed critical by the South African government in order to review the country's tariffs according to an effective-rate-of-protection calculus to promote domestic value-addition. This means cutting tariffs in key upstream capital-intensive sectors that are imposing import parity pricing (e.g. steel, aluminium, chemicals), while defending higher tariffs on dynamic or downstream sectors, particularly those that are strategic from an employment or value-addition perspective.[49] Further selective liberalisation is envisaged with the removal of tariffs on machinery and capital goods not produced in the Southern African Customs Union

---

[46] UNCTAD 2006.

[47] Mphalwa 2007.

[48] *Sunday Times Business Times* 5 August 2007.

[49] Critics of this sector-specific approach argue that reducing tariffs on inputs alone actually increases protection for the industries that use these inputs. Although lower tariffs on inputs help improve export profitability, the retention of tariffs on final goods fosters inefficiency and promotes an anti-export bias (Edwards and Lawrence 2006).

(SACU) and a review of tariff peaks and 'nuisance' tariffs. In the next section, we consider how these domestic imperatives and drivers of trade policy reform have translated into the second level game of the WTO's Doha negotiations.

3   SOUTH AFRICA AND THE DDA: A MIDDLE POWER OR MUDDLING ALONG?

Popular and academic treatments of South Africa's role, interests and identity in the WTO have conventionally cast the country as a middle power facilitator or mediator between the industrialised and developing worlds. This is a recurring motif in the country's broader post-apartheid international relations. From this perspective:

> Pretoria's overall policies vis-à-vis the WTO have sought to promote the organisation's regime (a regime built upon firm neoliberal foundations) while also putting forward propositions that would aid developing countries to cope with the liberalising agenda of the organisation. By doing so, South Africa pursues a bridge building role aimed at developing 'confidence' in the system...[50]

This balancing act suggests that policymakers' acceptance of global hegemonic 'realities' and the normative prescriptions of globalisation are tempered by a reformist agenda that aims to promote greater participation, influence and equity for developing countries in multilateral trade. In practice, this strategy involves transforming developing countries into 'competition states' that are attractive to global capital (hence former President Thabo Mbeki's promotion of the continental New Partnership for Africa's Development), whilst highlighting the inequities engendered by skewed trade liberalisation and Northern hypocrisy over free trade. In one school of thought, this pragmatic posturing explains the perceived contradictions between South Africa's system-supporting and change-agency roles within the WTO: 'This policy not only serves the interests of important South African industries (the government believes), but it also acts to flag to its constituency on the Left that the government is attempting to promote the interests of the disempowered'.[51]

This middle power thesis is a fair representation of South Africa's multilateral trade diplomacy in the initial post-apartheid years, which was broadly accommodatory, pragmatic, and even technocratic to the North's offensive demands.[52] This approach first took shape during Alec Erwin's

---

[50] Taylor 2001, 112.
[51] Taylor 2005, 306.
[52] Keet 2006.

tenure as the country's trade minister from 1996 to 2004, when South Africa sought to burnish its new multilateral credentials as an interlocutor between Africa and the industrialised world. During this period, Erwin wielded strong ideas about South Africa's position in the world economy as a major Southern player; he personally privileged a strategy of 'trade-offs' rather than 'stand-offs' with the North. Starting at Seattle in 1999 – where efforts to launch the Millennium Trade Round collapsed (inter alia, following protests from African trade ministers who were excluded from opaque 'green room' bargains) – to the eventual adoption of the DMD two years later, South Africa played an instrumental role in brokering consensus for an ambitious new trade round. Pretoria's position was informed by three objectives: first, to relocate global production and investment from the North to the South, especially in sectors of actual or potential comparative advantage; second, to correct the imbalances and asymmetries in existing trade and trade-related agreements (e.g. anti-dumping, subsidies and intellectual property rights); and third, to enhance the provisions for special and differential treatment (SDT) and aid-for-trade for the developing world, especially Africa.[53] Erwin therefore plied his influence among African trade ministers to acquiesce to the DDA, contrary to the formally agreed African position. The latter held that without a full review of the existing Uruguay Round agreements (including attention to almost 100 specific implementation concerns), there could not be any launch of a major new round.

In recognition of South Africa's role as a middle power interlocutor between the developed and developing countries, Erwin was officially appointed as one of six 'Friends of the Chair' at Doha and tasked with facilitating the rules negotiations. This established South Africa's credibility as a positive partner in global trade. However, through his prominence in these processes, Erwin was criticised by civil society – and even some African trade ministers at Doha – for colluding with the WTO's undemocratic modalities.

This middle power agency has essentially served to promote and legitimise the WTO's liberalisation agenda and its neoclassical model of development. Given Africa's factor abundance in land and comparative advantages in agriculture and agro-processing, South Africa together with the Group of 20 (G20), Group of 90 (G90) and Africa Group have sought to promote farm trade reform as the centrepiece of the DDA. Not only is this sector the most distorted globally with egregious trade barriers and farming subsidies[54], but agriculture is the economic lifeblood for most

---

[53] Department of Trade and Industry 2000/2001.
[54] Notwithstanding limited exports, South Africa's labour-intensive, resource-based and rural deciduous fruit canning industry has been hard hit by global protectionism and *(continued)*

sub-Saharan African countries that are locked into commodity-exporting development paths:

> Agriculture is a major source of employment in the region and accounts for about 70 percent of total employment. It also plays a key role in economic growth, accounting for roughly 24 percent of the region's GDP and 40 percent of its foreign exchange.[55]

While commercial agriculture is not a significant contributor to the South African economy, comprising only 4 per cent of the country's GDP and employing 10 per cent of the formal labour force (although one third of the South African population are still rural), there are growing defensive concerns linked to land reform and future small-scale agriculture.[56] In the agriculture negotiations, South Africa has pressed its developed country partners to, inter alia, reduce overall domestic support to at least US$13 billion, minus any peace clause; reduce tariff peaks and adopt product-specific caps; eliminate export subsidies by 2013, as pledged by Europe at Hong Kong; ambitiously and expeditiously address the cotton issue; and tighten rules on non-emergency food aid, since the latter has previously distorted local production (e.g. Zambia). In sum, South Africa has held firm to the principled position that agriculture is the locomotive at the front of the Doha negotiating train: if there is going to be any movement, this has to move first. Even though actual agricultural exports are not so significant, the fact that South Africa has prioritised agriculture in this manner suggests that its commitment to developmental concerns operates not just at the individual level, but also the collective, particularly the G20, G90 and Africa Group (see Chapter 10).

At Cancún in 2003, South Africa joined key developing countries in blazing a new trail of resistance politics to the North with the formation of the G20 for greater equity in global farm trade (discussed in detail in Maria Lima's chapter, Chapter 4). The emergence of the G20 was an important moral and political victory for developing countries: not only did it significantly strengthen the group's bargaining power, but it fundamentally shifted the terms and terrain of the agriculture negotiations (which subsequently stabilised around the G20's purported 'middle ground' position). Although the Cancún Ministerial Conference signalled a break in South Africa's strict middle-power-ship mould when the country joined the frontline ranks and resistance of the G20, the politics of the conference also

---

market distortions, and exporters are often priced out of third country markets by subsidised EU goods (Kaplan and Kaplinsky 1999).

[55] African Trade Policy Centre 2004, 20.

[56] Kirstenn 2007.

revealed key differences between South Africa and its continental neighbours vis-à-vis the Singapore Issues – i.e. trade facilitation, government procurement, competition policy and investment – as well as agricultural reform.

The Singapore Issues

At Cancún, African countries (as part of the G90) collectively resisted negotiations on the Singapore Issues for three reasons: legitimate concerns over the potential resources required to implement any new agreements; unrealistic demands for prior progress on the implementation agenda; and an understandable desire to restrict intrusions into governments' policy space.[57] In contrast to the Africa Group's blocking strategy, South Africa adopted a more pragmatic calculus towards the deep trade agenda proposed by the European Union (EU) (discussed by Manfred Elsig in Chapter 2). Pretoria was therefore prepared to consider a modified, less ambitious and carefully defined agenda. Some observers contend that this 'naïve' preparedness to seek compromises and pursue integrative strategies in the round constrained Pretoria's ability to develop defensive positions and its willingness to play a more proactive role in developing country coalitions.[58]

South Africa's position on the Singapore Issues was motivated by two considerations. On the one hand, it was argued that a broad negotiating agenda with reciprocity principles permitted trade-offs to extract implementation commitments from industrialised countries. On the other hand, because of its diversified and sophisticated economy (including an outward investor), South Africa had to consider and pursue negotiating issues and concerns in the WTO that most of its Southern African Development Community (SADC) and African partners were not yet ready to grapple with, or demonstrated little material interest in. In a bid to rescue the round at Cancún, Erwin had thus lobbied for a pragmatic trade-off between agriculture, cotton and the Singapore Issues. However, the G90 rejected this intervention, which left South Africa isolated within Southern ranks, particularly Africa.[59]

Agricultural reform and preferences

Although the Singapore Issues emerged as the proximate deal-breaker at Cancún, the negotiating endgame exposed the intricacies of agricultural reform in the WTO. While also a beneficiary of privileged

---

[57] Draper and Khumalo 2005.
[58] Keet 2006.
[59] Lee 2006.

access into Northern markets (e.g. African Growth and Opportunity Act), South Africa blamed the deadlock on the perversity of preferences and the dependencies they generate.[60] African countries are broadly split between liberalisers that seek competitive markets (e.g. South Africa and the four West African cotton producers) and protectionists, which seek to rationally defend their trade preferences in Northern markets or rely on subsidised imports for their food security. Although African countries had adopted common positions prior to Doha and Cancún, continental unity was exposed as precarious when the preference-dependent economies – including Mauritius, which led the Africa Group – sided with the EU and the protectionist Group of 10 (G10) led by Norway, Switzerland and Japan.

The debate over the Singapore Issues and preferences points to a challenge for South African trade diplomats, namely balancing pragmatic self-interest (particularly ensuring greater market access for the country's manufacturers and service exporters in SADC, the continent and abroad) and politically supporting the defensive, dependent and developmental interests of the G90. Some scholars therefore argue that South Africa's middle power facilitation role in the DDA is limited to co-optation by the major trading powers, since Pretoria has not been able to deliver Africa, the G20 and other Southern formations to the North's agenda.[61] Although South Africa's initial integrative trade diplomacy in the WTO has recently shifted to the distributive end of the negotiating spectrum, the government has exercised leadership to broker common ground on the WTO's development agenda. Two examples illustrate this system-supporting agency.

First, in August 2003 South Africa helped to facilitate a deal in the Agreement on Trade-related Aspects of Intellectual Property Rights (TRIPS) and Public Health negotiations. This established a mechanism that would allow countries with no or insufficient manufacturing capacity to import medicines for public health reasons under compulsory license (although many NGOs see this as too leaky). Second, as chair of the WTO's Committee on Trade and Development Special Session (CTDSS) from 2004 to 2006, South Africa played an instrumental role in shaping the norms of a DDA development package, including fair trade, capacity-building, balanced rules and good governance.[62] The CTDSS deliberated extensively on the aid-for-trade agenda to address adjustment costs and supply-side constraints in the developing world, and drew attention to the particular exigencies of small, weak and vulnerable economies (SVEs) in

---

[60] Erwin 2003.
[61] This view is expressed by Lee 2006.
[62] See Ismail 2005.

the world trading system.[63] Since March 2009 following the height of the global credit crisis, South Africa has also chaired the WTO's Committee on Trade in Financial Services (CTFS). With global finance dominated by OECD states and circuits, few developing countries have previously held this position. Pretoria's planned agenda for its CTFS tenure includes examining Northern financial bailouts and stimulus packages in response to the crisis, particularly their externalities on the developing world.

4   RECLAIMING DEVELOPMENT IN THE DOHA NEGOTIATIONS

Compared to the country's offensive, yet limited interests in agriculture, the South African government has adopted more defensive positions in NAMA and services. Guided by the domestic imperatives of its industrial policy process, South Africa has argued that local industries and jobs are most vulnerable in the NAMA negotiations. For this reason, South Africa led the formation of the NAMA-11 at Hong Kong in 2005, which drew eight of the G20 protagonists to its cause.

The formation of the NAMA-11 followed several related processes. In November 2005 nine developing countries submitted a document to the CTDSS, entitled 'Reclaiming Development in the WTO Doha Development Round'.[64] These countries reasserted the centrality of agriculture as the lodestar for the DDA negotiations and argued that the demands of industrialised countries in industrial tariffs and services threatened to invert the development content and logic of the round. Recalling the tone and principles of the 2001 DMD (particularly paragraph 16 enjoining less-than-full-reciprocity in NAMA reduction commitments for developing countries and LDCs), these countries sought to play a change-agency leadership role:

> We for our part are committed to work for a genuine development outcome of the round that is fair and balanced and that will create new opportunities for all Members, developed and developing, to grow their economies and foster their development... It is thus timely to reclaim the developmental objectives and trajectory of the negotiations (emphasis added).[65]

A number of countries also submitted a second document on the issue of the flexibilities in NAMA and their interpretation of the latter as outlined in the 2004 July Framework. These countries rejected the notion that the

---

[63] See Ismail 2006.
[64] WTO 2005c.
[65] WTO 2005c.

flexibilities were linked to the tariff reduction formula (i.e. higher flexibilities should imply a lower coefficient).[66]

In light of this heightened activism in the negotiations, South African Trade and Industry Minister Rob Davies noted: 'The NAMA-11 has become a force in the process: we don't shape the text but cannot be ignored...'.[67] The NAMA-11's impact on the industrial tariff negotiations has been threefold. First, the coalition successfully resisted the attempts by developed countries to force a premature agreement on modalities in NAMA ahead of any significant agreement on the main issues in agriculture. South African trade negotiators have routinely argued that the sequencing of the Doha Work Programme is not incidental: development issues are to be addressed first; agricultural modalities second; and finally NAMA modalities. In other words, substantial reform of agricultural protectionism by rich countries should set the benchmark for NAMA tariff liberalisation.

Second, at the behest of the NAMA-11, the Hong Kong Ministerial Declaration endorsed the need to ensure a balanced outcome to the round as a whole, consistent with SDT. South Africa was partly instrumental in securing the adoption of paragraph 24, which states that there will be a 'comparably high level of ambition in market access for Agriculture and NAMA'.[68] This is not the exact wording proposed by the NAMA-11, which sought a higher level of adjustment in agriculture than in other areas (e.g. NAMA and services) and higher levels of adjustment borne by developed rather than developing countries. Although the NAMA-11 did not win that textual format during the negotiating endgame, there is now agreement on proportionality between the levels of ambition.

Finally, the NAMA-11 has promoted a more pragmatic formula for balancing industrial tariff reductions in order to preserve developing countries' domestic policy space. This follows the views of progressive scholars that the demands of the developed country majors in the WTO will further kick away the ladder of development[69], since: 'The principles espoused by developed countries in current negotiations on NAMA do not conform to their historical experience regarding the use of tariffs for industrial development'.[70] The Hong Kong Ministerial Conference endorsed a Swiss formula to reduce each individual tariff line, rather than the more flexible Uruguay Round modality of reducing the average of total

---

[66] WTO 2005b.
[67] Comment by then Deputy Trade and Industry Minister Rob Davies at the DTI's Pre-WTO Ministerial National Consultative Conference, Johannesburg, 10 April 2008.
[68] WTO 2005a.
[69] See Chang 2002.
[70] Akyüz 2005, 8.

industrial tariffs. Since developing countries historically have higher bound tariffs than their industrialised peers[71], the use of this formula will result in proportionately steeper cuts for the South. Some WTO analysts have criticised this approach, since it practically portends more-than-full-reciprocity. For this reason, the NAMA-11 initially called for a spread of at least 25 points between the coefficients for developed and developing countries as well as additional flexibilities. The latter have included a higher number of tariff lines and larger trade coverage for developing countries so as to accommodate their development needs.

South Africa has raised its own unique concerns arising from the 'historical injustice' of its developed country status during the Uruguay Round (discussed earlier). The latter applies not only to South Africa, but also SACU through its common external tariff. Formed in 1910, SACU is the world's oldest functioning customs union. Its membership consists of one developing country (South Africa), three SVEs (Botswana, Namibia and Swaziland) and an LDC (Lesotho). As a result of the Uruguay Round, SACU's bound tariffs rates (17 per cent) are almost half the average for comparable developing countries such as Argentina and Brazil (30 per cent) as well as India (40 per cent). According to South African negotiators, the Swiss formula will result in SACU undertaking applied tariff cuts on a scale far greater than any commitments made by all WTO members in either NAMA or agriculture.[72] In October 2007, SACU for the first time developed a common position on NAMA, which highlighted the diverse nature of its membership and cautioned that further liberalisation threatened local industries, particularly labour-intensive sectors that are dominated by small and medium-sized firms (e.g. clothing, textiles, leather and footwear).[73] The labour federation COSATU cried foul too, insisting that South Africa would be '[s]eriously de-industrialised, lose a significant part of our manufacturing sector, and become simply a producer of primary products and a destination for tourism'.[74]

As a consequence of these historical, political and socioeconomic dynamics within SACU, South Africa has called for additional flexibilities and an implementation period of not less than ten years, since: 'Any outcome cannot be at the expense of our industrial development prospects

---

[71] The average weighted bound tariffs for NAMA in developing countries are close to 14 per cent, compared to 3 per cent in industrialised countries.

[72] A Swiss formula with a coefficient of 22 as provided for in the July 2008 package will result in 23 per cent of South Africa's industrial tariff lines taking a cut of 30 per cent or more at applied rates even after applying the flexibilities provided for developing countries accepting formula cuts (Davies 2009a).

[73] WTO 2007.

[74] Vavi 2006.

or at the expense of deepening unemployment and poverty in our country'.[75] There has been some sympathy from the WTO membership for SACU's conundrum, which was recognised in the May 2008 NAMA modalities text.[76] South Africa has also raised concerns about Northern insistence on including an anti-concentration clause and mandatory sectoral bargaining in NAMA. The former would essentially limit the use of agreed flexibilities to protect vulnerable jobs and industries, and fully expose sectors with highly-substitutable products to competition.[77]

In sum, the challenge for South Africa in the Doha negotiations since the time of Hong Kong in 2005 has been to ensure a balanced rate of exchange between agriculture and NAMA. The popular mercantilist imagery in government – as well as local business, labour formations and Parliament, which Pretoria has successfully enrolled to its cause[78] – is that South Africa is offered little new market access in agriculture, but expected to sacrifice the country's manufacturing sector, including future industrial development opportunities, in order to conclude the Doha deal. With regard to the former, trade negotiators argue that the generous flexibilities permitted in agriculture would allow European and North American farmers to continue protecting their markets against exports from South Africa (including the same sensitive products excluded under bilateral trade agreements). Under this business-as-usual scenario, South Africa is not guaranteed any new direct or indirect commercial advantage in agriculture to compensate the country for losses in industry. This strict distributive bargaining strategy in NAMA was succinctly expressed by a COSATU delegate to the Geneva mini-ministerial in July 2008 (which is worth quoting at length):

> What is at stake is the very future of manufacturing on the African continent. If passed in their current form, we will lose our industrial base and become simply a supplier of raw materials to the factories of Asia and Europe and a destination for tourism. Our domestic debates on policy choices will be rendered irrelevant if we are trapped in commitments that are poorly designed and damaging to the interest of our country. With the highest unemployment rate in the world of any medium-sized country (those with a population in

---

[75] Davies 2009a.

[76] Section 7d states: '[As an exception, South Africa shall have recourse to [1-6] additional percentage points in the flexibility provided under paragraph 7(b)(i).]' (WTO 2008:4).

[77] Davies 2009a.

[78] See statements by Business Unity SA (BUSA) and the NAMA-11 trade unions at Geneva in July 2008. The National Assembly also adopted a resolution on 26 June 2008 setting a strict mandate for Geneva. This enjoined South Africa's trade negotiators to seek a balanced, fair and developmental outcome.

excess of 40 million), we have no space to make concessions that will destroy jobs.[79]

5   SOUTH AFRICAN TRADE DIPLOMACY IN PERSPECTIVE: BALANCED PRIORITIES?

Like most of its WTO partners, South Africa has pursued multiple tracks of trade policy reform: multilateral, regional and bilateral. The latter has involved the negotiation of various regional trade agreements (RTAs) as part of the government's broader 'butterfly' export growth strategy.[80] Although this global economic strategy was further refined in 2001 with the identification of 'strategic' and 'priority' trading partners, there has been little liberalisation this millennium beyond the Trade, Development and Co-operation Agreement with the EU and the SADC Trade Protocol. Although SACU has embarked on trade negotiations with China and India, these initiatives are progressing at glacial speed, while the United States (US) has formally withdrawn the offer of a free trade agreement (FTA) with the region.[81] The stalled multilateral juggernaut and its leadership vacuum do not inspire confidence either. While Pretoria's trade negotiators remain committed to reaching an agreement, they are on record that South Africa will not rush to sign an imperfect and imbalanced deal.[82]

As a developing country in the WTO, South Africa has limited negotiating capacity, diplomatic resources and market power to ensure a fair and balanced outcome in the negotiations. For this reason, South Africa has rationally joined Southern bargaining coalitions to collectively pursue developmental gains (see Chapter 8). Pretoria has also pursued a soft power strategy that seeks to shift the debate, focus and norms of the round from a neoclassical market exchange perspective to one that places development and policy space at the heart of the DDA.[83] South Africa's negotiators therefore argue that:

---

[79] Comment by Ebrahim Patel of the Southern African Clothing and Textile Workers Union, *Business Day* 23 July 2008.

[80] In 1996 the government adopted a trade strategy premised on the metaphor of a butterfly, largely aimed at strengthening South-South trade, investment and technological linkages. This conceived of Africa as the continental body of the butterfly, opening up its trading wings to the dynamic growth poles of Asia in the East (especially China and India) and Latin America (especially Mercosur) in the West.

[81] The focus will now switch to the more limited Trade and Investment Development Co-operation Agreement.

[82] *Business Report* 25 May 2009; see Davies 2009b.

[83] See Rodrik 2001.

Development and increased trade are not synonymous, although trade growth can contribute to development. In this regard, we must be attuned to the fact that a single-minded focus on trade and market opening can also be detrimental to broader development considerations. The construction of the agenda and process of negotiation must take these considerations into account.[84]

South Africa negotiating position is based on a principled linkage between agriculture (where exports are not so significant) and NAMA – where the country has key interests, alongside services (see figure 1) – with the former determining the speed at which the trade bicycle travels. Some commentators suggest that this negotiating puzzle represents a 'Faustian bargain' for the country, since: 'South Africa's bets are hedged on growing its knowledge and services economy, and protecting and expanding markets for its key industries and capital investments'.[85] The NAMA premium is appreciable and appears to fit with the Harvard panel's recommendation to strengthen the real economy as the basis for low-skilled employment creation. However, there is still considerable debate about the role of trade policy vis-à-vis export competitiveness, as earlier discussed. By contrast, agricultural policy arguably enjoys greater weight than it deserves: South African commercial farming contributes only 4 per cent of the county's GDP, employs about 10 per cent of the formal labour force and contributes about 8.4 per cent of export earnings. South Africa has nonetheless invested considerable diplomatic capital in the WTO's farm trade negotiations, particularly through its role in the G20 (subsidies), Cairns Group (tariffs) and since 2007 as a third party to the Canadian-Brazilian dispute against US corn subsidies, which has since petered out. Much of this agency has been in pursuit of collective gains for the South, since South Africa has relatively less to gain in agriculture than Brazil, China and India. The latter have the largest agricultural production capacities and agrarian industrial interests within the G20.[86] South Africa could potentially have struck an easy deal with the North by making concessions on agriculture to gain greater flexibilities in NAMA. The fact that it has not done so reinforces the point about its commitment to developmental concerns that operate not just at the

---

[84] Government of South Africa 2008b.

[85] Pillay 2006.

[86] Sandrey and Jensen (2007) calculate that South Africa stands to gain approximately US$223 million from the Doha Round, with only US$37 million of this from agricultural reform and the remainder from NAMA reforms. For agriculture, the big local winners would be beef, mutton and dairy products, while wheat and sugar exports would probably decline.

individual level, but also the collective (particularly Africa, where agriculture is critical). Some critics have therefore questioned why South Africa does not more actively subscribe to the Group of 33 (G33). Like most African countries, South Africa also has growing defensive concerns linked to the country's land reform programme and the state's support for emerging black farmers and rural development.[87]

Most striking, however, is the relative neglect of the services sector in South Africa's multilateral trade diplomacy, since this sector contributes more than two-thirds to the country's GDP and employment. Notwithstanding clear or potential export interests (see figure 2), South Africa has yet to develop and articulate strong offensive positions vis-à-vis OECD markets, but also the Southern African region and wider continent, where barriers still remain high. In one view, this lack of offensive positions stems from the DTI's erstwhile capacity and resource constraints to negotiate trade in services deals, as well as difficulties in mobilising the business community (although the DTI is now supporting the establishment of a Coalition of Services Industries). The DTI moreover lacks the authority to determine domestic policy in this sphere, which constrains what it can negotiate at the multilateral level. Politics have also trumped economics: South Africa is reluctant to purse aggressive services market openings in Africa, reflecting its foreign policy ambitions to be regarded as a regional 'partner' not 'hegemon', but also owing to the political dynamic between developed and developing countries in the Doha Round.[88]

Although South Africa has tabled an offer in the WTO's services negotiations (essentially locking-in the status quo) and has received several plurilateral requests[89], the country's position is broadly defensive. The DTI argues that it is imperative to preserve the country's policy space to first develop a national and regional services strategy, while not foreclosing the scope to support sunrise services industries in the future. Reflecting these concerns, South Africa joined Cuba, Indonesia, Philippines and Venezuela in a so-called 'Annex C' coalition at Hong Kong in 2005. The latter opposed Northern demands

---

[87] This community of black smallholder or peasant farmers supports nearly 2.5 million households located largely in the former rural homelands (Kirstenn 2007).

[88] Draper, Khumalo and Stern 2009.

[89] South Africa has already received requests for plurilateral negotiations on energy, environmental services (e.g. water, sanitation, irrigation, etc), construction, telecommunications and computer-related services, financial, maritime transport, legal, postal/courier (including express delivery), audiovisual, air transport, logistics, cross-border trade, distribution and mode three.

for greater market access in services, whether by mandatory
quantitative, qualitative, sectoral or modal targets.

Figure 1. South Africa's defensive interests in the WTO

Agriculture	*Goods*	*Services*	*New generation issues*
Land reform (incl. emerging farmers) Agro-processing Grains Cotton Dairy	Textiles and clothing Leather Footwear Furniture Metal products, machinery and vehicles	Education Healthcare Transport Energy Logistics Audio-visual Services related to agriculture	Market access WTO-plus Domestic and regional policy space (incl. SACU common institutions and regulatory regimes)

Source: Own compilation.

Figure 2. Potential South African export interests in services

Sector	
Business and professional Computer and related services Other business services Communication Construction and related-engineering services Distribution Environment Tourism and travel-related services Finance	*Legal and architectural* *Services incidental to mining* *Telecommunications* *Retailing and franchising* *Insurance and related services* *Banking and other financial services*

Source: Own compilation.

There are parallel developments on the other tracks of the
country's bilateral and regional trade diplomacy, where South Africa has
strongly promoted developmental principles and emphasised the need for
policy space and flexibilities that are commensurate with the country and
the region's respective levels of development. Curiously, while South
Africa had previously demonstrated support for the deep integration
agenda in the WTO, the country's trade negotiators have adopted more
defensive postures in regional and bilateral trade negotiations where the
country's bargaining power is weaker. Trade commentators suggest that
this reflects four concerns: fear of conceding market access; possible
closure of domestic and regional policy space; an in-principle objection
to extending regulatory commitments beyond the WTO; and the stated
lack of common policy regimes, institutions and regulations in SACU.[90]
The collapse of the SACU-US FTA negotiations in April 2006 was

---

[90] Draper and Qobo 2007.

symptomatic of this paradigm, since Washington's negotiating template was deemed too inflexible and anti-developmental. In the Economic Partnership Agreement (EPA) negotiations with the EU, the SADC configuration initially adopted a similar defensive stance: trade in services, investment and the new generation trade issues would be negotiated in a cooperative manner, with no region-wide binding obligations. However, not unlike the WTO, these negotiations have also unfolded in the 'shadow of power'.[91] Presently only South Africa remains outside of the SADC Interim EPA, largely on principled but also pragmatic grounds. The smaller regional states – namely Botswana, Lesotho, Mozambique and Swaziland – have all signed the agreement, whereas Namibia has only initialled, with reservations. South-South RTAs, such as the trade agreements being negotiated with India and China (which in 2009 ranked for the first time as South Africa's biggest trading partner) have also been re-conceptualised from extensive tariff liberalisation negotiations to cooperative agreements aimed at facilitating trade and addressing non-tariff barriers, complex customs administration and rules of origin. South Africa has also encouraged trade arrangements that promote sectoral cooperation (including specific manufacturing capabilities) and investment in minerals beneficiation.[92]

6   CONCLUSION

Three factors will be important in shaping the future direction of South Africa's multilateral trade diplomacy. First, the impact of the global financial crisis on the South African economy will further constrain the space for bargaining in the negotiations, particularly in NAMA. While the country's financial institutions have been relatively insulated from the economic downturn, several real sectors have been hard hit by falling export demand and greater risk aversion (e.g. mining, manufacturing and cyclical labour-intensive industries). The economy has entered its first recession in seventeen years and is expected to shed up to 500,000 jobs. This will further compound the country's unemployment and poverty crises. Set against these externalities, new Trade and Industry Minister Rob Davies has set ambitious benchmarks for the government:

De-industrialisation is therefore the central challenge we must address frontally and arrest. Indeed, our performance will be measured by the extent to which we succeed in preventing the further erosion

---

[91] See Steinberg 2002.
[92] Department of Trade and Industry 2007a.

of the economy's strategic productive capacity in key industries and sectors.[93]

South Africa is one of the few G20 countries to not resort to trade protectionism to shield domestic investments and jobs from the global economic downturn.[94] For this reason, Pretoria has raised concerns about the negative externalities of Northern financial bailouts and stimulus packages on developing countries, and called on industrialised countries to provide leadership in resisting protectionism. South Africa has argued for a broad definition of the latter, not only as traditional trade and investment barriers but all national-specific measures that countries can take, within WTO disciplines and beyond, that impose costs on others (particularly developing countries that have weaker fiscal bases) and that distort international trade and investment flows.

In March 2009, the National Economic Development and Labour Council (NEDLAC) – the corporatist bargaining council that consists of government, business and labour – developed South Africa's response to the global crisis. This crisis compact has five pillars: continued public investment in infrastructure (R787 billion, with greater emphasis on localisation to develop domestic supply capacities and stem import leakage); countercyclical macroeconomic policy; social and employment-supporting measures; and industrial and trade policies. The latter includes potential rescue packages for vulnerable sectors (e.g. clothing and textiles and the automotive industry). Critics have charged that any tariff increases, even to WTO-legal bound levels, may raise domestic costs and undermine the country's competitiveness. This policy orientation may even precipitate SACU's disintegration, since some member states, especially Botswana, are net importers of goods and hence support greater openness.

The second important factor for South Africa involves greater inclusiveness and transparency in the process of the WTO's negotiations. To be fair, since the collapse of Seattle in 1999, there have been reform initiatives led by the Director-General to ensure fairer representation in 'green room' consultations and mini-ministerial gatherings. However, formal participation and more 'voice' have not necessarily translated into greater procedural or substantive impact on the DDA. South Africa has argued that future small group bargaining (such as the G7) must include the mandated representatives of recognised groups – including the G20, G33, NAMA-11, LDCs and Africa Group – as well as sufficient time and space for intra-coalitional consultations and compacts to ensure greater

---

[93] Davies 2009b.

[94] In October 2009, following an application by the Southern African Clothing and Textile Workers' Union, South Africa raised customs duties on a range of garments and textiles from the currently applied rate of 40 per cent to the bound rate of 45 per cent.

legitimacy of outcomes. The exclusion of Africa from the inner locus of bargaining during July 2008, coupled with an apparent revival of the old Principal Supplier Principle, meant that the African continent's agenda – e.g. cotton, bananas and duty-free quota-free market access for LDCs – was simply discarded during the negotiating endgame.

South Africa has also called for better consultation within and among the WTO's various negotiating groups. Compared to the more accommodating 'bottom-up' process of the agriculture negotiations, South Africa has long argued that NAMA has been highly circumscribed and prescriptive, with the chair consistently ignoring the positions of the NAMA-11 and wider informal groupings, such as the Group of 110 (G110) (see Faizel Ismail's chapter, Chapter 9). South Africa will demand greater sensitivity and consultation in future industrial tariff negotiations, since: 'We have now won acceptance of South Africa's need to be accorded additional flexibilities, but these negotiations are not yet complete and what is currently available to us is completely unacceptable to our government and constituencies'.[95]

The final factor is the inauguration of President Jacob Zuma in May 2009, whose administration is likely to strengthen and consolidate the South African developmental state and its associated industrial policy and planning paradigms. In particular, the promotion of Rob Davies to the trade and industry portfolio and the establishment of a new Economic Development Ministry under former trade unionist Ebrahim Patel may portend greater distributive bargaining in the DDA. In the view of the financial press:

> The combination of Patel and Davies in the economic cluster could have its biggest effect on trade policy. With the world economy taking strain and protectionism growing, SA is looking for ways to raise tariffs and tighten trade. Both Patel and Davies appear in step with this tendency, which often pays limited attention to the rest of Southern Africa.[96]

Economic policy will continue to be contested terrain, particularly within government where the mandates of key economic ministries overlap. A National Planning Commission led by Trevor Manuel has been appointed to coordinate government planning. This could pit Manuel's outward-looking philosophy against the inward-looking approach of Davies and Patel. The latter have also signalled the possibility of forum-shopping in international trade, with greater emphasis on South-South cooperation that extends from the India-Brazil-South Africa (IBSA) Dialogue Forum

---

[95] Davies 2009a.
[96] *Financial Mail* 15 May 2009.

and China, to exploring commercial and cooperative ventures with Bolivia, Cuba and Venezuela. Nonetheless, South Africa remains committed to the multilateral process of securing a developmental Doha agreement. With an economy that relies heavily on global trade and investment inflows, and a low point of defection from the WTO, South Africa will in the long run find it difficult to reject a Doha compromise, should Brazil, China and India accept the deal.

REFERENCES

African National Congress. 2007. Economic Transformation for a National Democratic Society. Policy discussion document prepared for the National Policy Conference, Polokwane, March.

African Trade Policy Centre. 2004. *Trade Liberalisation under the Doha Development Agenda: Options and Consequences for Africa.* Addis Ababa: ATPC.

Akyüz, Yilmaz. 2005. The WTO Negotiations on Industrial Tariffs: What is at Stake for Developing Countries? Geneva: Third World Network.

Alves, Phil and David Kaplan. 2004. South Africa's Declining Export Shares: The Developing Country Challenge. *Trade and Industry Monitor* 30:2-6.

Amsden, Alice H. 2001. *The Rise of 'The Rest': Challenges to the West from Late Industrializing Economies.* Oxford: Oxford University Press.

Bell, Trevor. 1997. Trade Policy. In *The Political Economy of South Africa's Transition,* edited by Jonathan Michie and Vishnu Padayachee. London: Dryden Press.

Cerny, Philip G. 2000. Globalisation and the Restructuring of the Political Arena: Paradoxes of the Competition State. In *Globalization and Its Critics,* edited by Randall R. Germain. Basingstoke: Palgrave Macmillan.

Chang, Ha-Joon. 2002. *Kicking Away the Ladder – Development Strategy in Historical Perspective.* London: Anthem Press.

Congress of South African Trade Unions (COSATU). 2006. Industrial Strategy Document. Mimeo.

Davies, Rob. 2006. Budget Vote Speech by the Deputy Minister of Trade and Industry, National Assembly, Cape Town, 30 March.

Davies, Rob. 2007. Input to Budget Vote Debate by the Deputy Minister of Trade and Industry, National Assembly, Cape Town, 29 May.

Davies, Rob. 2008a. Input to Debate on Budget Vote 32 on Trade and Industry by the Deputy Minister of Trade and Industry, National Assembly, Cape Town, 28 May.

Davies, Rob. 2008b. Address by the Deputy Minister of Trade and Industry to the 5th Anniversary of the International Trade Administration Commission (ITAC), Pretoria, 17 October.

Davies, Rob. 2009a. Reclaiming the Development Dimension of the Multilateral Trading System. Special Address, Geneva Lectures on Global Economic Governance, Oxford University, 2 March.

Davies, Rob. 2009b. Budget Vote Speech by the Minister of Trade and Industry, National Assembly, Cape Town, 30 June.

Department of Trade and Industry. 2000/2001. Multilateral Trade Strategy. Pretoria.

Department of Trade and Industry. 2007a. National Industrial Policy Framework. August.

Department of Trade and Industry. 2007b. Implementation of Government's National Industrial Policy Framework: Industrial Policy Action Plan. August.

Draper, Peter and Nkululeko Khumalo. 2005. Friend or Foe? South Africa and Sub-Saharan Africa in the Global Trading System. In *Reconfiguring the Compass: South Africa's African Trade Diplomacy*, edited by Peter Draper. Johannesburg: South African Institute of International Affairs.

Draper, Peter, Khumalo, Nkululeko and Matthew Stern. 2009. Why isn't South Africa more pro-active in international services negotiations? In *Opening Markets for Trade in Services. Countries and Sectors in Bilateral and WTO Negotiations*, edited by Juan A. Marchetti and Martin Roy. Cambridge: Cambridge University Press.

Draper, Peter and Mzukisi Qobo. 2007. Rabbits Caught in the Headlights? Africa and the 'Multilateralizing Regionalism' Paradigm. Paper presented at the Conference on Multilateralizing Regionalism, 10-12 September, Geneva.

Draper, Peter and Phil Alves. 2007. Déjà Vu? The Department of Trade and Industry's National Industrial Policy Framework. Occasional Paper 2. Parktown, Johannesburg: Business Leadership South Africa.

Draper, Peter and Andreas Freytag. 2008. South Africa's Current Account Deficit. Trade Policy Report 25. Johannesburg: South African Institute of International Affairs.

Edwards, Lawrence and Paul Dunne. 2006. Trade and Poverty in South Africa: Exploring the trade-labour linkages. Paper prepared for the South African Trade and Poverty Research Project. Cape Town: Southern Africa Labour and Development Research Unit (SALDRU).

Edwards, Lawrence and Robert Lawrence. 2006. South African Trade Policy Matters: Trade Performance and Trade Policy. Working Paper 135. Cambridge, Mass.: Harvard Centre for International Development, Harvard University.

Edwards, Lawrence and Matthew Stern. 2006. Trade and Poverty Research Project in South Africa: Lessons and Policy Recommendations. Cape Town: Southern Africa Labour and Development Research Unit (SALDRU).

Erwin, Alec. 2003. Statement on the Outcomes of the 5th Ministerial Meeting of the WTO to Parliament, Cape Town, 26 September.

Fine, Ben and Zaverah Rustomjee. 1997. *South Africa's Political Economy: From Minerals-Energy Complex to Industrialisation?* London: Hurst.

Gelb, Stephen. 2007. Strategy for Developmental State Needs Revamping. *Sunday Times*. 4 July.

Government of South Africa. 2008a. Statement to the WTO Trade Negotiating Committee, Geneva, 22 July.

Government of South Africa. 2008b. Statement to the WTO Trade Negotiating Committee, Geneva, 30 July.

Hausmann, Ricardo and Bailey Klinger. 2006. South Africa's Export Predicament. Working Paper 129. Cambridge, Mass.: Harvard Centre for International Development, Harvard University.

Hirsch, Alan. 2005. *Season of Hope. Economic Reform Under Mandela and Mbeki.* Scottsville and Ottawa: University of KwaZulu-Natal Press and International Development Research Centre.

International Monetary Fund. 2007. South Africa: 2007 Article IV Consultation. IMF Country Report 07/274.

Ismail, Faizel. 2005. Mainstreaming Development in the World Trade Organization. *Journal of World Trade* 39(1):11-21.

Ismail, Faizel. 2006. How Can Least Developed Countries and Other Small, Weak and Vulnerable Economies Also Gain from the Doha Development Agenda on the Road to Hong Kong? *Journal of World Trade* 40(1):37-68.

Kaplan, David and Raphael Kaplinsky. 1999. Trade and Industrial Policy on an Uneven Playing Field: The Case of the Deciduous Fruit Canning Industry in South Africa. *World Development* 27(10):1787-1801.

Keet, Dot. 2004. South Africa's Official Position and Role in Promoting the World Trade Organisation. Cape Town: Alternative Information and Development Centre (AIDC).

Keet, Dot. 2006. Challenges and Strategies Post Hong Kong'. Economic Policy Issues 8. Cape Town: Alternative Information and Development Centre (AIDC).

Kirstenn, Johann. 2007. Socio-Economic Dynamics of the South African Agricultural Sector. Trade Policy Briefing 10. Johannesburg: South African Institute of International Affairs.

Lee, Donna. 2006. South Africa in the World Trade Organisation. In *The New Multilateralism in South African Diplomacy*, edited by Donna Lee, Ian Taylor and Paul Williams. Houndmills: Palgrave Macmillan.

Lee, Donna, Taylor, Ian and Paul Williams, eds. 2006. *The New Multilateralism in South African Diplomacy.* Houndmills: Palgrave Macmillan

Marais, Hein. 1998. *South Africa: Limits to Change. The Political Economy of Transformation.* London and Cape Town: Zed Books and University of Cape Town Press.

Mpahlwa, Mandisi. 2006. Budget Vote Speech by the Minister of Trade and Industry, National Assembly, Cape Town, 30 March.

Mpahlwa, Mandisi. 2007. Proposal to go it alone on trade misreads the evidence. *Business Day*, 7 November.

Narlikar, Amrita and Diana Tussie. 2004. The G20 at the Cancun Ministerial: Developing Countries and Their Evolving Coalitions in the WTO. *The World Economy* 27(7):947-966.

Nel, Philip, Taylor, Ian and Janis van der Westhuizen, eds. 2001. *South Africa's multilateral diplomacy and global change: The limits of reformism.* Ashgate: Aldershot.

Nel, Philip, Ian Taylor and Janis van der Westhuizen. 2000. Multilateralism in South Africa's Foreign Policy: The Search for a Critical Rationale. *Global Governance* 6:43-60.

Nye, Joseph. 2004. *Soft Power: The Means to Success in World Politics.* New York: Public Affairs.

Taylor, Ian and Philip Nel. 2002. 'New Africa', globalisation and the confines of elite reformism: 'Getting the rhetoric right', getting the strategy wrong. *Third World Quarterly* 23(1):163-180.

Odell, John. 2000. *Negotiating the World Economy.* Ithaca and London: Cornell University Press.

Organization for Economic Cooperation and Development (OECD). 2008. South Africa – Economic Assessment. OECD Economic Surveys Volume 2008/15. Paris.

Pillay, Morgenie. 2006. SA in Faustian bargain with India, Brazil after Doha. *Business Report.* 29 October.

Rodrik, Dani. 2001. The Global Governance of Trade As If Development Really Mattered. New York: United Nations Development Programme.

Sally, Razeen. 2008. *Trade Policy, New Century: the WTO, FTAs and Asia Rising.* London: Institute of Economic Affairs.

Sandrey, Ron and Hans G. Jensen. 2007. South African agriculture: a possible WTO outcome and FTA policy space – a modeling approach. In *South Africa's way ahead: trade policy options*, edited by Ron Sandrey, Hans G. Jensen, Nick Vink and Taku Fundira. Stellenbosch: Trade Law Centre for Southern African (TRALAC).

Seboni, Violet. 2005. Speech delivered by the Second Deputy President of COSATU to the SANGOCO workshop on non-agricultural market access (NAMA), 24 June.

Steinberg, Richard H. 2002. In the Shadow of Law or Power? Consensus-Based Bargaining and Outcomes in the GATT/WTO. *International Organization* 56(2):339-374, Spring.

Taylor, Ian. 2001. *Stuck in Middle GEAR. South Africa's Post-Apartheid Foreign Relations*. Westport: Praeger.

Taylor, Ian. 2005. The Contradictions and Continuities of South African Trade Policy. In *The Politics of International Trade: Actors, Issues, and Regional Dynamics*, edited by in Dominic Kelly and Wynn Grant. Basingstoke: Palgrave.

Thurlow J. 2006. Has Trade Liberalisation in South Africa Affected Men and Women Differently? DSDG Discussion Paper 36. Washington: International Food Policy Research Institute (IFPRI).

Tregenna, F. 2007. The contribution of manufacturing and services sectors to growth and employment in South Africa. Pretoria: Employment Growth and Development Initiative, HSRC.

Wilkinson, Rorden. 2006. *The WTO. Crisis and the Governance of Global Trade*. New York: Routledge.

United Nations Conference on Trade and Development (UNCTAD). 2006. *Trade and Development Report 2006. Global Partnership and National Policies for Development*. New York and Geneva: UNCTAD.

Vavi, Zwelinzima. 2006. COSATU Open Letter: Request for Actions on NAMA Negotiations at the WTO.

World Bank. 1993. *The East Asian Miracle. Economic Growth and Public Policy*. New York and Oxford: Oxford University Press.

World Trade Organization (WTO). 2005a. Hong Kong Ministerial Declaration, 18 December, WT/MIN(05)/DEC.

WTO. 2005b. Flexibilities for Developing Countries. 3 November, TN/MA/W/65.

WTO. 2005c. Reclaiming Development in the WTO Doha Development Round. 1 December, WT/COMTD/W/145.

WTO. 2007. Communication from the Southern African Customs Union. 29 October, TN/MA/W/92.

WTO. 2008. Draft modalities for non-agricultural market access. Second Revision. 19 May, TN/MA/W/103/Rev.1

Part III

Bargaining Coalitions in the Doha Negotiations

AMRITA NARLIKAR[1]

8. A THEORY OF BARGAINING COALITIONS IN THE WTO

The current round of trade negotiations – the Doha Development Agenda (DDA) – irrespective of its outcome, has already proven itself to be unique and unprecedented, and not for its emphasis on development or its proclivity to deadlock alone. The round has seen a dramatic increase in the participation of countries through coalitions; one list, produced by the World Trade Organisation (WTO)'s Trade Negotiations Committee in December 2006, numbers them at 62.[2] Moreover, an overwhelming majority of these coalitions have representation from developing countries. These groupings matter first and foremost because of the empowerment that they offer to some of the most marginalised members of the organisation. Second, for international organisations under fire for their lack of accountability and legitimacy, greater involvement of some of the smallest and weakest via coalitions offers a new route to legitimisation. Third, and somewhat paradoxically, insofar as the growing activism and influence of the developing world has contributed to the recurrence of deadlock in the Doha negotiations,[3] bargaining coalitions necessitate closer analytic attention to ensure the continued working, survival and improvement of the multilateral trading system. Targeting research efforts at coalitions therefore is now important not only for the empowerment that they offer for developing countries or the improved legitimacy that they might impart to the system, but also because such research helps us

---

[1] The author thanks Pieter van Houten, Diana Tussie, and particularly Sonia Rolland for their invaluable inputs. She is grateful to Brendan Vickers and the Institute for Global Dialogue team for inviting her to present this paper at a conference in Pretoria, 4-5 August 2008. The usual caveats apply.

[2] *Formal and Informal Groupings or Coalitions in the DDA Negotiations*, C.TNC, 08-12-2006 (Unpublished WTO Document). It is worth noting that the majority of the coalitions on the list fit the definition of 'bargaining coalitions' (i.e. a group of countries that explicitly work together to defend a common interest). But it also includes a small number of groupings, such as the G4, the FIPs, the FIPs-plus, and the G6, which are akin to the old 'Quad' (i.e. key players, sometimes from different coalitions, who try to take the lead on building consensus).

[3] Baldwin 2006.

A. Narlikar, B. Vickers (eds.), Leadership and Change in the Multilateral Trading System, 183–201.
© *2009 Republic of Letters Publishing. All rights reserved.*

analyse changes – within the institution or in certain features of the coalitions – that might restore the efficiency of the organisation without undermining its improved inclusiveness.

In this chapter, I present a theoretical analysis of coalitions in the WTO, drawing on recent examples to illustrate the argument. The argument proceeds in three steps. In the first section, I address the logic of coalition formation in the WTO using some simple insights from game theory, and apply these insights specifically to bargaining coalitions involving developing countries in the WTO. The second section applies these theoretical insights to recent cases of coalitions in the WTO. These coalitions, while much stronger and longer-lasting than their predecessors, come with new and unanticipated problems. In the third section, I present an overview of types of reform measures that could be taken on to retain the opportunities but overcome the problems presented by coalitions today. The findings of the chapter are summarised in the fourth and concluding section.

1   THE LOGIC OF COALITION FORMATION

In this chapter, I focus explicitly on bargaining coalitions, i.e. those based on an explicit coordination among countries that seek to defend a common position in a negotiation. Note that these are to be distinguished from decision-making groups that form a part of the WTO's informal institutional machinery, such as the Quad (comprising the EU, US, Japan and Canada) in the past, or indeed even the more diverse groupings that have formed a part of the Doha consensus-building process such as the Group of 4 (G4) or the 'New Quad' comprising EU, US, Brazil and India, or the Group of 7 (G7) constituted at the Director-General's initiative in the July 2008 talks that included the EU, US, Australia, Japan, Brazil, India, and China. Developing countries privy to such small group consultations, whether at the ministerial level or the technical level, are consistently active players in the bargaining coalitions that are studied in this chapter. In contrast to bargaining coalitions, groupings such as the New Quad or the G7 come together to hammer out a consensus from the differing positions of individual countries and coalitions, rather than defend a collective position.

Even though bargaining coalitions in the WTO do not enjoy formal standing in the WTO, in contrast to the group-based diplomacy of the United Nations Conference on Trade and Development (UNCTAD), they do find institutional recognition in the organisation on its website and they leave a paper-trail of proposals that reveals their importance. These coalitions are of different types. The membership of some is limited to developing countries (or indeed the developed world), whilst others cross the North-South divide. They can be issue-based alliances or bloc-type coalitions.[4] The former, clustering at one end of the coalition spectrum, are formed in response to shared concerns over a particular issue, and dissipate after the issue has been resolved. At the other end of the spectrum are bloc-type coalitions of like-minded countries, which are bound together by shared ideas or even identities, usually address multiple concerns rather than a single issue. Further, coalitions can serve a variety of functions: at a minimal level, they can facilitate information-sharing, and can progress to burden-sharing through a division of labour and collective representation for agenda-setting, the negotiation of modalities, and even legal representation in filing disputes.[5]

Coalitions are of particular importance to developing countries. Some lack the technical capacity to negotiate effectively, while most seldom enjoy the significant trade shares that could allow them individual bargaining power.[6] In theory, consensus-based decision-making allows even the smallest country de jure veto power; in practice, the small and the weak are reluctant to incur the wrath of the large by single-handedly blocking consensus.[7] Moreover, the threat of a larger number of countries to walk away from a negotiation carries greater credibility and consequence than a similar threat exercised by an individual developing country. Finally, insofar as international institutions have had to fight back accusations of suffering from a democratic deficit and a lack of legitimacy, demands backed by the power of large numbers carry extra normative weight. But exactly what mechanisms underlie the search for improved bargaining power via coalitions?

There are two possible mechanisms to gaining benefits through coalitions, which are discussed in this section in terms of the 'Defection Hypothesis' and the 'Collective Gains Hypothesis'.

Defection Hypothesis: The purpose of belonging to a coalition lies in being able to attract side-payments: countries join coalitions with the purpose of being bought off.[8]

---

[4] Narlikar 2003.

[5] For an overview of the different coalition types and their functions, see Narlikar 2003 and Rolland 2007.

[6] The concept of bargaining power here draws on the work of Thomas Schelling: 'The power to hurt is bargaining power'. In the case of the WTO, this effectively translates into the potential ability of countries to cause major disruption to the trade process if they were to walk away from the negotiating table, and similar levels of disruption to the trading system if they were to close their markets. Few developing countries enjoy such power.

[7] Steinberg 2002; Narlikar 2005.

[8] Tussie 2003, 14.

As per the Defection Hypothesis, countries join coalitions not in pursuit of the professed collective aim but particular, individual interests. They are more likely to secure these interests in the form of side-payments if they first demonstrate their power by joining coalitions and thereby also establish their worth of being bought off to the outside party, than if they were acting on their own.

If we accept this logic, the central puzzle, for those of us who study coalitions and also those who belong to them, then becomes: what is the optimal point of defection, as opposed to what strategies should be used to preserve the unity of the coalition? For instance, countries may wish to hold out against side-payments in the hope of acquiring more concessions from the outside party, and this can be best achieved by demonstrating loyalty to the coalition. But each country also fears being isolated in the endgame, which generates the 'sucker's payoff' as it is the only one still adhering to the collective position at a time when the coalition has collapsed. As such, the timing of defection will depend centrally on the expectations of coalition members about how their allies will behave. Additionally, it will also depend on the size of particular allies and the types of side-payments that they can realistically expect. Hence for instance, we might expect smaller countries to defect before the larger ones; defection by larger countries is likely to trigger many more defections. However, even though the temptation to defect affects all coalitions, three fundamental problems explain why this does not form the primary logic driving coalition formation:

First, the Defection Hypothesis as the driving logic for coalition formation may be countered by examining the internal dynamics of the coalition, and conceptualising the collective action facing coalitions in terms of a one-off, multiple-person prisoner's dilemma. Each country is best off being the sole defector, i.e. playing {D,c} (and thereby procuring the maximum side-payment), and the worst off being the last one to defect, i.e. playing {C,d} (see figure 1). To ensure that one's own country is not the last one left standing in the coalition, countries enter into a competitive race to defect, and a downward spiral ensures.[9] In other words, if everyone makes this calculation, the result is non-cooperation. Unless the game is repeatedly infinitely, all players would indeed make this calculation, and coalitions would not form in the first place. Observation – for instance the 62 coalitions listed in the WTO's 2006 list – however, firmly contradicts this prediction.

---

[9] Note that ideally, countries would prefer also not to be the first to defect (i.e. there is an optimal point of defection when the country can maximise its gains from a bilateral deal). And if this were the only concern, coalitions would not be prone to easy unravelling. But as early defection generates some gains, which significantly outweigh the certain cost of being isolated in the endgame, the spiral of unravelling is likely.

Figure 1. The Two Games

Outcome

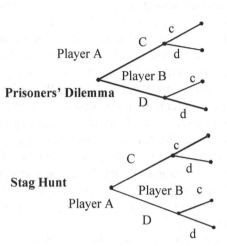

Equal Payoff for both, with more than the sucker's payoff but less than the optimal payoff (e.g. 7,7)

Sucker's Payoff for A, optimal payoff for B (e.g. 0,10)

Optimal Payoff for A, sucker's payoff for B (e.g. 10,0)

Sub-optimal Equilibrium but generating payoff higher than sucker's payoff for both parties (e.g. 5,5)

Optimal Payoff Equilibrium (e.g. 10,10)

Sucker's Payoff for A, payoff between Optimal-payoff and Risk-averse payoff for B (e.g. 0,7)

Sucker's Payoff for A, and pay-off between Optimal payoff and risk-averse payoff for B (e.g. 7,0)

Risk-averse Equilibrium (e.g. 5,5)

Second, factors external to the coalition also defy the Defection Hypothesis. The outside party would also be aware of the outcome of non-cooperation that is likely to result from the internal politics of the coalition. And it is difficult to see why the outside party would choose to invest in any meaningful side-payments if it knows that the coalition is likely to unravel anyway. To be bought off thus cannot be the driving logic of coalition formation.

Third, were a coalition formed based on the logic of defection, repeated defections over several iterations by a country would undermine its credibility. For the outside party, the knowledge that it has repeatedly defected in the past would lead it to reduce the value of bilateral offers to buy it off. The country's credibility would also decline amongst its members, resulting in its declining ability to influence the collective agenda.

Of course defections happen, coalitions collapse, and no coalition lasts forever. But these facts should not be interpreted to mean that the defection route provides the central mechanism for coalition formation. If potential defection formed the guiding spirit behind coalition formation, all coalitions would suffer from problems of both internal and external credibility. The fact that coalitions are formed at all, and further survive, suggests that an alternative logic may be at work, which is captured in the Collective Gains hypothesis.

Collective Gains Hypothesis: The main purpose of joining coalitions for countries is the promise of collective gains (rather than side-payments).

While the temptation to defect affects all coalitions, it can and has been overcome through effective agenda-setting. If the coalition structures and frames its agenda in such a way that its collective demands, if successfully met, would significantly outweigh the gains that an individual member would make through defection, then the likelihood of defection declines. Through such agenda-setting to ensure a big collective gain or a basket of gains, the benefits of defection are reduced. Unlike the finitely repeated Prisoners' Dilemma where defection is the dominant strategy resulting in mutual defection, we now see a Stag Hunt at work among the coalition members. In Rousseau's Stag Hunt, if all members cooperate, they will hunt stag and eat well; if one defects in pursuit of a rabbit, the others will go hungry and he will eat rabbit (which he likes less than venison).[10] Mutual cooperation {C,c} generates highest possible payoff in the Stag Hunt for all players. It is also one of two equilibria present, the other one being mutual defection {D,d}).[11]

How can negotiators ensure that they and their allies take the collective gains route rather than the redundant defection route to successful outcomes? Based on the analysis above, trade negotiators aiming to ensure that their allies do not defect have two mechanisms available to them. First, they can try to improve the odds that their coalition partners end up playing the Stag Hunt, where mutual cooperation is one of the two equilibria, as opposed to the Prisoners' Dilemma where mutual defection is certain. Second, to further increase the likelihood of collective gains, within the Stag Hunt, they can try to further create conditions that lead members to choose {C,c} over {D,d}. To achieve these ends, the following steps are useful.

First, the agenda can be set such that the collective payoffs from cooperation {C,c} significantly outweigh the gains from individual defection {D,c} and defection is no longer the dominant strategy. This would help towards ensuring that the game being played is a Stag Hunt and not a Prisoners' Dilemma. Second, smaller members tend to be more risk averse,

---

[10] We can work with several variations of this model and add frills to it. For instance, the defection of just one player may not lead to the failure to hunt stag, depending on how big the hunting party is, and how plentiful stag are, i.e. as long as a critical mass is available that does not defect and the agenda is realistic, the collective goals are likely to be met. This, in turn, will reduce the temptation of at least some otherwise risk-averse players to defect in favour of rabbit. See Skyrms 2001 for an analysis on variations within the Stag Hunt.

[11] Jervis 1978 uses the insightful intuitions of these simple games to analyse the Security Dilemma.

and a preponderance of small allies in a coalition may heighten the risk that within a Stag Hunt, they end up going for the risk-averse equilibrium of $\{D,d\}$.[12] The probability of this happening increases if levels of trust among coalition allies are low. This risk, however, can be reduced if larger members are able to offer side-payments to smaller allies, for instance through provisions of special market access. By acting as a strong and united coalition, all the members have greater likelihood of extracting concessions on the collective (and most-preferred) agenda. Third, while the previous two measures refer specifically to the internal dynamics of the coalition, to ensure the gains of cooperation are met, we must also take the actions of the opposing party into account. This could be the North in North-South negotiations, or any external party with whom negotiation is crucial if the potential gains of mutual cooperation are to be realised. Here a large membership of the coalition and also the presence of large economies within it can help: the likelihood that the outside party will make concessions and help the coalition achieve its collective (and most preferred goal) increases in direct proportion to the weight of the coalition. The refusal of a large coalition, which has large market economies as members, to sign an agreement has a bigger detrimental impact on the outside party than a similar refusal by a smaller coalition. The reliability of such a coalition is also likely to provide more reassurance to the risk-averse members and keep them committed to the group.

The logic outlined in this section explains how coalitions can overcome the risk of defection within them, and thereby use the second route to making gains through coalitions (i.e. through the collective agenda, as opposed to side-deals). But having successfully established their unity and commitment to the collective agenda, these coalitions must face another hurdle. To reach an agreement, having demonstrated their strength, all coalitions (and especially those from the South involved in North-South negotiations as they involve smaller and weaker countries), must make some concessions. If they continue to stand firm, and use a strictly distributive strategy, there is a risk that the outside party (i.e. the North) decides that a situation of deadlock is preferable to an agreement based exclusively on the terms of the coalition. And herein lies the paradox. The coalition must somehow be able to show a willingness to make concessions, without these concessions being interpreted as a sign

---

[12] 'If the failure to eat that day – be it venison or rabbit – means that he will starve, a person is likely to defect in the Stag Hunt even if he really likes venison and has a high level of trust in his colleagues. (Defection is especially likely if the others are also starving or if they know that he is). By contrast, if the costs of CD are lower, if people are well-fed or states are resilient, they can afford to take a more relaxed view of threats.' (see Jervis 1978, 172).

of weakness from the outside party. And historically and in recent negotiations, this has been a particularly difficult task.

Why is it difficult for strong, united coalitions to make concessions, particularly when the coalitions comprise developing countries? The collective agenda of large coalitions is arrived at through considerable logrolling that incorporates the diverse interests of all its members. Were the agenda not far-reaching and ambitious, the benefits of defection would outweigh those of cooperation, leading to the unravelling of the coalition. But an ambitious agenda that brings together diverse interests also makes it difficult for the coalition to negotiate with flexibility. Compromise, under such circumstances, becomes especially difficult to make because a concession on any one issue area, or a sub-issue, risks antagonising the member/s of the coalition and acting as a trigger for defection. Bernard Hoekman has also commented on this: 'The move towards the creation of negotiating coalitions of groups of countries may reduce the number of 'principals' but possibly at the cost of greater inflexibility and a higher risk of breakdown, especially in a setting where there is little time to consult'.[13]

What does this add up to? Coalitions can successfully overcome the defection risk to benefit from the gains of collective action by converting the Prisoners' Dilemma into the Stag Hunt, and by further creating conditions that lead their members in the Stag Hunt to arrive at the payoff-maximising, mutual cooperation equilibrium, rather than the risk-averse equilibrium of mutual defection. But coalitions that manage to do this successfully also heighten the risk of deadlock. The following section illustrates this problem. Through the use of empirical examples, it shows how coalitions of developing countries in the WTO, having learnt the ways of maintaining their unity, have also heightened the frequency and scale of deadlock in the WTO.

2   EMPIRICAL ANALYSIS: EVOLVING COALITIONS IN THE WTO

In the run-up to both the launch of the Uruguay Round and the DDA, we find some evidence for the Defection Hypothesis. In the case of the G10 in the pre-launch of the Uruguay Round,[14] and the Like Minded Group in the

---

[13] Hoekman 2003.

[14] At the time of the preparatory meetings for the Uruguay Round in 1986, this group comprised Argentina, Brazil, Egypt, India, and the former Yugoslavia, plus Cuba, Nigeria, Nicaragua, Tanzania and Peru. The G10's central agenda was to ensure that the 'new issues' of services, TRIPs, and TRIMs were not included in GATT negotiations (see Narlikar 2003).

pre-negotiation phase of the DDA,[15] at least some members in both coalitions received side-payments, and ended up defecting from the coalition. India, in both instances, stood firm on the collective demand, and ended up isolated in the endgame. Negotiators from both coalitions – those that defected and also those that stood firm – agreed in interviews that the agreement that was eventually arrived at was highly sub-optimal from their perspectives.[16] In no interview did they identify the route of defection as the preferred method one to make gains. This reinforces the argument that was made in Section 1: defection may happen, but coalitions are seldom built with the end of defection (and gains via that route) in mind.

Coalitions and countries learn. The DDA has seen the formation of several coalitions along the lines of the second hypothesis, i.e. coalitions manage to stand firm and pursue the collective agenda through effective agenda-setting. The Group of 20 (G20),[17] Group of 33 (G33),[18] NAMA-11,[19] Cotton-4, LDC group,[20] and the Small and Vulnerable Economies

---

[15] The LMG was founded under Indian leadership, and originally included Cuba, Egypt, India, Indonesia, Malaysia, Pakistan, Tanzania, and Uganda. It was initially formed to oppose the inclusion of the Singapore Issues – trade and investment, competition policy, trade facilitation, and government procurement at the Singapore ministerial conference in 1996. Subsequently, the group turned its attention to the problems that developing countries had encountered in implementing and securing the promised benefits of the Uruguay Round agreements – the so-called 'implementation issues' – and was joined in its cause by the Dominican Republic, Honduras and Zimbabwe (see Narlikar and Odell 2006).

[16] Narlikar 2003; Narlikar and Odell 2006.

[17] The G20, since November 2006, comprises 22 members: Argentina, Bolivia, Brazil, Chile, China, Cuba, Egypt, Guatemala, India, Indonesia, Mexico, Nigeria, Pakistan, Paraguay, Peru, Philippines, South Africa, Tanzania, Thailand, Uruguay, Venezuela, Zimbabwe; http://www.wto.org/english/tratop_e/agric_e/negs_bkgrnd04_groups_e.htm, accessed on 12 September 08.

[18] The so-called 'Friends of special products' grouping, or the G33, has since November 2006 comprised 46 countries: Antigua and Barbuda, Barbados, Belize, Benin, Bolivia, Botswana, China, Congo, Cote d'Ivoire, Cuba, Dominica, Dominican Republic, El Salvador, Grenada, Guatemala, Guyana, Haiti, Honduras, India, Indonesia, Jamaica, Kenya, Korea, Madagascar, Mauritius, Mongolia, Mozambique, Nicaragua, Nigeria, Pakistan, Panama, Peru, Philippines, St Kitts and Nevis, St Lucia, St Vincent and the Grenadines, Senegal, Sri Lanka, Suriname, Tanzania, Trinidad and Tobago, Turkey, Uganda, Venezuela, Zambia and Zimbabwe; NAMA-11 Ministerial Communiqué, Geneva, 20 July 2008, http://www.wto.org/english/tratop_e/agric_e/negs_bkgrnd04_groups_e.htm, accessed on 12 September 08.

[19] This coalition, which focuses on non-agricultural market access, includes (as of 2008) Argentina, Brazil, Egypt, India, Indonesia, Namibia, Philippines, South Africa, Tunisia and Venezuela; http://www.thedti.gov.za/downloads/nama.pdf, accessed on 12 September 2008.

[20] Angola, Bangladesh, Benin, Burkina Faso, Burundi, Cambodia, Central African Republic, Chad, Congo, Democratic Republic of the, Djibouti, Gambia, Guinea, Guinea Bissau, Haiti, Lesotho, Madagascar, Malawi, Maldives, Mali, Mauritania, Mozambique, Myanmar, Nepal , Niger, Rwanda, Senegal, Sierra Leone, Solomon Islands, Tanzania, Togo, Uganda *(continued)*

(SVE) group.[21] The LDC group and the SVE predate the DDA; the G20, G33, and Cotton-4 were formed around the Cancún Ministerial Conference in 2003; NAMA-11 was formed around the Hong Kong Ministerial Conference of 2005. All these coalitions have withstood the test of time for sufficiently long to throw the Defection Hypothesis into question and reinforce the Collective Gains Hypothesis.

Let us take the G20 example.[22] Based on defections by developing countries from their coalitions in the past, many outsiders predicted that the G20 would collapse at the Cancún Ministerial. They pointed to the rifts within the coalition, and argued that political will is a weak force to act as a cement for a coalition that brings together such diverse economic interests (from Brazil and India as agriculture exporters on the one hand, to India with its defensive interests in agriculture on the other). But the coalition did not collapse at Cancún. It built close links with other coalitions of developing countries, and also generated new coalitions. Most of the NAMA-11 members are also members of the G20, for instance, and there is also significant overlap between the membership of the G20 and the G33. The fact that two of its leaders – Brazil and India – have become a part of the 'New Quad' (and other key consensus-building groups such as the G4, Group of 6 (G6), the FIPs and the G7) bears testimony to the influence that the group has achieved.

The central explanation behind the survival and power of the G20 lies in its ability to get all its members to commit to the collective agenda on agriculture. Specifically, this agenda logrolls two sets of demands: an aggressive set of demands on greater market access in the North, along with a dramatic reduction in export subsidies and domestic support mechanisms, and a defensive set of demands that seeks to protect the agricultural markets of developing countries. The recognition by the G20 members that potential collective gains will outweigh individual payoffs is explicit, so $\{C,c\}>\{D,d\}$. On being asked about the likelihood of his country defecting from the G20 at Cancún in 2003, a negotiator from a small country stated that the collective gains that could be had if the G20 were successful significantly outweighed any gains that the US or EU

---

and Zambia; http://www.wto.org/english/tratop_e/agric_e/negs_bkgrnd04_groups_e.htm, accessed on 12 September 08.

[21] For the early history of the SVE group, see Narlikar 2003. In November 2005, it included Barbados, Bolivia, Cuba, Dominican Republic, El Salvador, Fiji, Guatemala, Honduras, Mauritius, Mongolia, Nicaragua, Papua New Guinea, Paraguay, and Trinidad and Tobago; http://www.wto.org/english/tratop_e/agric_e/negs_bkgrnd04_groups_e.htm, accessed on 12 September 2008.

[22] This section draws on and develops the argument presented in Narlikar and van Houten 2010.

could offer him through preferential market access.[23] Additionally, there is some evidence that leaders of the group, particularly Brazil and India, have tried to reduce the fear of smaller powers that they might get isolated in the endgame and end up with the sucker's payoff, i.e. reduced the costs of {C,d} by offering them some immediate concessions in the form of preferential market access for LDCs, and also regional trade arrangements (political and economic) with each other (e.g. IBSA, or India's Africa Forum) and with other members. By incorporating the defensive concerns of members, the G20 also guards against a defection of members to the G33. Having established a collective agenda that addresses the major concerns of all its members, the G20 has repeatedly shown its commitment to its cause and has stood firm in the face of several attempts to break it (which include bilateral offers, but also other kinds of pressure that are inevitably brought to bear upon a coalition that stands in the way of achieving consensus). But in this collective agenda, to which the G20 has shown repeated and firm adherence, also lie the problems facing the group. These problems in turn have important implications for the proclivity of the trading system to deadlock and its sustainability.

The diversity of interests represented in the logrolled agenda make it very difficult for the group to make any concessions. Brazil for instance, may well be willing to concede on granting reciprocal market access to the North, but will risk triggering the defection of several members (including India). Attempts by Brazil and Argentina to concede to the North by scaling down the demands for special products would similarly risk antagonising members such as the Philippines, Indonesia, India, and others who form a part of the G33.[24] Concessions by the sub-set with defensive interests in agriculture would in turn jeopardise the allegiance of many members of the G20 who are also Cairns Group members and attach priority to an all-round lowering of barriers to agriculture (by the developed world in particular).

The risks of making concessions on a particular issue when a coalition combines diverse interests came dramatically to the fore in the July talks of 2008. Brazil, driven by its powerful lobby of agricultural exporters, urged its G20 allies to accept the negotiated July Package. Unsurprisingly, China and India with their defensive interests in agriculture, along with other allies both within the G20 as well as part of the G33,

---

[23] Interview, Cancun, September 2003.
[24] Indeed, the dangers of this came to the fore and the G20 came to a breaking point when in the G7 consultations as part of the July 2008 talks, Brazil showed considerable willingness to accept the concessions offered by the US on the Special Safeguard Mechanism, and China and India firmly refused.

firmly refused to accept a deal until the North improved its offer. Deep differences over the adequacy of the proposed trigger for the Special Safeguard Mechanisms provided the immediate cause for the rift within the G20, along with disagreements within the G20 on the adequacy of the US offer to cap its overall trade-distorting support (OTDS) to US$14.5 billion and further demand a peace clause in exchange for this cap (for a detailed analysis of the collapse of the July 2008 talks, see Faizel Ismail's discussion in Chapter 9).

Had the G20 actually fractured with other countries following Brazil's lead, and had agriculture been the only source of the deadlock, it is entirely plausible that members of the organisation would have finally been able to reach the elusive Doha deal. But the coalition, in fact, did not collapse; Chinese and Indian leadership of the defensive agenda appear to have reinforced the trust of other coalition allies and their willingness to stand firm, rather than make concessions and let the coalition unravel. Even Brazil was brought round rather quickly to resume a negotiating position that was sensitive to the concerns of its more defensive G20 allies. Immediately after the failure of the July talks, several statements were made by leading members of the coalition emphasising the unity of the group. In subsequent meetings, the group has further attempted to maintain its unified position, and Brazil in particular has sought to distance itself from its July position to reinforce its commitment to the collective stand.[25]

What the July episode demonstrates most patently is the difficulty that coalitions face in making concessions if they do manage to logroll multiple and diverse interests. The G20 came close to collapse at the July talks. Had other members of the coalition interpreted Brazil's willingness to make concessions as a signal of its declining commitment to the collective cause and the fragility of the coalition, and thereby resorted to the pursuit of side-payments (i.e. rabbits using the Stag Hunt model), a deal could have been reached. The gains of such a deal would have been some side-payments for the defectors and conciliators, no gains for those not defecting, and effectively sub-optimal gains for all members of the coalition as side-payments would be smaller than the collective gain that could have been achieved if the coalition had been sustained. On the other hand, by managing to preserve the unity of the coalition and not going along with Brazil's argument of actually accepting the US offer on agriculture, the G20 ended up contributing to deadlock. Effectively, the G20 faced a Hobson's choice: it could make concessions and risk unravelling, to get a deal with some small side-payments for some and no gains for others (rather than the prize of the

---

[25] Interview, senior trade negotiator from a leading G20 country, 12 December 2008.

collective gain). Or it could continue to build trust among its members, ensure that no one defects and all members work together to pursue the collective gain (i.e. the stag in the Stag Hunt), make no concessions, and risk another deadlock (i.e. no gains, so neither stag nor rabbit) in its negotiations with the outside party. This time, the coalition chose the latter.

The difficult choices faced by the G20 also affect other coalitions of developing countries. The fact that the North is aware of these difficulties further heightens the pressures facing the South. This means that any coalition of developing countries, including the G20, must devise ways in which it might negotiate integratively and constructively in order to not lock the system permanently into deadlock and lose the benefits of agreement. But it must simultaneously preserve its reputation as a strong coalition, both to preserve its own unity and trust among members (to reach the {C,c} equilibrium of the Stag Hunt), and to establish the credibility of its position and ensure as large a set of concessions from the outside party as is possible. The next section suggests how coalitions, and the institutions within which they operate, may achieve this fine balance.

3   PROPOSALS FOR REFORM

The demonstrated strength and newfound power of coalitions of developing countries in the WTO undoubtedly brings some important benefits. By assisting countries with research as well as representation, these coalitions have contributed to their empowerment. But, as we have seen in the last two sections, structural problems within these coalitions make it difficult for them to make concessions. A proliferation of such coalitions increases the proclivity of the WTO to deadlock. A highly inefficient WTO that finds it impossible to reach agreement inevitably strengthens regionalism and bilateralism, and works to the detriment of the developing world which has only recently begun to participate proactively in the institution. So what reform measures might help alleviate the problem of deadlock caused by coalitions, without undermining their newfound power? An answer to this question may improve the efficiency and sustainability of the system, but may effectively offer even greater power to developing countries. It promises to do so by moving coalitions of developing countries from veto-wielding blocking coalitions to the next level of negotiating coalitions, i.e. coalitions that are able to translate their power into influencing both process and outcomes.

I suggest two types of solutions, one at the level of the member countries and the other at the level of the institution. The first solution-set suggests measures that developing countries could adopt on their own, rather than having to rely on complementary structural changes beyond their control. As such, these solutions impart even greater agency to the weak. They also fit more easily within existing institutional structures and norms. The second solution-set, if adopted, is more radical, and is also likely to have greater and longer-lasting impact. Ideally the two sets would go hand-in-hand, but in the absence of circumstances conducive for institutional reform due to the preoccupation with resolving the Doha deadlock, a two step reform process could be launched. As a first step, developing countries took take it upon themselves to further improve the efficacy of their bargaining coalitions. Institutional changes could constitute the second step.

Reform measures for coalitions

To get their coalitions to work more effectively, developing countries could make some structural changes to facilitate their ability to make concessions without triggering defection. The simplest solution to this would be to build coalitions that are entirely issue-specific and thereby automatically cohesive. Unfortunately, this would amount to destroying the newfound power of coalitions: in the G20 case, for instance, this would involve dividing up the coalition into at least two groups of countries with aggressive vs. defensive interests in agriculture. Besides, one of the strengths of the recent coalitions lies in their ability to use their diversity as well as large country membership as a source of legitimacy, which in turn translates into some bargaining power. And as has already been argued elsewhere,[26] highly focused single-issue coalitions of developing countries lack external weight and are further prone to breakdown when they involve large economies with diversified interests. But a resort to issue-based coalitions is not the only option available on menu. A good alternative would be to persist with existing coalition types, but to develop credible signalling mechanisms.

Credible signalling mechanisms to demonstrate their commitment to particular positions can help developing countries overcome the problem of misinterpretation by allies as well as outside parties. One of the reasons why Cancún failed was that developed countries were simply not aware of the strength of the G20 or other coalitions. Similarly, there were several grounds for the North to assume that in later iterations, the G20 would be willing to make concessions (given that most coalitions in the North do make such concessions in the endgame). Were coalitions to improve signalling mechanisms, particularly using costly signals to credibly indicate their intentions, the probability of deadlock would be reduced. This would be true even if coalitions had no intentions of making

---

[26] Narlikar 2003.

concessions – as long as they credibly communicate their aims and strategies to the North, the likelihood of reaching agreement improves.[27]

One of the central ideas behind credible signalling is to demonstrate a willingness to incur costs to reach a particular, desired goal.[28] Even diversified coalitions of the weak have the ability to take on such costs.[29] Through effective issue linkage, the G20 for instance could have agreed to scale down its demands on Special and Differential Treatment, whilst simultaneously refusing to make any concessions on its prioritised area of agriculture which would have been the deal-breaker. The concessions on Special and Differential Treatment would not have represented a huge cost to the membership of the G20 or jeopardised the unity of the coalition, but would have been a sufficiently high cost insofar as the G20 would risk its relationship with other developing country coalitions such as the LDC group. Prioritisation of demands even with the same issue-area can have a similar effect. A visible and public refusal to accept bilateral deals and instead adhere to the coalition's position can also be effective signalling devices for reassuring allies and further demonstrating the strength of the coalition to the outside party.

Institutional Reform: Formalisation of coalitions

As previously discussed, coalitions find it difficult to make concessions because any concessions can (a) trigger the defection process; (b) concessions can be misinterpreted as a sign of weakness of the coalition by the outside party. To both these problems, there is a straightforward institutional solution: the formalisation of coalitions and a two-step negotiation. In the first step, countries would build alliances, and would need to credibly demonstrate the unity of the coalition (through cohesive coalition structures as well as the kinds of signalling mechanisms discussed in the first solution-set). In the second step however, these coalitions would receive formal recognition, and institutional guarantees would be placed against side-payments and attempts to buy members off. Alternatively, if such a moratorium could not be placed on bilateral and regional side-payments to divide and conquer the coalition, a most favoured nation (MFN) rule could be instituted such that side-payments offered to any one member of the coalition would have to be extended to all members of the group. Having such guarantees in place would help coalitions overcome the fear that any conciliatory gestures may be interpreted as a sign of the group's weakness, and would render the process of making concessions easier than it is today. Recognising that there are no permanent allies,

---

[27] This idea is formally developed in a model by Narlikar and van Houten 2009.
[28] On signalling, see Fearon 1994, and Banks 1991.
[29] On the use of signalling in trade negotiations, see Narlikar and van Houten 2009.

coalitions could be constituted for the duration of each new round, and subsequently re-constituted to ensure that they do not lock countries into dated loyalties.

Such a process of formalisation of coalitions with each new round would facilitate the negotiation process by narrowing the number of principals, without translating into the increasing inflexibility that is associated with coalitions today. Its benefits could be carried over into several negotiating formulae – in request-offer approaches, countries in a coalition would negotiate together, whilst developing countries could get to enjoy a prize place in the negotiation even with the Principal Supplier Principle if they were allowed to aggregate their market power through coalitions.[30] This is a significant advantage for small countries that would – and indeed have been – marginalised from the process due to the de facto return of the principal supplier approach in the choice of countries that are invited to the High Table of trade negotiations.[31] Eventually, the utility of the groups could also be extended to the Dispute Settlement Mechanism to improve its accessibility for developing countries as well as their retaliatory capacities.

The first step of the negotiation, wherein coalitions define themselves, iron out internal differences, and acquire recognition with the launch of a new round, may appear at first glance to add a new layer of complication to reaching agreement. But the formalisation of coalitions will help reduce the number of principals, while the moratorium (or alternatively extension) of side-deals will improve the flexibility of coalitions to negotiate meaningfully.[32] The result will be a more efficient WTO that is less prone to deadlock, and also a WTO where developing countries are able to translate their veto-player status into effective influence.

4   CONCLUSION

In this chapter, I have advanced the argument that developing countries form coalitions not guided by a spirit of potential defection, but in recognition of the high pay-offs to be had through the pursuit of collective

---

[30] Rolland 2007 also discusses a bargaining mechanism under the Principal Supplier Principle, using the aggregation practice developed by the EC as an example, p. 532.

[31] See Faizel Ismail's chapter in this volume on the use of the PSP in the recent talks, and the problems of legitimacy that this has generated for the organisation.

[32] Note that a system of groups operates in institutions like the IMF, and is less far-fetched than it might first year. The big difference between the system proposed here versus that of the IMF is that the latter institution is based on a weighted-voting system, whereas this system would continue to rely on the one-member-one-vote principle and consensus-based decision-making of the GATT and the WTO.

gains. Were defection from the coalition the primary motivation for joining it, common knowledge of this would ensure that coalitions would not form in the first place. This however does not mean that allies are not affected by the temptation to defect in the life of the coalition; they are. But this temptation to defect can and has been overcome, evidenced most patently in the creation of the strong coalitions of the DDA.

The chapter has further argued that the decision to cooperate (rather than defect), and also the strong coalitions that result from it, can be facilitated through two steps. First, through a variety of means including effective agenda-setting for the coalition, players can ensure that coalition dynamics reflect a Stag Hunt (which has two possible equilibria of mutual cooperation and mutual defection) over a Prisoners' Dilemma (where mutual defection is the only one equilibrium, and defection is the dominant strategy). Second, leaders of a coalition in particular can take steps to build trust amongst members, and thereby create incentives for allies to move towards the pay-off enhancing equilibrium of mutual cooperation and away from the risk-averse equilibrium of mutual defection.

While such strong coalitions have a greater chance of achieving the prize of the collective gain in their negotiations with the outside party, they also face the problem of making concessions for two reasons. First, any concessions made in a particular issue-area may be interpreted by some allies as a sign of potential defection, and trigger pre-emptive defection resulting in the unravelling of the coalition. Second, concessions may also be interpreted as a sign of weakness by the outside party, especially if the outside party is aware of the risk that concessions may lead to the unravelling of the coalition anyway. These difficulties in making concessions mean that the emergence of strong coalitions, while potentially of major benefit to developing countries if they do manage to extract concessions from the North, also make the system much more prone to delays in agreement and deadlock. Section 2 in the chapter discussed both the growing power of developing country coalitions in the recent Doha negotiations, as well as their contribution to the recurrence of deadlock in this round.

A permanently deadlocked multilateral system generates costs, and not only in the form of delayed gains for all parties. Developing countries, paradoxically as a result of their newfound coalition power, end up bearing a disproportionate share of the costs of these delayed gains. This is because they are the players that are much more dependent on the multilateral trading system and less able to strike regional and bilateral agreements on terms favourable to themselves. A deadlocked multilateral trading system that leads the developed world towards regional and bilateral alternatives does not advantage developing countries.

To overcome the unanticipated costs of strong coalitions of developing countries, while preserving and enhancing their benefits, I have suggested two solutions. The first is at the level of developing countries themselves, who could use signalling devices more effectively to counter the risk of misinterpretation of conciliatory moves as a sign of defection by members or as a sign of weakness by outsiders. The second is at the institutional level and would require the formal recognition of coalitions by the organisation. Each new trade round would be negotiated in two steps. The first step would involve the constitution of coalitions – comprising developed or developing countries – which would then become the principals for the actual multilateral trade negotiation in the second step. Formal recognition of these collective entities as principals could potentially significantly empower even small developing countries by elevating them into the role of principal suppliers as members of coalitions. A limitation placed on side-deals (be it through an outright moratorium or through an extension of such deals to all coalition members on an MFN basis) would allow these coalitions greater flexibility to make concessions.[33] Together, the two solutions offer gains to all parties involved in the negotiation process. They offer greater empowerment to developing countries via the coalitions that they have already developed, and thereby also improvements in perceptions of fairness of the multilateral trading system. Simultaneously, they are likely to improve the ability of the system to deliver results, and hence its efficiency, resulting in greater buy-in and engagement from the developed world. In coalition analysis thus lies the key to several problems that have challenged practitioners and scholars of trade governance.

---

[33] This institutional solution would also require an expansion in the role of the Secretariat, which would have to monitor the coalitions in Phase 1, and then the regulation of side-deals in Phase 2.

REFERENCES

Baldwin, Robert. 2006. Failure of the WTO Ministerial Conference at Cancun: Reasons and Remedies. *The World Economy* 29(6):677-696.

Banks, Jeffrey S. 1991. *Signaling Games in Political Science.* Chur: Harwood Academic Publishers.

Fearon, James D. 1994. Signaling versus the Balance of Power and Interests: An Empirical Test of a Crisis Bargaining Model. *Journal of Conflict Resolution* 38(2): 236-269.

Hoekman, Bernard. 2003. *Cancun: Crisis or Catharsis?,* September 20. http: //siteresources.worldbank.org/INTRANETTRADE/Resources/ Hoekman-CancunCatharsis-092003.pdf, accessed on 12 September 2008.

Jervis, Robert. 1978. Cooperation under the Security Dilemma. *World Politics* 30(2):167-214, January.

Narlikar, Amrita. 2003. *International Trade and Developing Countries: Bargaining Coalitions in the GATT and WTO.* London: Routledge.

Narlikar, Amrita. 2005. *The World Trade Organisation: A Very Short Introduction,* Oxford: Oxford University Press.

Narlikar, Amrita and John Odell. 2006. The Strict Distributive Strategy for a Bargaining Coalition: The Like Minded Group in the World Trade Organisation. In *Negotiating Trade: Developing countries in the WTO and NAFTA,* edited by John Odell. Cambridge: Cambridge University Press.

Narlikar, Amrita and Pieter Van Houten. 2010. Know the Enemy: Uncertainty and Deadlock in Trade Negotiations. Forthcoming in *Deadlocks in Multilateral Negotiations: Causes and Solutions,* edited by Amrita Narlikar. Cambridge: Cambridge University Press.

Rolland, Sonia. 2006. Developing Country Coalitions at the WTO: In search of legal support. *Harvard International Law Journal* 48(2): 483-551.

Skyrms, Brian. 2001. *The Stag Hunt.* Presidential Address, Pacific Division of the American Philosophical Association.

Steinberg, Richard. 2002. In the Shadow of Law or Power: Consensus-Based Bargaining and Outcomes at the GATT/WTO. *International Organisation* 56(2):339-374.

Tussie, Diana. 2002. Introduction. In *Trade Negotiations in Latin America: Problems and Prospects,* edited by Diana Tussie. London: Macmillan.

FAIZEL ISMAIL[1]

9. REFLECTIONS ON THE WTO JULY 2008 COLLAPSE:

Lessons for Developing Country Coalitions

The Doha Round negotiations of the World Trade Organisation (WTO) were launched in November 2001 in Doha, Qatar in the wake of the 9/11 terrorist attack on the United States (US). The event was a significant success for the newly formed WTO after the dramatic failure of the Seattle Ministerial Conference in December 1999 to launch the new round. However, this initial success was to be marred by several subsequent failed ministerial meetings[2] and missed deadlines. The Doha mandate called for modalities[3] in agriculture to be agreed by March 2002 and in NAMA, by the end of May 2002. By December 2008, the establishment of full modalities, in the agriculture and non-agricultural market access (NAMA) or industrial tariff negotiations, was still to be achieved by the WTO.

The attempt by WTO members to secure a 'framework agreement' by the time of the Cancún Ministerial Conference in September 2003 was frustrated by the collapse of that meeting. The limited objective of

---

[1] This paper is written in the author's personal capacity. He is indebted to Amrita Narlikar and Rorden Wilkinson for the challenging comments and suggestions made on earlier versions of the paper.

[2] The WTO has formal Ministerial Conferences that are required to take place at least once in two years. Since its formation at the Marrakesh ministerial meeting, the WTO has held five Ministerial Conferences, with the last being the sixth Ministerial Conference held in Hong Kong in December 2005. However, there are other informal ministerial gatherings of the WTO that have taken different forms, including so-called mini-ministerial meetings that were held to discuss the launch of the Doha Round; small groups of ministers meeting among themselves (e.g. G4, G5 and G6) and larger groups of ministers (approximately thirty) convened by the Director-General to negotiate breakthroughs in the negotiations, sometimes referred to as the 'green room'. These smaller informal ministerial meetings have no legal status and any 'breakthroughs' arrived at in these must be taken to the broader membership for decision.

[3] 'Modalities' are not clearly defined in the WTO. The concept refers to the technical formulas that are utilised to develop a schedule of commitments (on tariff reductions or subsidy reductions) that members have to finally agree to. A 'Framework Agreement' falls short of this objective and develops the architecture for the modalities agreement without fully agreeing the technical formulas that will be used to determine the legal commitments of members.

A.Narlikar, B.Vickers (eds.), Leadership and Change in the Multilateral Trading System, 203–230.

WTO members to at least agree on a 'framework' for modalities was finally achieved in the July 2004 Framework Agreement. Building on this success and learning from the Cancún collapse, the WTO reduced its expectation to achieve full modalities at the next WTO ministerial conference held in Hong Kong, China, and merely made some incremental advances on the July 2004 Framework Agreement. However, since then the various attempts to achieve full modalities in agriculture and NAMA have proved elusive. A Group of 6 (G6) WTO members (US, EU, Japan, Australia, Brazil and India) attempted to advance the modalities negotiations among themselves in early 2006, only to result in another failure for the WTO by July 2006. WTO Director-General (DG) Pascal Lamy who hosted and chaired the G6 ministerial meetings in July 2006 in Geneva decided to suspend the Doha negotiations.

A smaller group of four members (EU, US, India and Brazil, the so-called G4) then began a process of negotiation amongst themselves in an attempt to make a breakthrough on the vexed issues of agriculture and NAMA modalities during the first half of 2007. The G4 ministerial meeting held in Potsdam, Germany from 19-23 June 2007 collapsed on the third day of the scheduled four to five day meeting. After the collapse of the Potsdam G4 ministerial meeting, the WTO Director-General called on the Chairs of the WTO negotiating groups to resume the multilateral negotiating process of the Doha Round.[4]

The Chairs of Agriculture and NAMA had produced several draft texts since June 2007, leading to their third draft texts that they produced on 10 July 2008. These texts were to become the basis for the finalisation of the negotiations on agriculture and NAMA modalities at the end of July 2008. After several missed informal deadlines, the Chair of the WTO Trade Negotiating Council (TNC), Pascal Lamy, called for a final negotiating process based on the Chairs' Texts. This would be held in Geneva from 21 July 2008, with about 30 to 40 ministers invited to participate in the process. However, this attempt to conclude the negotiations on agriculture and NAMA was to fail yet again with the collapse of the Group of 7 (G7) (EU, US, Japan, Australia, India and Brazil) ministerial. The WTO consequently failed to conclude the negotiations on modalities for agriculture and NAMA. The G7 ministers and several other small groups that met in July 2008 produced some incremental, but very controversial advances on the agriculture and NAMA modalities negotiations.

This chapter is divided into four sections. Part one will briefly discuss the 'Lamy Package' that emerged out of the G7 ministerial meetings and the subsequent reports of the Chairs of Agriculture and NAMA on

---

[4] See WTO doc. 'Informal TNC Meeting at the level of Head of Delegation', Job (07)/ 105, 22 June 2007.

the July 2008 modalities negotiations. Part two assesses the collapse of the July 2008 ministerial meetings and advances three reasons for the deadlock. The first reason ascribes the failure to the imbalanced nature of the texts, both within NAMA and between NAMA and agriculture. The promise of the Doha Round was that the trade-distorting subsidies and prohibitive tariff barriers in developed countries that undermined developing country agriculture would be substantially reduced. In NAMA, the industrial tariffs of developed countries still retained high peaks and tariff escalation but were relatively low, whilst developing countries had relatively high bound tariffs. Developed countries were thus expected to make a major contribution by reducing their farming subsidies and opening their agriculture markets; and developing countries were expected to reciprocate in a proportionate manner by reducing their relatively higher bound tariffs in NAMA. However, with each revised set of texts produced by the Chairs, the agriculture text was perceived to contain only insignificant commitments by the developed countries in agriculture, whilst the NAMA text provided for relatively onerous market opening into developing countries, particularly the larger emerging economies. This was partly ascribed to the role of the Chair of the NAMA negotiating group who by his own admission decided at the very outset, in his first draft text, to determine the level of ambition himself.[5] The chapter argues that the inefficient role of the Chairs in the July 2008 ministerial meetings was to become a significant contributory factor for the collapse of the July 2008 ministerial meetings.

The second reason offered for the failure is increasing protectionism within the European Union (EU) and the US, and their attempts to raise the bar of the level of ambition for developing countries, particularly the major emerging markets that have been perceived as significant competitors with the EU and US. It will be argued that the EU and US have increased their collaboration in the Doha Round, accommodating each others' interests, while pursuing an aggressive market opening agenda vis-à-vis the major emerging markets that are perceived to be their competitors in global markets. This chapter thus contributes to the thesis advanced by several scholars of the persistence of an 'asymmetry of economic opportunity' in favour of developed countries in the WTO.

The third reason that is offered for the failure is the resurrection – in the form of the G7 – of the old Principal Supplier approach and power politics that had characterised much of the General Agreement on Tariffs and Trade (GATT) period. This resulted in the collapse of each phase of the process: at Potsdam in June 2007 (G4); in July 2006 when the failure of the G6 ministers led to the suspension of the round; and at the collapse

---

[5] See WTO 2007 doc. Draft NAMA Modalities Job (07)/126, 17 July 2007.

of the Cancún Ministerial Conference, where the majority of members were not represented in the green room.[6] The moving deadlines for the date of the ministerial meetings from before Easter to after Easter, to the third week of May, to mid-June and then end-July 2008 created a great deal of uncertainty. By contrast, the July 2004 Framework Agreement was negotiated in a more inclusive multilateral process resulting in a successful outcome. Similarly, the green rooms, chaired by Pascal Lamy, at the Hong Kong Ministerial Conference in December 2005 were able to make some incremental advances on the July 2004 Framework Agreement, due to the inclusiveness of the meetings.

Part three of the chapter analyses the collapse of the July 2008 ministerial meetings and makes some recommendations for WTO members to address the underlying causes of the collapse. It considers the situation of different developing country groups at the end of the July 2008 ministerial meetings and the challenges that confront these groups on the way forward. A discussion on the lessons that can be learnt from this experience for each developing country group in the WTO is undertaken with reference to the theoretical framework presented by Amrita Narlikar in Chapter 8. The chapter supports the thesis advanced by Narlikar that the basic rationale for the creation of coalitions is captured by the Collective Gains Hypothesis. The chapter concludes by calling on developing countries to continue to work for a successful conclusion of the Doha Round based on its development mandate.

1   THE WTO JULY MINISTERIAL MEETINGS AND THE 'LAMY PACKAGE'

This section starts by describing the events that led to the collapse of the G7 ministerial meetings at the end of July 2008. It then sets out the main elements of the 'Lamy Package'. The subsequent reports of the Chairs of Agriculture and NAMA are then briefly summarised.

What happened during the nine days of the Geneva negotiations?

After two days of opening statements in the WTO TNC and green room, WTO DG Pascal Lamy constituted the G7 ministerial, which was to dominate the negotiations until they collapsed on 29 July 2008. The negotiations were held in different formats, beginning with the TNC, followed by green rooms (approximately 31 members were invited) and then the creation of the G7 on Wednesday, 23 July 2008. The TNC and the green rooms were held daily. However, on Monday, 28 July 2008 WTO members waited all day and night for a green room meeting, which

---

[6] See annexure 1. For a discussion of the Cancún Ministerial Conference, see Ismail 2004.

did not materialise. The G7 had met throughout the night. When the latter convened again the next day, the negotiations finally collapsed over their inability to agree on the Special Safeguard Mechanism (SSM).[7] The last TNC gathering after the collapse of the ministerial meetings was held on Wednesday, 30 July 2008. The DG reported on the failure of the negotiations to reach full modalities.[8] Lamy argued that the G7 were not able to find convergence on the SSM and thus were not able to get to the next set of issues, which would have begun with the cotton issue. He stated that the failure was a collective responsibility and that the progress made by all groups should be preserved. In this regard, he stated that the Chairs of the negotiating groups would be submitting their reports.

The Lamy Package

The Lamy Package[9] that was submitted to the green room on the evening of Friday, 25 July 2008 proposed compromise numbers in several elements of the agriculture and NAMA modalities texts. On the overall trade-distorting support (OTDS) for the US, Brazil, India and China proposed that the US should go to the bottom of the range (US$13 billion). The US offered US$15 billion and then later US$14.5 billion (about the middle of the range). In exchange, the US called for a new 'peace clause' (i.e. assurances that their programmes would not be subject to legal challenges) and significant market access in agriculture, NAMA and services.[10] Brazil accepted the US offer on OTDS.

On NAMA, the Lamy Package proposed coefficients in the middle of the NAMA Chair's ranges.[11] The package proposed a coefficient of 8 for developed countries. For developing countries, it proposed a coefficient of 20 for the first group of developing countries that opt for a lower coefficient and higher flexibilities; 22 for the second group of countries that take the normal flexibilities; and a coefficient of 25 for the third group of countries that opt to take no flexibilities. In the G7, Brazil negotiated hard for the flexibilities provided to the first group of developing countries to be extended from 14 per cent of lines and volume, to an extra 2 per cent of trade volume. This was included in the Lamy Package.

---

[7] The SSM is a mechanism that was agreed to be created in Hong Kong for poor farmers in developing countries to protect their domestic markets from import surges (particularly from highly subsidized US and other developed country exports).

[8] Washington Trade Daily, 31 July 2008.

[9] See Washington Trade Daily, 28 July 2008.

[10] See Kaushik, Kaukab and Kumar 2008.

[11] The Lamy Package adopted the proposed middle ground of the NAMA Chair's 10 July 2008 Draft Text.

On anti-concentration, the EU and US (together with Japan and Australia) insisted that 30 per cent of lines per chapter be exempted from flexibilities, whilst Brazil, India and China were only prepared to accept a 10 per cent exclusion.[12] The Lamy text proposed that 20 per cent of lines be excluded or 9 per cent of value per chapter. On sectorals, the Lamy Package changed the language from the 10 July 2008 NAMA draft text that called for sectorals to help 'balance the overall results of the negotiations on NAMA', to providing a carrot of increased coefficients for those countries that participate in sectorals (coupled with calls for these countries to commit to participate in at least two sectoral initiatives). This proposal was opposed by both India and China and thus re-negotiated.[13] The new language restates the non-mandatory nature of sectorals and that participation in the negotiations of the terms of at least two sectorals of their choosing shall not prejudice the decision of the member to participate in such a sectoral. The resistance of India and China to make sectorals mandatory did succeed in preventing the attempts by the US and the EU to create a mandatory linkage between the participation of developing countries in sectorals and the core NAMA modality (formula and flexibilities).

The Agriculture and NAMA Chairs report on the collapse

The Chairs of the Agriculture and NAMA negotiations submitted their reports of the July 2008 modalities negotiations on 12 August 2008. In his report, the Chair of Agriculture stated that whilst there was a credible basis for concluding many issues, there was still disagreement on other very significant issues.[14] He went on to state that he was not in a position to record the convergences in precise textual language as the circumstances have changed. Therefore, he stated that the existing texts remain. The Chair throughout refers to the reports of the G7 and green room discussions – as well as the Lamy Package, which was reported on – without attempting to convert any of this into textual language.

By contrast, the Chair of NAMA stated that the G7 had reached convergence on the NAMA modalities; indeed, '[t]he majority of members meeting in Green Room format indicated that, while they had reservations over particular issues, they could live with the proposed compromise outcomes on these elements of the NAMA modalities'.[15] However, he states that some members did not provide explicit support to all NAMA

---

[12] Washington Trade Daily, 4 August 2008.
[13] See WTO doc, Job(08)/96, 12 August 2008.
[14] WTO doc, Job (08)/95, 12 August 2008.
[15] WTO doc, Job (08)/96, 12 August 2008.

elements of the package. The Chair then only cites three members (i.e. South Africa, Argentina and Venezuela) that did not provide explicit support. He then goes on to include in textual format the Lamy Package's proposed numbers for all the issues: coefficients, flexibilities, anti-concentration and sectorals. On the sectorals, the new negotiated language after the first Lamy text was negotiated with India and China is included.

2   ASSESSING THE COLLAPSE OF THE JULY 2008 GENEVA MINISTERIAL MEETINGS

What caused the collapse?

The Lamy text (produced on the evening of Friday, 25 July 2008) proposed a 140 per cent trigger on the SSM for developing countries – allowing developing countries to exceed their current bound rates by 15 per cent only if imports on a product increased by 40 per cent or more.[16] India rejected this proposal and insisted on a 115 per cent trigger instead. Another compromise text tabled on the morning of Tuesday, 29 July 2008 proposed a 115 to 120 per cent trigger for India (with 33 per cent increase in bound tariffs) and another trigger of between 130 and 140 per cent (with 50 per cent increase in tariffs). India was prepared to accept the 120 per cent trigger. However, China could not accept this compromise and the US refused to move from the 140 per cent trigger. WTO DG Pascal Lamy could take the process no further and the meeting collapsed. The US stated that '[a]ny safeguard must distinguish between the legitimate need to address exceptional situations involving sudden and extreme import surges and a mechanism that can be abused'.[17]

The proximate cause of the collapse was the SSM, although the negotiations could have broken down on several other issues: cotton; NAMA; new tariff quota creation; tariff simplification; bananas; geographical indications; the Agreement on Trade-related Aspects of Intellectual Property Rights (TRIPS) and the Convention on Biological Diversity (CBD); fishery subsidies; rules (e.g. anti-dumping); preference erosion; tropical

---

[16] It was reported that India and China wanted a trigger of 110 whilst the US demanded 155 and Australia 165. The report states that Lamy's first proposal put forward on Thursday night proposed a figure of 120 per cent of imports, but on Friday morning the Lamy Package changed this figure to 140 per cent. This prompted Indian Commerce Minister Kamal Nath to state that he would not be party to the package and he threatened to walk out of the talks. However, the WTO DG left the figure of 140 in the text, which was then presented to the green room for consideration on the Friday night (Washington Trade Daily, 7 August 2008).

[17] Washington Trade Daily, 30 July 2008; WTO Reporter 2008.

products; or duty-free quota-free market access (DFQFMA) for LDCs. *So what was the real cause of the breakdown?* I present three main reasons for the failure of the July ministerial meeting: first, the imbalanced nature of the texts and the role of the chair; second, the increasing protectionism within the EU and US, and their attempts to raise the bar of the level of ambition for developing countries; and third, the resurrection of the Principal Supplier Principle and power politics of the earlier GATT period. In the following section, I discuss the theoretical issues and concepts that that have emerged in the academic literature to describe each of these concerns and then discuss them in the context of the failed July ministerial meetings.

Imbalanced texts and the role of the Chairs: theory and practice

Theory on the role of the chair
In a recent comprehensive study of the role of the chair in international negotiations, Tallberg[18] attempts to develop a 'rational institutionalist theory' of the role of the chair in international negotiations and describes this role as 'formal leadership'. In his consideration of the three roles of the chair in WTO negotiations – i.e. agenda management, brokerage and representation – he argues that the role of representation is seldom required. Thus the role of the chair in the WTO negotiations is adequately described as that of agenda management and brokerage. He argues that the chairs that play these roles are vested with 'asymmetric' power to influence the negotiations. This power comes from their privileged access to information about the real preferences of members and the support of the Secretariat, and their control over the negotiating process. However, this asymmetric power is conditioned by the rules governing decision-making and the design of the chairmanship. He argues that the chair's scope to influence the negotiations is much wider if the method of decision-making is that of majority voting, than the tougher methods of consensus or unanimity, where the interests of all parties have to be considered.

     After applying his theory to the three different institutional settings of the EU, the WTO and the multilateral environmental agreements, Tallberg argues that in both the latter cases, formal leaders positively enhanced the efficiency of the negotiations by transforming competing proposals into single texts and forging agreements. In addition, in these cases he argues that there was '[n]o evidence of the chairs having

---

[18] Tallberg (forthcoming).

systematically biased outcomes...'.[19] However, the extensive research undertaken by Odell[20] of decision-making in the GATT/WTO provides several examples of sub-optimal or inefficient outcomes as a result of injudicious use of the brokerage methods or the bias of the chair.

In a study[21] on the role of the NAMA chair, Ambassador Don Stephenson of Canada, in the NAMA negotiations between the Potsdam G4 ministerial meeting in June 2007 and the July 2008 ministerial meeting, it was argued that his role reflected all the above errors. His failure to provide efficient formal leadership was contrasted with that of the Chair of Agriculture, Ambassador Crawford Falconer of New Zealand, in the agriculture negotiations. Falconer displayed a capacity to listen carefully to the views of different members, to act in an objective manner, to make judicious use of the tools of brokerage (providing alternative options, single texts, etc) and appropriate timing of single texts, and a fierce independence from the influence of any of the major developed or developing country groups in the WTO.

Evaluation of the role of the Chairs in the July 2008 meetings
The NAMA-11 coalition of developing countries, which represents a significant group of emerging market economies, criticised the various draft texts of the NAMA chair that emerged prior to the July 2008 ministerial meeting for ignoring their views and reflecting the preferences of the chair. South Africa (the coordinator of the NAMA-11, as Brendan Vickers explores in chapter 7) raised these concerns in a statement to the TNC on 22 July 2008: 'Our experience in the NAMA negotiations over the last two years is that the texts that have emerged at various points have consistently ignored the positions and views we have expressed as the NAMA-11'. South Africa went on to note that whilst '[t]he agricultural negotiations have been conducted through a carefully constructed "bottom-up" process through which the positions of all WTO Members are found in the agricultural modalities text, the NAMA modalities text is highly circumscribed and prescriptive. The text sets out a narrow range of coefficients, and offers flexibilities that have a double constraint in terms of the percentage of tariff lines and trade volumes that can be covered'. The South African statement continued that: '[w]e have witnessed a range of demands that would result in an outcome where many developing countries that are required to reduce their tariffs are being required to accept reduction commitments that are deep and in excess of the cuts to be borne by developed countries. These demands are inconsistent with

---

[19] Tallberg (forthcoming).
[20] Odell 2005.
[21] Ismail 2009 (forthcoming).

the Doha development mandate and cannot be a basis for concluding the Round'.[22]

In a statement to the TNC on 26 July 2008, Argentina said that without significant changes to the Lamy Package, it would be very difficult for Argentina to support the proposals. Argentina argued that the package was 'poor in agriculture and substantially unbalanced in NAMA'. Argentina furthermore argued that the implications of the proposed formula in NAMA would mean less-than-full-reciprocity in reverse for developing countries, as the formula required developing counties to make a deeper cut in their tariffs than developed countries.[23] The Foreign Minister of Brazil, Celso Amorim, also criticised the imbalances between the agriculture and NAMA texts and within NAMA. Summing up Brazil's view of the agriculture text, Amorim argued that the text was '[b]uilt on a logic of accommodating exceptions rather than seeking ambition, with almost 30 paragraphs in the text establishing specific carve-outs for specific countries'.[24] By contrast, he argued that '[t]he NAMA text was built on the logic of forcing countries, especially developing ones, out of comfort zones' and he referred to the attempts to extract an 'additional price' in the NAMA negotiations from developing countries through the anti-concentration clause and 'disguised mandatory sectorals which would overload the negotiations and make a conclusion impossible'.[25]

The above statements point to significant dissatisfaction[26] amongst some major developing countries and developing country groups on the lack of balance between the agriculture and NAMA texts. In particular, developing countries were perturbed by the 'additional price' or increased level of ambition that they were asked to pay in the NAMA negotiations, compared to the relatively lower level of obligations that developed countries were willing to commit to in the agriculture negotiations. In NAMA, the chair was seen to have taken sides with the developed country *demandeurs* by setting the level of ambition in NAMA even before the level of ambition in agriculture had been agreed, and by adding the anti-concentration clause and 'disguised mandatory sectorals', when the Doha mandate called for sectorals to be voluntary. In sum, the perception shared

---

[22] Government of South Africa 2008.

[23] Government of Argentina 2008.

[24] Government of Brazil 2008.

[25] See Brazilian Permanent Mission to the UN and WTO 2008; G20 Statement on the State of Play, 20 June 2008; G20 Statement to the WTO Committee on Agriculture Special Session, 26 May 2008.

[26] South Africa represents the NAMA-11 in the WTO and Brazil is the coordinator of the G20. Whilst the Ministers made the above statements in their own country names, their views largely reflect the views of the NAMA-11 and the G20 respectively.

by a large number of developing countries was that the texts were imbalanced against the interests of developing countries, and that the NAMA and TNC Chairs had committed serious errors of judgment that would bias the outcomes in favour of the developed countries. The discussion next turns to the second reason that we advance for the collapse of the July 2008 ministerial meetings: increasing protectionism in the US and EU and the assertion of their narrow mercantilist interests. We begin with an historical overview of this trend and proceed to evaluate the July 2008 ministerial meetings in that context.

Increasing protectionism and aggressive EU/US demands

EU/US protectionism in the GATT / WTO and asymmetrical outcomes
The history of the GATT suggests that the interests of developing countries were largely ignored, which led to imbalanced texts that reflected the interests of the dominant economic powers. The original GATT 1947 was based on the most favoured nation (MFN) principle (i.e. all members shall be treated equally); thus no special provisions were made to accommodate the different levels of economic development of developing countries. Developing countries had, however, raised these concerns during the negotiations on the International Trade Organisation (ITO) Charter, which was later rejected by the US Congress.[27] Developing countries continued to urge developed countries to address their particular development concerns in the GATT. A study of these issues and concerns led to the Haberler Report in October 1958. The Haberler Report found that there was some substance to the disquiet expressed by primary producing countries that the rules and conventions about commercial policies were relatively unfavourable to them.

Rorden Wilkinson observes that by the mid-1960s the evolution of the GATT led to two different experiences.[28] For the industrialised countries, liberalisation under the GATT had seen the volume and value of trade in manufactured, semi-manufactured and industrial goods increase significantly. In addition, the North had also managed to protect their agricultural and textile and clothing sectors from international competition through a blend of formal and informal restrictions. To give effect to this there were a number of GATT waivers to protect developed country agricultural markets and the exclusion of textiles and clothing from liberalisation in developed countries. For developing countries, however,

---

[27] WTO 1999.
[28] Wilkinson 2006a.

this meant that the products of export interest to them were excluded from liberalisation.

US perceptions of the increasing competitiveness of the EU, Japan and East Asia and their economic 'convergence' with the US led to increasing US protectionism in the 1970s and the 1980s. Ostry[29] calls the arsenal of non-tariff measures that were put in place in the 1970s mainly against Japan (but which had the effect of blocking other developing country exports into the US and the EU) the 'new protectionism'. The 1980s saw increasing use of trade remedy laws in the US and the EU and increasing resort to unilateral trade measures by the US. By the time of the Uruguay Round, the US and the EU had begun to establish a common agenda visà-vis the rest of the world. During the Uruguay Round, the US and EU were able to find an accommodation of each others' interests in the Blair House Accord, which was agreed in November 1992. Even in the final stages of the Uruguay Round negotiations, during the first week of December 1993, the EU and the US continued to negotiate among themselves in Brussels, prompting then GATT DG Peter Sutherland to urge the EU and the US to report to the other 'over 100 participants' in Geneva 'whose interests must also be assured and accommodated'. By the formal conclusion of the round on 15 December 1993, many other members, especially developing countries, still complained that they were not in a position to assess the offers the EU and US were making against their own. They added that the agreements reached between the EU and US continued to reduce the ambition in many issues of interest to developing countries, particularly agriculture, textiles, leather, cotton and tropical products.

Another close observer of the Uruguay Round argued that the lack of real market access gains for developing countries in the Northern majors' agriculture markets and the onerous commitments they undertook in TRIPS led to the perception that developing countries 'had given more than they got' and therefore the Uruguay Round agreements were imbalanced in favour of developed countries.[30] Wilkinson argues that this imbalance was endemic to the GATT system; moreover, with each ministerial conference of the WTO since the Doha Round was launched, this asymmetry of economic opportunity in favour of the major developed countries has been reinforced.[31] In other words, the failed ministerial conferences and missed deadlines are perceived to be a symptom of this basic asymmetry of economic power that is embedded in the institutions

---

[29] See Ostry 1997. The increasing use of Section 301 of the 1974 Trade Act sanctioned unilateral action against unfair trade practices by foreign trade partners.

[30] Finger 2007.

[31] See Wilkinson 2006b

of the system.[32] It is next necessary to evaluate the validity of the above trends in the context of the Doha Round negotiations during the period up to July 2008.

Assessing the Doha Round to the July 2008 ministerial meetings
Since the launch of the Doha Round and the lead up to the Cancún Ministerial Conference in 2003, WTO members missed the deadlines to agree on the modalities in the agriculture and NAMA negotiations. This was mainly due to their failure to meet the Doha mandate to substantially reduce agricultural protection. As the Cancún Ministerial Conference approached, the EU and US began to negotiate a bilateral agreement to accommodate each others' interests. This resulted in the EU-US joint text, which was tabled on 13 August 2003. The latter galvanised developing countries into action to prevent another 'Blair House' type agreement that would accommodate the interests of the EU and the US and reduce the ambition of the round yet again. In addition the joint text agreed by the EU and the US on agriculture took the negotiating process a step back by agreeing to a mere 'framework' for the agriculture negotiations just a few weeks prior to the Cancún ministerial. This transatlantic pact on agriculture was challenged by a range of countries, including Australia, Brazil, Argentina, South Africa and many other former US allies, who had coalesced around the common objective of securing freer global agricultural markets. Developing countries led by Brazil, China, India and South Africa established a broad-based alliance that grew into the Group of 20 (G20) of developing countries coalition on agriculture.

In addition, a group of developing countries[33] argued that the real danger of a joint push by the EU and other developed countries (notably the US)[34] to seek additional extensive concessions from developing countries in the NAMA and services negotiations was that the development content of the round would be turned on its head. Developed countries would make more inroads into developing country markets, while developing countries would still face high levels of protection and distortions in global markets for products of export interest to them. This united front was further consolidated at Hong Kong in 2005, where ministers of the NAMA-11 group presented joint proposals in the negotiations on NAMA. In the final text of the Hong Kong Ministerial Declaration (specifically paragraph 24), this group was able to

---

[32] Wilkinson 2006a.
[33] Government of South Africa 2005.
[34] Washington Trade Daily, 17 July 2008.

establish a strong linkage between the levels of ambition in NAMA and agriculture.[35]

The closing of ranks by the EU and the US was further visible at the Potsdam G4 ministerial meeting in June 2007, where Brussels and Washington accommodated each others concerns' and jointly pressured Brazil and India. Reflecting on the collapse of the Potsdam negotiations, Brazilian Foreign Minister Celso Amorim remarked that the collaboration of the EU and US during the meeting reminded him of the EU-US joint text in the pre-Cancún period. Amorim thus referred to Potsdam as 'Cancún II'.[36] Following Potsdam the EU and US intensified the joint coordination of their positions, particularly on agriculture, NAMA, services[37] and environment[38]. On agriculture, the EU began to work more closely with the US bilaterally to build convergence in their positions on specific issues. On NAMA, the EU and US presented two new proposals on 5 December 2007. The first proposal[39] called for a high level of ambition for developing countries. The second proposal aimed to further restrict the existing flexibilities that were already provided for developing countries in paragraph 8.[40]

The lack of political support in the EU and the US (and other developed countries) for agricultural reform and the rise of protectionism was a major contributing factor to the collapse of the ministerial meeting. To this must be added their perceptions of the increased economic power of the emerging markets, which gave rise to increased collusion between them to raise the level of ambition for developing countries in NAMA and services. Part of this was due an increasing clash of paradigms between the developed and developing countries, namely the increased assertion of commercial interests or the need for 'new trade flows' against the livelihoods of farmers in developing countries and the industrial development prospects and jobs of workers in developing countries.

---

[35] WTO 2005.

[36] Washington Trade Daily, 22 June 2007.

[37] See WTO doc. Services Special Session, Report of the Chair, Job. This group consists of Australia, Canada, EU, Japan, Korea, New Zealand, Norway, the Separate Customs Territory of Taiwan, Penghu, Kinmen and Matsu, Switzerland and US.

[38] See WTO doc, CTESS Job (07)/193, 3 December 2007.

[39] WTO doc. A communication by Canada, the European Communities, Iceland, Japan, New Zealand, Norway, Switzerland and the United States titled 'Joint Paper on Revised Draft Modalities for Non-Agricultural Market Access'. 5 December 2007.

[40] By prohibiting more than half of six digit sub-headings to be excluded from any four digit sub-heading subject to a full formula cut or any combination of six-digit sub-headings (under a four digit) representing more than 50 per cent of the total value of imports.

An additional factor for the current tension in the Doha negotiations stems from the perceived threat to the competitive positions of the traditional industrial economies from the emerging economies, particularly the rise of the so-called 'BRICs' (Brazil, Russia, India and China). To these economies could be added several more, including Mexico, South Africa, Argentina and Malaysia. At the UNCTAD XII conference held in Accra, Ghana in April 2008, United Nations Secretary-General Ban Ki Moon stated that the share of developing countries in world exports has grown from 30 per cent to almost 40 per cent. A recent report by Goldman Sachs[41] notes that since 2001, the US share of world gross domestic product (GDP) has fallen from 34 per cent to 28 per cent, whilst the BRICs' share has risen from 8 per cent to 16 per cent. During the same period, China's reserves have rocketed from US$200 billion to US$1,800 billion; Brazil's from US$35 billion to US$ 200 billion; and India's from US$50 billion to US$300 billion (see the three country chapters in this volume).

In sum, the attempts by the US and the EU to coordinate their positions, accommodating their own interests between themselves and then seeking aggressive gains from other economies (particularly the emerging markets) has been a strong feature of the Doha Round negotiations since Cancún. This strident Northern agency must be regarded as a major contributing factor to the collapse of the WTO July 208 ministerial meetings. Thus Wilkinson's observations (discussed above) of the persistence of asymmetry of economic opportunity in the GATT/WTO since the early GATT rounds retains its validity up to the end of July 2008 ministerial meetings. We now turn to the third reason for the collapse of the July 2008 ministerial meetings. The historical debate on the methods of decision-making in the GATT will be briefly assessed and the Principal Supplier Principle method of negotiations employed in the GATT will be evaluated. We will then analyse the method of negotiations employed in the July 2008 ministerial meetings in this historical context.

The Principal Supplier Principle

The debate in historical perspective
The issue of voting method is an old debate in the GATT and has it origins in the early negotiations on the proposed ITO that was to be part of the Bretton Woods institutions following the Second World War. During the negotiations on the proposed ITO, the issue of the voting

---

[41] Goldman Sachs 2007.

method was one of the few issues on which developing country lobbying was more successful. For decision-making in the ITO the US delegation proposed the same method of weighted voting that was used in the recently created International Monetary Fund (IMF). A similar proposal was made by Britain to take into account the economic size of the country in its share of the vote – i.e. a system of weighted voting. Developing countries voiced their opposition to such a system of voting as they feared that this would institutionalise their secondary status. A number of developing countries[42] voiced strong opposition to weighted voting and came out in favour of consensus. As a consequence, the ITO did not adopt a system of weighted voting. This decision was to be adopted by the GATT, which also employed the consensus approach to its decision-making.

The Principal Supplier approach also had its origins in the early ITO/GATT debates. During the negotiations on the ITO, many members had preferred a system of bargaining that was formula-based (i.e. across the board tariff negotiations), but the US Congress indicated that this would not be acceptable. Britain supported this method as it would have led to the levelling of high US tariffs. The US delegation however argued for a system of reciprocal bargaining over specific tariff lines that required a product-by-product, Principal Supplier method of tariff negotiations. A country could only be requested to make tariff cuts on a particular product by the principal supplier of that product to that country. This meant that for any particular product the importing country negotiates its tariff rate with its principal supplier and not with all suppliers of the same product. Developing countries at the time were seldom principal suppliers of any product, except raw materials that entered industrialised countries duty-free. Only at the fourth Geneva Round of GATT in 1956 was this rule modified to allow developing countries to negotiate collectively in requesting concessions. However, they were still effectively prevented from requesting concessions in any products that they did not produce in large quantities. Thus the Principal Supplier rule had the effect of locking-out developing countries from the tariff cutting negotiations. The current debate in the WTO on the formation of small informal groups that become the main decision-making forums or that shape the main content of the deals has significant resonance in the debate in the GATT since its inception. The negotiating method employed in July 2008 harked back to the Principal Supplier approach utilised in the old GATT. We discuss this further in the section below.

---

[42] These countries included Czechoslovakia, Turkey, Lebanon, Iraq, El Salvador, Venezuela and Mexico.

Evaluating the G7 in the July 2008 ministerial meetings

The third reason for the collapse of the ministerial meetings is ironically due to the 'medieval process'[43] that saw the EU/US sticking to their old habits of setting up imbalanced small groups that cut the main deals, without consideration for the smaller players, and the marginalisation of their issues in the negotiations. The formation of the G7 was a surprise after the failure of the G4 (and earlier G5 and G6 informal ministerial groups) in Potsdam. The package that emerged on the evening of 25 July 2008 (see discussion above) was not agreed and did not address the issues of interest to the majority of WTO members. It was supported by neither India nor China and gained no legitimacy amongst the majority of members.

The African ministers who were not represented in the G7 issued a statement that read: '[w]e are deeply concerned that in the Group of Seven (G7) not one African country was represented in a round that purports to be about development'. The statement continued that '[m]ost of the issues of importance to the African continent were not even discussed, especially cotton'.[44] Reflecting their dissatisfaction with the G7 process, the Group of 33 (G33) of developing countries, whilst they continued to support the positions that India and China expressed on the SSM (India and China were represented in the G7), they called for the issue of SSM to be returned to the WTO Agriculture Negotiating Group, chaired by Crawford Falconer as soon as possible.[45]

Thus the G7 ministerial meetings called by WTO DG Pascal Lamy during the July 2008 ministerial meetings failed to achieve the objective of negotiating the breakthrough in the agriculture and NAMA modalities negotiations that Lamy had hoped for. Some agreements reached in the G7 on elements of the modalities – the so-called 'Lamy Package' – did not have the support of all the members of the G7.[46] Neither did the G7 enjoy the support of the majority of the WTO members that felt that their issues were marginalised in the negotiations. In addition, the WTO DG did not succeed in resolving any of the issues of interest to the smaller developing countries in smaller side meetings that were on his so-called 'to-do' list.[47] Cotton did not get onto the

---

[43] Then-EU Trade Commissioner Pascal Lamy blamed the collapse of the WTO Cancún Ministerial Conference in 2003 blamed on the 'medieval process' of the negotiations.

[44] Press Statement issued by the Deputy Prime Minister and Minister for Trade of Kenya, 30 July 2008.

[45] See Washington Trade Daily, 15 September 2008.

[46] See Letter by Kamal Nath, Minister of Commerce of India, to the WTO DG Pascal Lamy, dated 24 September 2008 and 17 October 2008.

[47] WTO DG Pascal Lamy's 'to-do' list included the issues that were not in the Lamy Package (including cotton, bananas, DFQFMA, preference erosion, etc).

agenda at all. The banana negotiations unravelled. The issue of DFQFMA for LDCs was not addressed. There were several more complex issues on NAMA that affected South Africa (see Chapter 7), Argentina and Venezuela, which also remained unresolved. In the conclusion below, we summarise the three reasons advanced for the collapse of the July 2008 ministerial meetings and then propose some policy recommendations for the WTO membership.

3   POLICY RECOMMENDATIONS FOR THE DDA

We make three recommendations to address the underlying causes of the collapse of the July 2008 ministerial meetings. First, the studies by Tallberg and Odell (discussed earlier) on the role of the chairs suggest that formal leaders can positively enhance the efficiency of the negotiations by transforming competing proposals into single texts and forging agreements. This positive and efficient role of the chairs can be restored in the WTO negotiations by studying the more successful efforts of previous chairs that enjoyed wide support amongst the membership. A case in point is the Chair of the agriculture negotiations in the period before and including the WTO July 2008 ministerial meetings. In addition, the WTO could develop a code of conduct for the chairs of the negotiating groups, based on its own rich experience of the performance of previous WTO chairs. Second, the success of the next attempt to advance the Doha negotiations will also require that the EU and US take account of the development interests of the large and smaller developing countries and not simply try to advance their own commercial interests. Fairness and balance in the negotiations requires that the large number of exemptions the developed countries have demanded to accommodate their agriculture sensitivities are reciprocated in providing similar flexibilities to developing countries to protect their poor farmers and industrial workers. Third, the WTO should think carefully about how it constitutes small groups to advance the negotiations in the future. Because of their size, China, India, the US and the EU can claim to be part of any small group that is created to broker a deal. However, the interests of the rest of the membership have to be represented in any negotiating group too. The model of small groups that includes members simply on the basis of their economic and political weight or Principal Supplier approach is not suited to the diversity of economic interests and the political expectations of members to be represented and included at every stage of the negotiating process.

Since the onset of the Doha Round, and particularly after Cancún, the WTO has evolved a rich tapestry of alliances or groups, especially amongst the majority of developing countries. These groups can play a key role in building joint negotiating positions and convergence among the membership. As then-EU Trade Commissioner, Pascal Lamy had acknowledged the positive role of developing country groups in the WTO. After Cancún, he compared the G20 to a trade union that legitimately represents its members' interests. Subsequently at Hong Kong, a deal was brokered in a green room gathering that included the representatives of different groups, including the G33, the Africa Group, the LDCs and the African, Caribbean and Pacific (ACP) countries. It is therefore only fair that the ACP, Africa Group, the G33, the NAMA-11, the Cotton-4 and the LDCs are also represented in any future negotiating group. We next turn to consider the lessons of the collapse of the July 2008 ministerial meetings for the different developing country coalitions. We begin by setting out the theoretical framework that is employed to evaluate the role of these developing country coalitions.

4   CONCLUSION: LESSONS FOR DEVELOPING COUNTRY COALITIONS

Theoretical contributions to the debate on coalitions

In theorising about bargaining coalitions in the WTO (see Chapter 8), Amrita Narlikar distinguishes between two types of coalitions: issue-based alliances (formed around concerns for a particular issue) and bloc-type coalitions (shared ideas on multiple concerns). She considers two possible hypotheses for the creation of coalitions, namely the 'Defection Hypothesis' and the 'Collective Gains Hypothesis'. The strategic rationale for the former is based on narrow individual interests, where countries join a coalition to first establish their power and then to be bought-off by the outside party in the form of side-payments (i.e. the Prisoners Dilemma). In this scenario, each party to the coalition fears being isolated during the endgame, where it could be the only member left adhering to the collective position after the collapse of the coalition (thereby generating the 'suckers payoff'). However, Narlikar asserts three arguments against the Defection Hypothesis as an explanation for the primary logic of coalition formation. She argues that countries will not cooperate if they all are aware that everyone else is driven by this logic; outside parties too will not take the coalition seriously; and repeated defections by a member will in any event result in a lack of credibility of a coalition member. Instead, Narlikar argues that a more convincing rationale for coalition formation is captured by the concept of the 'Stag Hunt', where parties recognise that their collective interests are more likely to be achieved if they cooperate (see Chapter 8 for a fuller discussion of this theory).

Narlikar provides three recommendations to strengthen developing country coalitions in the WTO and to reduce the temptation of members of the coalition to defect: a) effective agenda-setting that addresses the concerns of all the members; b) larger members making side-payments to smaller members (e.g. increased market access); and c) the building of a large coalition (including large and smaller members) that increases the reliability of such a coalition achieving its goals and provide reassurance to its own members. Narlikar also suggests that a negotiating posture that displays a willingness to negotiate is more likely to generate concessions from the other side and prevent defections and the collapse of the coalition, rather than a negotiating posture of simply standing firm (i.e. strict distributive strategy).[48] In the section below we discuss the lessons of the July 2008 ministerial collapse for developing country coalitions, with specific reference to this theoretical framework.

Lessons for developing country groupings

The G20
There are three important lessons to be drawn from the July 2008 ministerial meetings for the G20 group of developing countries. First, the G20 has been the main force that has shaped the architecture of the Agriculture modalities text. Whilst this has been partly due to its willingness to compromise and offer pragmatic solutions to accommodate developed country protectionist needs, these concessions have largely been 'pocketed' by the developed countries. These concessions have not been meaningfully reciprocated by the developed countries in the agriculture and NAMA negotiations, where developing countries have sought flexibilities to accommodate their development needs.[49] Thus, a negotiating posture that is too pragmatic and too early without gaining reciprocal concessions from the developed countries will risk being unreciprocated by the developed country partners.

Second, the failure of the G20 to find a solution on special products and the SSM, leaving the deal to emerge at the end between the G33 and the US (and Cairns Group) was probably unwise. In the future, the G20 should strive to better balance commercial and development issues. The G20 will need more effective agenda-setting to address issues

---

[48] For a discussion of a strict distributive strategy, see Narlikar and Odell 2006.

[49] Brazilian Foreign Minister Celso Amorim submitted a long list of flexibilities in Agriculture where the G20 had accommodated the needs of the developed countries for additional flexibilities. The list included 6 specific flexibilities for the US, 2 for the EU and 4 for the G10 countries in the Domestic Support Pillar. Similarly, the US had obtained 3 specific flexibilities, the EU 4 and the G10 countries had obtain 11 flexibilities in the Market Access Pillar. In the Export Competition pillar the EU and US had each obtained 1 specific flexibility.

within itself and trade-offs between its members. A failure to address the need for trade-offs between its own members early enough could have a high cost for the capacity of the group to maintain its unity during an intense negotiating process. Thus Narlikar's second recommendation of negotiating internal trade-offs to strengthen the G20 coalition is relevant.

Third, the unity of the G20 was tested when it met during the July ministerial meetings to discuss the Lamy Package. Brazil, as the coordinator of the G20, had accepted the Lamy Package, which included a US$14.5 billion offer on OTDS for the US.[50] The G20 was divided on this issue, with some members arguing that the package was imbalanced. The G20 will need to reflect on how the coordinator of the group should behave, balancing its own interests and the interests of the group. In addition, making concessions too early, without consultations or support of the group would be perceived as a defection to obtain side-payments and lead to divisions and the collapse of the group. In future, the coordinator should exercise greater discipline by reporting back and consulting with the members before any decisions are taken.

The NAMA-11

The NAMA-11 (including South Africa as the group's coordinator) was not included in the G7 negotiations and neither was it consulted on the Lamy Package. Whilst Brazil was willing to accept the compromise language on industrial tariffs outlined in the Lamy Package, India had some reservations. Other members of the NAMA-11 were not consulted and were faced with a take-it-or-leave-it package. Argentina, Venezuela and South Africa continued to negotiate for a better deal. The group will need to reflect on how to maintain its solidarity in spite of the different negotiating positions and interests of its members. An early compromise by a major member of a coalition could be perceived as a defection to obtain a side-payment, thus weakening the coalition and precipitating its collapse. This puts pressure on the remaining members of the coalition to ensure that they do not end up with what Narlikar refers to as a 'suckers pay-off'.

The G33

The coordinator of the G33, Trade Minister Marie Penguestu of Indonesia, was also not represented in the G7 negotiating group. However, India and China (both members of the G33) maintained close

---

[50] See Washington Trade Daily, 28 July 2008. It was reported that Brazil was canvassing support for the Lamy Package, although this was opposed by India, South Africa and Argentina. Foreign Minister Celso Amorim was reported to have stated that Brazil was willing to press ahead, notwithstanding the differences within the G20 and Mercusor on the Lamy Package.

links and consultations with the group. Notwithstanding the exclusion of the coordinator, the G33 continued to support the positions of India and China in the G7 on the SSM. The G33 called for the issue of the SSM to be returned to the WTO Agriculture Negotiating Group, chaired by Crawford Falconer as soon as possible.[51] The group also maintained a posture of negotiation and a unified front. This group has clearly emerged as the most united and powerful of the developing country coalitions. There are lessons here for both the G20 and the NAMA-11 on how to maintain the cohesion and unity of a coalition.

The Cotton-4

The Cotton-4 (i.e. Burkina Faso, Benin, Chad and Mali) were not involved in the negotiations, although the cotton issue was to be next on the G7's agenda following the resolution of the SSM. The Trade Minister of Burkina Faso, Mamadou Sanou, lamented the failure of the ministerial meeting, stating that if there was no respite from the negative impact of US trade-distorting subsidies, the cotton farmers in his country '[w]ould soon disappear in the next couple of years because of global cotton subsidies'. At the press conference on 29 July 2008, the WTO DG admitted that the cotton issue was not taken up because it was linked to product-specific caps in the 'amber' and 'blue' boxes of farm spending, as well as the reference period and the size of the 'blue' box.[52] WTO members will have to reflect on how and why an issue of such vital interest and importance to some of the world's poorest countries could have been left to the end of the agenda and not addressed during the ministerial meetings.

The Africa Group

The Africa Group ministers made several statements during the end-July ministerial meetings. The Africa Group present in Geneva (including Burkina Faso, Cameroon, Egypt, Gabon, Lesotho, Mauritius, South Africa and Kenya) issued a press statement on 20 July[53] and 25 July 2008 to signal their concern that issues of interest to Africa should be addressed in the ministerial meeting.[54] The trade ministers expressed their frustration

---

[51] Washington Trade Daily, 15 September 2008.

[52] Washington Trade Daily, 30 July 2008.

[53] See Declaration of the Africa Group on the WTO Mini-Ministerial, Geneva, 20 July 2008.

[54] See Press Statement by the Deputy Prime Minister and Minister for Trade of Kenya, 25 July 2008. These issues included: real and effective substantial reduction of trade-distorting support by the developed countries in agriculture; agreement on a SSM that will effectively address import surges; a more ambitious outcome on cotton; a solution on bananas that does not impact negatively on African banana exporting countries; sufficient
(continued)

at being left out of the G7, stating that: '[w]e are deeply concerned that in the Group of Seven (G7) not one African country was represented in a round that purports to be about development. This does not augur well for the future of global governance'. On 30 July 2008, the Deputy Prime Minister and Minister for Trade of Kenya, speaking on behalf of the Africa Group stated that:

> [t]aking into consideration the two weeks we have been here in Geneva... we are deeply disappointed with the stalling of the negotiations. It should be known that most of the issues of importance to the African continent were not even discussed, especially cotton.[55]

Whilst the Africa Group could easily have objected to the process and outcome of the G7 at the end of the July 2008 ministerial meetings, they instead reflected their goodwill by calling upon the membership to 'capture the progress made' and 'consider resumption as soon as is feasible and continue with the negotiations'. In future, the Africa Group will need to strengthen its alliances with the major developing country coalitions so that it does not become marginalised and excluded from the negotiating process. It will do well to heed the third recommendation proposed by Narlikar, namely the need to increase the size of developing country coalitions so as to increase its bargaining power vis-à-vis the developed country majors.

The LDCs

The Minister of Trade and Industry of Lesotho, speaking on behalf of the LDCs at the TNC held on 29 July 2008, expressed disappointment that the issues of interest to LDCs – including 'the operationalization of Duty Free Quota Free Market Access and accompanying Rules of Origin in a manner that is commercially meaningful'; 'capacity building to address supply side concerns'; a 'simple and accessible Special Safeguard Mechanism'; and a 'fair and balanced outcome on cotton' – were not addressed. These issues will need to be prioritised by the membership to ensure that the development mandate of the Doha Round is adhered to. In addition, the LDCs will need to address the issue of how the differences between the Asian LDCs (that do not receive trade preferences in the US market) and the African LDCs that benefit from the trade preferences

---

flexibilities for African countries in the NAMA negotiations; the need to address the negative impact of preference erosion; the TRIPS Agreement to accommodate issues related to the CBD; and the development aspects of geographical indications.

[55] Press Statement by the Deputy Prime Minister and Minister for Trade of Kenya, 30 July 2008.

provided by the African Growth and Opportunity Act (AGOA) are dealt with in the modalities on preference erosion.

The LDCs had succeeded in securing an agreement at the 2005 Hong Kong Ministerial Conference that developed countries would grant LDC's DFQFMA for all their products. This would be complemented by an aid-for-trade package to strengthen production and supply capacity. Countries that could not immediately meet this DFQFMA commitment would provide at least 97 per cent access. The LDCs achieved this due to their internal unity (between the Asian and African LDCs) and the alliances they formed with the larger developing countries that had a common interest to build a larger coalition. The LDCs were also able to persuade the larger developing countries to provide them with DFQFMA as well, should they be 'in a position to do so'.[56] As Narlikar suggests, this internal bargain or 'trade-off' between developing countries is also crucial to strengthen the bargaining power and leverage of developing countries in the WTO negotiations.

Bananas and tropical products

The WTO DG Pascal Lamy used his offices to mediate between the tropical products group (mainly Latin American banana producers), the ACP banana producers and the EU. The DGs initial proposal on 16 July 2008 was rejected by both the Latin American producers and the ACP. Although several negotiating meetings were held by the DG and the parties concerned during end-July ministerial meetings in an attempt to resolve the issue, these did not result in an agreement. The EU thus announced that there will be no agreement on bananas outside of the Doha Round. Here too developing country groups will do well to heed the second and third recommendations proposed by Narlikar to strengthen their bargaining power vis-à-vis the EU. There have been many calls for the bananas issue to be resolved as part of an 'early harvest' to the DDA, together with the issues of interest to the LDCs (i.e. DFQFMA, cotton and aid-for-trade). Succeeding in including the bananas issue within an early harvest will require the tropical products group (mainly Latin American producers) and the ACP group of developing countries (concerned about preference erosion) to make 'trade-offs' between themselves and negotiating more effectively with the EU.

Developing countries must continue to strive to conclude the Doha Round on its development mandate. As a civil society conference on Global Partnerships for Development in August 2008 concluded: '[t]he Doha Round is not dead, it has simply paused.[57] At each stage of

---

[56] WTO 2005.
[57] See CUTS International 2008.

the round, developing countries have picked up the pieces of the failed ministerial meetings: after the collapse at Cancún in September 2003; after the suspension of the round in July 2006; and once more after the G4 Potsdam collapse in June 2007. They must do so again following the July 2008 deadlock and the cancellation of the ministerial meeting in December 2008. Developing countries must reflect and learn from their experiences. They must rebuild their technical and organisational capacity and strengthen their alliances. And they must march onto the next phase of the struggle to achieve a fair, balanced, inclusive and development-oriented outcome to the Doha Round. They should not rest until the promises of development in the Doha mandate have been fulfilled.

Annexure 1

Seattle 3rd WTO Ministerial Conference fails to launch Doha	December 1999
Doha 4th WTO Ministerial Conference succeeds and launches the DDA • Deadline for modalities in Agriculture • Deadline for modalities in NAMA	November 2001 End March 2003 End May 2003
Cancún 5th WTO Ministerial Conference collapses	Seattle 2003
WTO July 2004 General Council succeeds in adopting 'Framework Agreement'	July 2004
Hong Kong 6th WTO Ministerial Conference makes incremenetal progress	December 2005
Failure of G6 ministerial results in suspension of the DDA	July 2006
Failure of G4 ministerial at Potsdam	June 2007
Failure of the G7 ministerial at Geneva	July 2008
Cancellation of proposed ministerial	December 2008

REFERENCES

Brazilian Permanent Mission to the UN and WTO. 2008. *G20, Five Years of Activities of the G20: Moving Forward the Doha Round.* July 2008. Geneva: Brazilian Permanent Mission to the UN and WTO.

CUTS International. 2008. Cuts-FICCI Conference on Global Partnership for Development. Where do we stand and where do we go? A Report of the Proceedings. New Dehi, 12-13 August.

Finger. Michael. 2007. Implementation and the imbalance: dealing with hangover from the Uruguay Round. *Oxford Review of Economic Policy* 23(3):440-460.

Goldman Sachs. 2007. *BRICs and Beyond.* Goldman Sachs Global Economics Group.

Government of Argentina. 2008. Statement of Argentina to the WTO Trade Negotiating Committee, 26 July.

Government of Brazil. 2008. Statement by Minister Celso Amorim to the Informal Trade Negotiating Committee, 21 July (as delivered).

Government of South Africa. 2005. Statement by South Africa to the 55th session of the Committee on Trade and Development on behalf of Argentina, Brazil, India, Indonesia, Namibia, the Philippines and Venezuela. 28 November.

Government of South Africa. 2008. Statement to the WTO Trade Negotiating Committee, Geneva, 22 July.

Kaushik, Atul, Rashid Kaukab and Pranav Kumar. 2008. A Brief Analysis of the July 2008 Lamy Package. Jaipur: CUTS International. Mimeo.

Ismail, Faizel. 2004. Agricultural Trade Liberalisation and the Poor: A Development Perspective on Cancun. *BRIDGES* 8(1), January, pp. 4-5.

Ismail, Faizel. 2009. The role of the Chair in the WTO negotiations. From the Potsdam collapse in June 2007 to July 2008. *Journal of World Trade* 43(5), forthcoming.

Kaushik, Atul, Rashid Kaukab and Pranav Kumar. 2008. A Brief Analysis of the July 2008 Lamy Package. Jaipur: CUTS International. Mimeo.

Narlikar, Amrita and John Odell. 2006. The Strict Distributive Strategy for a Bargaining Coalition: The Like Minded Group in the World Trade Organization. In *Negotiating Trade: Developing countries in the WTO and NAFTA,* edited by John Odell. Cambridge: Cambridge University Press.

Odell, John. 2005. Chairing a WTO Negotiation. *Journal of International Economic Law* 8(2):425-448.

Ostry, Sylvia. 1997. *The Post-Cold War Trading System. Whose on first?* London and Chicago: University of Chicago Press.

Tallberg, Jonas. The Power of the Chair: Formal Leadership in International Cooperation. *International Studies Quarterly* (forthcoming).

Wilkinson, Rorden. 2006a. *The WTO. Crisis and Governance of Global Trade*. London: Routledge.

Wilkinson, Rorden. 2006b. The WTO in Hong Kong: What it Really Means for the Doha Development Agenda. *New Political Economy* 11(2), June.

WTO. 1999. Background Document – High Level Symposium on Trade and Development. Geneva, 17-18 March.

WTO. 2005a. Hong Kong Ministerial Declaration, 18 December, WT/MIN(05)/DEC.

WTO Reporter. 2008. Negotiations, Doha Talks Collapse Over US-India Dispute on Ag Safeguards; Future of Round in Doubt. 30 July.

10. CONCLUSION:

WHAT LEADERSHIP AND WHAT CHANGE?

Recurrent deadlock in the Doha Development Agenda (DDA) may, at first glance, appear to be symptomatic of the lack of any change in the multilateral trading system. As much of the preceding analysis in this book suggests, however, a great deal has changed. Indeed, the persistent deadlock in the World Trade Organisation (WTO), the shift of trade negotiations to alternative forums at the regional and bilateral level, and the sense of crisis surrounding the multilateral trading system, may well be attributed to these changes. In this concluding chapter, we draw on the contributions made in this volume to highlight the changes that have occurred in the course of the Doha negotiations, analyse why members of the WTO have been so reluctant to assume the mantle of leadership, and present some solutions.

We see the insights of this book as contributing to the growing scholarship on the multilateral trading system and the problems that it faces today.[1] A major contribution of our collection is its country-specific analysis: with six of the ten chapters focusing on the motivations driving the behaviour of the key players, we are able to offer new insights into explaining the negotiation strategies of the established and emerging leaders of the organisation, and further how their actions have brought the WTO to a point of stasis today. While Part I of the book focuses on the traditional leaders of the organisation – the European Union (EU) and the United States (US) – Part II investigates the rise of new players that have emerged in an increasingly multi-polar WTO, namely Brazil, China, India, and South Africa. A major intervening variable between the levels of individual countries and the institution is that of inter-state coalitions. Especially when they involve developing countries (including the BICS – Brazil, India, China and South Africa – which we study in this volume), coalitions offer a source of empowerment to them whilst also increasing the level of uncertainty in the organisation. Part III of the book comprises two chapters on coalitions in the WTO, which investigate the impact that coalitions have had in facilitating a more equitable distribution of power in the WTO, as well as new challenges that they pose to the organisation.

---

[1] See, for instance, the Warwick Commission Report 2007.

A.Narlikar, B.Vickers (eds.), Leadership and Change in the Multilateral Trading System, 231–249.

While this book is primarily about the old and new/potential *leaders* in the WTO, Part III also pays some attention to the 'followers' i.e. the smaller members who constitute the majority of the membership of the WTO, and without whose consent any exercise of leadership would be meaningless.[2]

1   CHANGE AMIDST STASIS

The DDA presents us with a paradox: while the negotiations themselves have been in a state of overall stagnation,[3] major changes have in fact occurred within the WTO. Three are critical, and are outlined below.

First, Brazil, India, China and South Africa – the BICS – have emerged as key players in the organisation, both as leaders of coalitions and in their own right. This rise is due partly to their growing trade shares. For instance, as leading exporters of merchandise trade in 2007, China ranked 3rd (contributing to 8 per cent of world merchandise exports), Brazil 16th (contributing to 1.1 per cent), India 21st (contributing to 1 per cent) and South Africa 39th (and contributing to 0.5 per cent of world exports). When intra-EU trade was excluded, China and Brazil retained their ranks of 3rd and 16th respectively, although their shares in world merchandise exports increased to 10.7 per cent and 1.5 per cent respectively. India and South Africa emerged as the 20th and 25th largest exporters. As exporters of commercial services, the ranks of the BICS are higher still: China ranked 4th (contributing to 4.5 per cent of exports in commercial services), India 5th (contributing to 3.6 per cent), Brazil 19th (contributing to 0.9 per cent) and South Africa 23rd (comprising 0.6 per cent share of services exports). Admittedly, the EU and the US continue to occupy the first and second rank positions, but the rapid catch-up of the BICS with them is obvious in their declining trade shares relative to those of the rising powers. For example, over ten years ago, in 1997, the US contributed 12.6 per cent of world merchandise trade. By 2007, the US share had declined to 11.5 per cent. Amongst the BICS in 1997, China was the highest ranking as the 10th largest exporter of merchandise, with 3.3 per cent of world exports (in contrast to 8 per cent in 2007), while Brazil, India and South Africa did not even feature in the list of top

---

[2] The importance of followers in the exercise of leadership is borne out in Joseph Nye's analysis, where he conceptualises the leadership process as comprising three key components: leaders, followers, and contexts; see Nye 2008.

[3] The first major deadlock of the DDA was at the Cancún Ministerial Conference in 2003. Bar the one major breakthrough that was achieved in the July Package of 2004 and a lackluster, face-saving Hong Kong Ministerial Declaration in December 2005, the negotiations have been marked by recurrent deadlock at all levels: within Geneva at the ambassador level as well as the ministerial and mini-ministerial levels.

25 merchandise exporters.[4] In other words, the rise in their weight simply as major trading nations has been rapid and dramatic.[5]

Second, the expanding trade shares of the BICS have been accompanied by their growing activism in the WTO. It is worth noting that the two are not necessarily co-related: Brazil and India, even with miniscule trade shares in the GATT years, were vociferous participants in its Green Room and corridor diplomacy, whereas other developing countries with historically much larger trade shares maintained a low profile both in the GATT and the WTO. A combination of growing confidence as a result of economic growth, along with institutional adaptation and learning,[6] has contributed to the bigger voice of the BICS in the DDA. All four chapters in Part II illustrate this rising activism, which is often framed in terms of developmental concerns.

Third, while we see signs of learning by the BICS, it is equally important to acknowledge the adaptation of the WTO to these changing balances of power. The old Quad has been replaced by new core groups that take the shape of the Group of 4 (G4), Group of 6 (G6), Group of 7 (G7) and others. In all the variants of these key consensus-building groups, Brazil and India have been regular invitees. At the Geneva negotiations in July 2008, China was also included in the deliberations of the G7 (which comprised the EU, US, Australia and Japan, along with Brazil, China and India). South Africa, while still not at the High Table of the trade negotiations, has also acquired greater prominence since the onset of the DDA negotiations in 2001. Not only is South Africa the largest and most industrialised economy in Africa – providing a voice for a continent often marginalised from the inner locus of trade bargaining – but South Africa has also exercised middle power leadership as an interlocutor between the advanced developed countries of the North and the developing nations of the South. At Doha in November 2001, South Africa was therefore appointed as one of six 'Friends of the Chair' to facilitate the rules negotiations. Since then, the country has played an increasingly active and visible role in the WTO's deliberations, in particular chairing the Committee on Trade and Development Special Session (CTDSS) from 2004-2006 and since 2009 following the height of the global credit crisis, the Committee on Trade in Financial Services (see Chapter 7). With the high politics of global finance dominated by the

---

[4] World Trade Statistics, www.wto.org.

[5] See Goldman Sachs 2007.

[6] This argument is made specifically for Brazil and India in Hurrell and Narlikar 2005, but could be extended easily to the cases of China and South Africa (both of which are relatively newer members of the WTO, have only recently learnt the ways of the institution, and have begun to use this learning to exercise their clout).

OECD core and circuits, few developing countries have previously held the latter position.

Compare the WTO against other international organisations, such as the World Bank, the International Monetary Fund (IMF) or the United Nations Security Council, and it becomes obvious that the organisation stands out in its ability to reflect the changing ground reality of increasing multipolarity.[7] It is also worth noting that these changes are fairly recent, having occurred in tandem with the Doha negotiations: until as late as 2001, India had led the Like-Minded Group (LMG), a coalition whose agenda included improving the transparency and inclusiveness of the WTO for developing countries.[8] Interestingly, however, these significant changes in the balance of power of the WTO as well as reform of the institution have not resulted in a greater buy-in from the members of the organisation – developed or developing. The Doha negotiations have run into repeated deadlock; not only has a 'Doha-lite' proven elusive, but members have been unwilling to make face-saving concessions to secure even a 'Doha super-lite'. Members have further signalled their effective disengagement from the DDA by turning to alternative regional and bilateral trade agreements.[9] From the old players within the organisation as well as new ones, acting alone or in concert, there is little evidence of any willingness to facilitate the provision of the global public good of free trade. Such a lack of commitment from its members is likely to raise problems in any organisation; it becomes critical in a member-driven organisation like the WTO. Drawing on our case studies, we analyse the sources of the problem.

2   DISENGAGEMENT AND RELUCTANT LEADERSHIP

Given that the key decision-making processes of the WTO have been adapted to the changing balance of power, what explains the stasis in the organisation? We argue that the answer lies in the leadership vacuum in the WTO: neither the established leaders nor the emerging ones are willing to take on the responsibilities of leadership. To know exactly why this is the case, we need to return to the comparative insights offered by the country-specific case studies of Part I and Part II. Given that the existence of coalitions can decrease the predictability of the negotiation process and increase its proclivity to deadlock, we also draw on the insights of Part III to discuss the importance of leadership with specific reference to collective bargaining in the WTO.

---

[7] Subacchi 2008.
[8] Narlikar and Odell 2006.
[9] See Bhagwati 2008; Sally 2008.

The Old Guard: the EU and the US

Traditionally, a key role in the negotiation process in the GATT was played by the EU and the US. This was partly a result of the negotiating practice of using the Principal Supplier Principle (where concessions reached between the principal suppliers and *demandeurs* were subsequently multilateralised). But even after this practice was discontinued, the EU and the US continued to play a prominent role in GATT and WTO negotiations as members of the old Quad. While the EU and the US today no longer occupy the same prominence as they did in the past in an increasingly multipolar WTO, they remain major players in international trade. Given the very significant actual and potential market shares that they still represent, any Doha deal without their involvement and agreement would be meaningless. And yet, far from providing leadership for the new round, both powers have shown increasing disengagement. The two chapters by Manfred Elsig and Geoffrey Pigman on the EU and the US respectively explain the declining enthusiasm of the EU and the US for the Doha negotiations. While the two chapters highlight case specific reasons for disengagement, equally important is the common theme of the rise of the BICS that emerges in their analyses. The growing power of the BICS has led both the EU and the US, albeit guided by different motivations, to turn away from the leadership that they had provided for the multilateral trading system in previous decades.

Elsig uses Albert Hirschman's framework of exit, voice, and loyalty to argue that in the course of the Doha negotiations, '… enthusiastic leadership turned towards a partial exit in the form of pragmatic forum-shopping vis-à-vis other venues to regulate trade'. The rise of the BICS contributed to this 'partial exit' as the EU, particularly in the DDA, found it difficult to translate its voice into influence: with the emergence of developing countries, acting alone and in coalitions, 'it was no longer sufficient for the EU to agree with the US to push the agenda forward'. The EU encountered unprecedented resistance over the Singapore Issues, and was thus unable to push its 'deep trade' agenda, nor was it able to secure tangible concessions in other issue areas (which may have persuaded its domestic constituencies) in return for its own concessions on agricultural market access.

Elsig's argument of the EU's declining loyalty, and therefore declining leadership, as a result of the changing balance of power in the WTO may also be extended to the US to explain its declining leadership of the DDA. Pigman however traces two additional influences of the rise of the BICS on the US commitment to multilateralism in trade. First, going back to the Clinton administration's response to the end of the Cold War and the rise of 'Big Emerging Markets', the separation between economic and security policy was replaced by a strategy that treated trade policy as an integral part of foreign policy. Second, replacing its 'one-size-fits-all' approach to developing countries (which had been in place since 1964 with the Johnson administration agreeing to Part IV of the GATT), the US began to take an increasingly differentiated approach to various developing countries (including the BICS). This trend, whose origins lie in the Clinton years, has become stronger over the years, especially with the launch of the 'Global War on Terror'. Pigman provides a brief overview of US bilateral relations with each of the BRICs to argue '...with respect to each of the BRICs, US trade policy has become one tool in the larger toolkit of US foreign policy instruments, and, despite similarities between the four BRICs, US policy towards each has become increasingly differentiated'. Effectively, Pigman's argument translates into one about declining American leadership at least at the multilateral level, and the subordination of the goal of trade liberalisation (which had greatly facilitated the dramatic tariff reductions secured in the GATT years in the Cold War era) to broader foreign policy goals that are specific to the particular bilateral relationship.

While the rise of the BICS has effectively, in the case of both the EU and the US, contributed to a decline in their willingness to bear the costs of leadership in the WTO, factors specific to their domestic polities have further exacerbated this tendency towards disengagement. In the case of the EU, Elsig identifies three factors: the role and timing of agricultural reform; the implications of the enlargement process; and the lack of support by export-oriented industries. First, common knowledge that the European Commission had strong incentives to lock-in the CAP 2003 reforms meant that concessions offered on the back of the reform process were seen as quasi-automatic by the rest of the WTO's membership; the fact that the Commission was reluctant to offer additional concessions on market access did not help the negotiating dynamic. Second, while the EU enlargement process could have potentially created a new momentum for limiting CAP spending and also assume greater leadership by virtue of its expanded market, this has not been the case. The new members of the EU represent a new constituency within it who risk the erosion of their newly-acquired preferences through multilateral trade liberalisation. The EU thus faces an added set of constraints in taking on WTO-based liberalisation, let alone leading the way on it. Third, in contrast to the Uruguay Round (1986-1994), export industries have been largely silent. This is partly because in the face of limited progress on the NAMA or services negotiations (along with the disappearance of the Singapore Issues from the negotiation agenda), export industries have lost interest in the DDA. Instead, they have turned to alternative means of securing market access. Elsig mentions examples of multinational firms resorting to tariff-jumping, acquisitions, lobbying activities, and bilateral trade and investment deals. Add to these the availability of a wide range of regional alternatives[10] and it is not surprising to see why in this trade round, exporting interests no longer balance the protectionist lobbies at home in the EU, and why EU negotiators in turn have thus been unwilling to lukewarm in pushing for a completion of the DDA.

The US too faces a different set of domestic constraints that result in its similar disengagement. Given the divided nature of US government, good relations between the White House and Capitol Hill are essential if pro-trade legislation is to be passed. Pigman's chapter demonstrates the tensions in this relationship under the George W. Bush administration. As the number of Democrats grew in both Houses and the further the 'Fair Trade' protectionist agenda gained in strength, the US Congress refused to renew Fast Track for the remainder of the Bush presidency. Additionally, the US faced similar problems to the EU in that export-oriented industries were far less vociferous than import-competing ones.[11] This particular configuration of domestic interests and institutions made it very difficult for the US to take on any leadership initiatives in the WTO. Notwithstanding the multilateralist orientation of the Obama administration (as reflected in the Group of 20 (G20) summits and the new administration's economic diplomacy), Pigman rightly points out that: 'The WTO was the ghost at this feast of multilateral cooperation and compromise, with the conclusion of multilateral negotiations to complete the DDA far from prominent on the London G20 agenda'. While peering into the future, Pigman specifies the conditions under which the Congress might renew Fast Track for President Obama. But it is clear that, at least so far, there are strong international and domestic forces steering both the EU and the US away from the path of leadership that they had assumed naturally and willingly in the years of the GATT.

New powers but not yet leaders? The BICS

While there is a leadership vacuum in the WTO resulting from the disengagement of the two leading members of the old Quad, the new members at the High Table of trade negotiations – the BICS – despite their increasing and improved participation, have still not shown themselves willing to take on the role of leaders. Recall that the EU and the US, as co-sponsors of the Uruguay Round, and indeed in the early years of the DDA, had demonstrated considerable leadership. For instance, Elsig, as evidence of EU loyalty and leadership, gives us the example of the Lamy moratorium of 1999, which placed a moratorium on

---

[10] Young 2010.
[11] Young 2010.

engaging in new preferential trade agreements at the bilateral level while the multilateral negotiations were still in progress. None of the BICS has shown a comparable willingness to bear the costs of the provision of global public goods. While more ready than ever before to block the negotiations, they are yet to translate their veto-player status into agenda-setting influence, as is illustrated by all our four case studies in Part II. Interestingly, however, we do see some variations in the types of negotiating strategies that the BICS are using. India occupies the most consistently and strictly distributive end of the negotiating spectrum; China and South Africa, whilst not quite as consistent nay-sayers as India, have undergone some change especially in the latter years of the DDA to move towards the more overtly distributive end; and finally Brazil has moved away from the strict distributive towards using a more mixed strategy with some integrative moves.

Brazil and India are the two most established powers amongst the BICS in the WTO in that they have a long history of active participation that dates back to the GATT. They are also the two consistently invited members of any core group that assumes the role of the new Quad (or its variants). While both have cooperated closely with each other in the DDA in attempting to guard what they see as the concerns of the developing world, and also leading coalitions of developing countries (as they did in the Uruguay Round),[12] India's position has been more consistently distributive throughout the Doha negotiations. Bar one episode at the Hong Kong Ministerial Conference in 2005, which Amit Ray and Sabyasachi Saha detail in their chapter, when India pushed for services with 'over-enthusiasm' and 'was seen as colluding with developed countries', India has been unwavering in advancing the cause of development in the WTO. This support for Third World-ist causes has been repeatedly borne out at all turning points in the DDA negotiations, including the Cancún Ministerial Conference wherein both Brazil and India (and to some extent South Africa) invited opprobrium from the US by being categorised into the 'won't-do' countries[13], as well as the July talks of 2008 when India's chief negotiator was termed 'Dr No'.

India's ability to stand its ground is important especially from the perspective of maintaining the unity of the coalitions that it leads (see Chapters 8 and 9 by Amrita Narlikar and Faizel Ismail respectively). However, as Narlikar argues in her chapter, strong coalitions that result at least partly from such leadership also contribute to the recurrence of deadlocks. As such, India's leadership of developing country coalitions generates a paradox. Its firm stance and group activism provide the

---

[12] Narlikar 2003.
[13] Zoellick 2003.

significant club good of coalition unity and strength. But this also means that India is not a provider of the public goods of free trade or the preservation and strengthening of the multilateral trading system. Successful coalition leadership has contributed greatly to India's newfound veto power, but the particular form that this coalition leadership takes has paradoxically also undermined its agenda-setting power in the system.

Brazil's trajectory, while overall similar to the Indian one in the early part of the DDA, with the two together (along with China) having led the powerful G20 coalition and further advocated a strongly developmentalist agenda, showed signs of developing a more conciliatory dynamic in the July 2008 talks. As coordinator of the coalition at the time, it is reported to have urged its allies within the G20 (unsuccessfully) – especially China and India – to compromise on the issue of the Special Safeguard Mechanism and accept the deal that was on offer, which included a cap on US domestic subsidies at US$14.5 billion (see Faizel Ismail's discussion of the July 2008 Lamy Package, Chapter 9). Brazil attracted considerable flak from many developing countries for taking this position. Several efforts were made to cover up the rift in the aftermath of the July talks.

While the differences between Brazil on the one hand, and China and India on the other – all members of not just the G20 but also the new G7 – came to the fore during 2008, it is important to note that this rift within the coalition was rooted in a fundamental and long-standing divergence of interests between the coalition members. Brazil's position in the coalition as an agricultural exporter with a particularly vibrant agribusiness sector was bound at some point to come into tension with Indian and Chinese concerns as food importers with sections of their populations dependent on subsistence farming.[14] The real puzzle in fact should be why Brazil (and indeed the other members of the G20 who were also members of the Cairns Group) did not fully defect in July 2008 or show signs of defection at an earlier stage of the negotiation. Chapter 4, by Maria Lucia Pádua Lima, offers us an important insight into why this was the case.

While the strategy of import-substitution industrialisation (ISI) came into question in Latin America in the aftermath of the debt crisis, the conversion to the Washington Consensus (including the prescription of unilateral trade liberalisation) did not generate the promised results either. Pádua Lima writes:

---

[14] These potential differences were recognised even at the time of the formation of the G20 (see Narlikar and Tussie 2004). Also see the country-specific chapters in this volume for an unpacking of the sector-specific goals of each of the BICS.

Growing disappointment at the outcomes of reform was intensified by the foreign exchange crisis that hit the country in 1999. The combination of external crisis and weak performance of the Brazilian economy broke once and for all the idea that quick and easy benefits would derive from a trade policy based on unilateral opening.

Learning this hard lesson, Brazil could have reacted to the Washington Consensus by developing a more protectionist policy. Interestingly however, and reflecting its unique historical development, its mixed experience with ISI and also external constraints precluded this option. Instead, Brazil came to emphasise the importance of reciprocity – as opposed to unilateral liberalisation – in the Doha negotiations, specifically in agriculture but also extending to NAMA. Here it differs from the positions taken by India, China, and indeed South Africa more recently, all of which have in one form or another emphasised the importance of qualified or non-reciprocity.[15] Brazil's notion of reciprocity, however, is also different from that advanced by the West in that it is firmly rooted in the notion of development as per the DDA mandate. It is this latter framing of reciprocity in terms of development that has allowed Brazil to be actively involved in the G20, adhere to the collective line taken by the coalition until July 2008, and further reaffirm its commitment to the coalition thereafter.

Besides Brazil and India, the two relatively new and rising key players are China and South Africa. Gregory Chin, in Chapter 6 of this volume, while recognising that China has not taken on a strong leadership role in the Doha negotiations, argues that 'it has been far from a passive actor'. This was evident from China's role in the G20, and also in its proposals for reform of the WTO. But this strategy evolved dramatically in the summer of 2008, when China's 'fairly low key, selective, somewhat aloof though generally supportive approach to the Doha Round' was transformed into high-profile and distributive diplomacy. Alongside India, China emerged as a much more vociferous player in the July 2008 talks. Not only was it included in the consultations of the G7, but it chose to exercise its influence visibly when it joined India in blocking the consensus that was being negotiated by refusing to concede on the Lamy Package. Chin explains China's 'self-identification with the developing world as motivated partly by national interests and by more

---

[15] China, on the grounds of its difficult accession process that required it to take on a disproportionate level of concessions; India because of its claims of the inadequately fulfilled promises of the Uruguay Round, plus its particular problems including a very large agrarian population that thrives on subsistence farming; and South Africa as a result of its transition domestically to an increasingly developmentalist state with high levels of unemployment, poverty and inequality.

enduring ideological legacies of 'Third Worldist' foreign policy self-identification from the Maoist period'. Whether China will continue to develop this role, particularly amidst the new challenges posed by the financial crisis, remains to be seen, and the recent transformation of its trade diplomacy certainly need not be interpreted as 'aggressively challenging' the system. But it is important to note that China's rise to more active participation in the Doha negotiations does not amount to leadership. If anything, China's recent turn brings it closer into line with India's negotiating behaviour in the WTO: it offers some direction to the other developing countries and empowers them, but it also makes the system more prone to deadlock.

South Africa shows a similar trajectory to that of China's. Brendan Vickers, in Chapter 7, traces the transformation of South African trade diplomacy from 'quintessential middle-power-ship' in the period 1995-2003 to an 'incipient "developmental state" paradigm' since Cancún in 2003 (and particularly Hong Kong two years later). While the former phase was associated with the 'cautious and integrative "middle power" agencies of facilitation, mediation and compromise positions between the industrialised and developing worlds', the new phase has been 'coupled with greater distributive or value-claiming bargaining'. South Africa's development activism in the WTO is driven by its industrial policy. This is legitimised and further developed by appealing to the 'historical injustice' of having had to negotiate the Uruguay Round with the status of a developed country, and also by framing its defensive demands (notably for NAMA and services) in terms of the need for greater domestic and regional 'policy space'. Importantly, since South Africa's main interests lie in NAMA (coupled with concerns over further 'de-industrialisation'), it could potentially have struck an easy deal with the North by making concessions on agriculture. The fact that it has not done so reinforces the point about its commitment to developmental concerns that operate not just at the individual level but also the collective (particularly Africa, where agriculture is critical). Akin to India and China, South Africa has also emphasised the importance of reforming negotiation processes in the WTO to address problems of lack of inclusiveness and transparency.

Any analysis of the BICS behaviour in the recent trade negotiations will be incomplete without some attention to the coalitions that they operate in. Part III of the book focused on the role of coalitions in both empowering the BICS (as well as other members of the coalitions) and in contributing to the stasis at the WTO. In Chapter 8, Amrita Narlikar offers a theoretical analysis of the dilemmas that confront trade coalitions involving developing countries, applies these insights empirically, and then offers proposals for reform. While the risk of defection affects all coalitions, Narlikar highlights the mechanisms whereby strong coalitions can be built such that members pursue the collective gains rather than the gains that could accrue individually through defection. Coalitions involving developing countries have indeed overcome this temptation to defect and thereby emerged as strong coalitions. However, Narlikar further suggests that strong coalitions, while a source of considerable empowerment to both their leaders as well as followers, also produce an unintended and serious cost. Having overcome the defection problem, they find it particularly difficult to make concessions for two reasons. First, internal to the coalition, members may read attempts to offer concessions as a sign of defection. Second, externally, the outside party may interpret concessions as a sign of weakness, especially if it is aware of the internal dissensions within the coalition. As such, while coalitions can greatly empower the weak and alter balances of power, they can also increase the proclivity of the system to deadlock. In other words, leadership of coalitions has shown an inverse relation with the leadership of the system, at least as far as the BICS in the WTO are concerned. Narlikar offers two solutions to the problem, which are discussed in Section 3 below.

In Chapter 9, Faizel Ismail examines the failure of the July 2008 talks and attributes it to three reasons: the imbalanced nature of the negotiating texts (within NAMA and also between NAMA and agriculture); increasing protectionism within the EU and the US; and the resurrection of the old Principal Supplier Principle. The first explanation – the imbalanced nature of the texts – is attributed to poor chairing, and the chapter calls for the establishment of a code of conduct for chairs. Ismail's analysis of EU and US protectionism further corroborates the findings of Elsig and Pigman in Part II: besides problems within their domestic polities, the transatlantic powers have attempted 'to raise the bar of the level of ambition for developing countries, particularly the major emerging markets that have been perceived as significant competitors with the EU and US'.[16]

In other words, the inability of the two to adapt to the changing balance of power within the WTO has contributed significantly to the stasis. The issue of the balance of power enters indirectly into Ismail's third explanation as well: substituting the Old Quad with a new G7 to reflect the WTO's growing multipolarity – as was done in the July 2008

---

[16] Writing elsewhere on the reasons for Doha's slow progress, Jeffery Schott also emphasises this point: there has recently been rampant 'China bashing' in the US and Europe, where policymakers face growing resistance to new trade liberalisation and renewed calls for economic nationalism, 'the blood brother of trade protectionism,' see Schott 2008.

talks – was effectively a return to a de facto Principal Supplier Principle, which led to considerable dissatisfaction on the part of many developing countries and threw the legitimacy of any proposed solutions via this mechanism into doubt. Finally, Ismail applies Narlikar's theoretical contributions to draw out the lessons that the July 2008 collapse generates for coalitions of developing countries.

Several common themes emerge from the case studies. Four are significant, and operate at four different levels. First, a part of the reason for the lack of leadership and resulting stasis in the WTO lies at the level of domestic politics. For the EU and the US, this takes the shape of disengaged political constituencies whose support for multilateral trade liberalisation has declined; for the BICS, this involves an emerging, often not clearly articulated, norm of development. The second theme that emerges from all the case studies is that of the evolving balance of power in the WTO, where both the old guard and the new pass the buck of leadership to each other. Third, and paradoxically, the same coalitions that empower the BICS and other developing countries also contribute to deadlock in the organisation and result in forum-shifting, thereby effectively undermining the newfound power of the developing world. Finally, even the cacophony of voices at the High Table of the WTO does not impart legitimacy to the organisation's decision-making, whereas it certainly impedes its efficiency and ability to deliver. If changes within the WTO are to be harnessed to produce effective leadership of the organisation, action at all these four levels will be necessary. In the next section, we identify possible solutions to the problems highlighted here.

3   LEARNING TO LEAD

Based on the insights of the case studies, we offer four sets of solutions to address the problems at the four levels: domestic, state, coalition and institutional.

Leadership begins at home

That leadership begins at home is a point that emerges most concretely from Manfred Elsig's chapter on the EU, but is further reflected in all the country-specific case studies. One of the key differences between the Uruguay Round and the DDA is that the former had strong support from export industries within the EU and the US; the absence of this support in the DDA has made the task of selling multilateral trade liberalisation at home very difficult for the US and EU governments (see Chapters 2 and 3). To overcome this problem, the importance of good leadership at home cannot be overemphasised.[17] Politicians and policymakers must recreate awareness about the benefits of trade and the costs of protectionism, especially in the context of the financial crisis where we have already seen an upswing in protectionism (see Chapter 1). Ideas matter as well. It is important to remember that even though the round has been framed in terms of development, the developed world stands to gain from concessions exchanged as much as the developing world. Charity is not the driver for this round, nor should it be; if the stakeholders in the North were to recognise this, they are more likely to also recognise the benefits that the round will bring them as well and their commitment to the DDA is likely to improve.[18]

In the case of the BICS, domestic concerns translate into trade negotiations in two ways. First, some very legitimate concerns about particular stakeholders (e.g. India's concerns about the impact that market opening would have on its millions of subsistence farmers or South Africa's concerns about the country's high unemployment rate and further 'de-industrialisation'), and second, new – but not yet fully articulated – ideas of an alternative pattern of trade and development, have together made the BICS reluctant leaders. Any deal on Doha will have to pay due respect to the first set of concerns. Note however that trade policy is no substitute for development policy at home and several of these concerns can only be addressed through effective domestic responses. Recognition therefore of the limits of trade policy for some of the problems facing these countries could translate into more negotiating space and an expansion of the zone of agreement. Second, all four of the BICS have, in different forms, expressed alternative visions of 'developmentalism', which go hand in hand with a commitment to the cause of Third World-ism (albeit in quite a different form from that of the 1970s).[19] All four chapters have emphasised that these ideas, while important, do not represent a wholesale, revolutionary challenge to the system so much as advance the cause of incremental reform. This is an important point and one that is worth driving home to the BICS that repeated deadlock of the multilateral trading system – a system in which they have only recently managed to establish themselves as major players – does not work to their advantage. The BICS themselves could reframe their agenda, domestically and internationally, bearing these costs in mind.

---

[17] See Warwick Commission 2007.
[18] Narlikar 2009.
[19] Hurrell and Narlikar 2006.

Inspiring countries to leadership

How could the EU, the US and the BICS be persuaded to fill the leadership vacuum in the WTO? As the chapters by Elsig and Pigman highlight, despite increasing multipolarity in the WTO, no agreement will be possible without the approval of the EU and the US. While their own governments can use several strategies domestically to sell the round to their stakeholders at home, other strategies can further be developed to ensure that the EU and the US re-embrace their responsibilities of leadership. First, the developing world can reframe its demands to emphasise the gains that both the EU and the US will make from this particular round, as well as the benefits that they derive from the existence of the multilateral trading system. Second, and perhaps more controversially, the zone of agreement could be expanded to bring at least some of the issue-areas of interest to the EU and the US back in. Third, the EU and the US could be brought back to the negotiating table if their regional and bilateral alternatives were to worsen, either simply as a consequence of the current financial crisis or more strategically through a conscious decision and credible signal by their partners to prioritise multilateralism.

While the indispensability of the EU and the US to reaching a meaningful agreement is not new, the newfound veto-player status of the BICS makes it just as important to persuade them to take a lead. As was argued in Narlikar's chapter on coalitions, if these countries are to transform their veto-player status into that of agenda-setters, two steps are necessary: first, they must be able to stand firm on certain issues (rather than simply cave in to pressure in the early stages of the game), and second, they must show themselves willing and able to make some concessions and not conflate the DDA with an 'entitlement policy'.[20] As has been further argued in this concluding chapter, this translates into an ability to provide not just club goods (in the case of the WTO, of coalition unity) but public goods (of free trade and the health of the multilateral trading system). While the BICS have, after years of learning and adaptation, finally shown themselves able to achieve the first step and provide the club good of coalition stability, they have not been able to make the necessary concessions and contribute to the provision of the public good of free multilateral trade. Indeed, their successful production of the club good has so far detracted from their ability to produce the public good. The solution lies at the coalition level and also at the level of the institution.

---

[20] Schott 2008.

Leadership at the coalition level

A key factor in the emergence of the BICS as veto-players in the WTO has been their successful participation in, and leadership of, coalitions. These coalitions were discussed in detail in Chapters 8 and 9, and also featured in the country-specific case studies. But while coalitions have greatly empowered these countries, they have also decreased their flexibility to offer concessions and reach an agreement. Narlikar offers two solutions to the problem. While the second solution is institutional and is hence discussed under the next sub-heading, the first requires the leaders of the coalition to employ signalling methods to effectively counter the risk of misinterpretation of conciliatory moves. These signals need to be internal and external. Internally, leaders of the coalition must reassure members that any concessions with the outside party are not symptomatic of defection on their part, while externally, they must ensure that the outside party does not misinterpret conciliatory moves as a sign of weakness.[21]

Institutional reform to facilitate effective leadership

While the last three solution sets operate at the level of the agents from whom leadership is expected, we must also taken into account the institution within which leadership is to be exercised and what shape reform here might take.[22]

Though the WTO has shown itself adaptable to the changed global balance of power by incorporating the BICS at the core of its decision-making, these changes have not worked. If anything, more diversity in the Green Room has increased the difficulty of reaching consensus and improved the legitimacy of the WTO only marginally at best. Moreover, while changes in balances of power are likely to be disruptive in any institution, the member-driven nature of the WTO makes it especially vulnerable to stasis if its members abdicate leadership in response to growing multipolarity. Chapters 8 and 9 offer some directions for institutional reform.

Faizel Ismail, in Chapter 9, identifies three main causes for the collapse of the July 2008 talks. The first – the imbalanced nature of the texts as a result of inadequate/inefficient/biased chairing – has attracted comment elsewhere as well from scholars and practitioners alike, and necessitates an institutional solution. Ismail highlights the importance of having a code on chairing in the WTO, which could overcome some of

---

[21] See Narlikar and van Houten 2010.
[22] See Wolfe 2008.

these problems.[23] While Ismail's second explanation deals with the rise of protectionism in the EU and the US, his third reason for the failure of WTO talks in 2008 is directly institutional. He argues that the G7 consultations that formed the core of the talks resulted in the marginalisation of the great majority of the WTO's membership; had the G7 actually managed to reach a consensus amongst themselves, it would have lacked legitimacy and ownership with a very large proportion of the WTO's membership. He thus recommends that: 'the WTO should think carefully about how it constitutes small groups to advance the negotiations in the future... the interests of the rest of the membership have to be represented in any negotiating group too'.[24]

Institutional action and reform may also be particularly useful to address the problem of the leadership of the BICS, insofar as these new powers find themselves bound into taking inflexible collective positions and are thereby unable to provide leadership to the system. Besides advancing a solution based at the level of the coalitions themselves, Chapter 8 advanced an institutional solution to the problem. Coalitions, as per this solution, would receive formal recognition and a limitation would be placed on side-deals (through an outright moratorium or through an extension of such deals on an MFN basis to all coalition members). Formal recognition of coalitions as principals in the negotiations could potentially significantly empower even some of the smaller countries (thereby addressing one of the problems that Faizel Ismail raised with the return of negotiations based on an implicit Principal Supplier Principle). Most importantly, such formalisation, by reducing the risks of misperception and misinterpretation of concessions, would mean that developing countries would no longer feel obliged to take entrenched positions. Greater flexibility and ability to compromise would help transform the veto-player status of the BICS into agenda-setters, from coalition leaders to leaders of the multilateral trading system.

It is a credit to the multilateral trading system that it has been able to facilitate and accommodate the rise of new powers. But this inclusiveness has not resulted in the new powers – the BICS – assuming the responsibilities of leadership, nor has it deterred the traditional powers – the EU and the US – from abdicating such responsibilities. By

---

[23] Odell 2005 presents another interesting perspective on the role and performance of chairs in the WTO negotiations. Like Faizel Ismail's chapter, Odell also points to lessons for future practice and suggests an informal innovation to enhance chairs' preparation for this task.

[24] Ismail's commentary on the use of the Principal Supplier Principle in recent times offers a powerful critique of the critical mass solution that has been advocated by the Warwick Commission Report, 2007.

analysing the specific constraints – and also opportunities – that these countries face on their leadership, this book has suggested ways in which the multipolarity of the WTO could be effectively harnessed to the advantage of all its members.

REFERENCES

Bhagwati, Jagdish. 2008. *Termites in the Trading System. How Preferential Agreements Undermine Free Trade*. Oxford: Oxford University Press.

Goldman Sachs. 2007. *BRICs and Beyond*. Goldman Sachs Global Economics Group.

Hurrell, Andrew and Amrita Narlikar. 2006. The New Politics of Confrontation: Developing Countries at Cancún and Beyond. *Global Society* 20(4):415-433, October.

Narlikar, Amrita. 2003. *International Trade and Developing Countries: Bargaining Coalitions in the GATT & WTO*. London: Routledge.

Narlikar, Amrita and Pieter van Houten. 2010. Know the enemy: Uncertainty and deadlock in the WTO. In *Deadlocks in Multilateral Negotiations: Causes and Solutions,* edited by Amrita Narlikar. Cambridge: Cambridge University Press.

Narlikar, Amrita. 2009. Reforming the multilateral trading system: Lessons of the Doha negotiations. In *Is free trade fair trade? New perspectives on the world trading system,* edited by Frank Trentmann. London: Smith Institute.

Narlikar, Amrita and John Odell. 2006. The strict distributive strategy for a bargaining coalition: The Like Minded Group in the World Trade Organization. In *Negotiating Trade: Developing Countries in the WTO and NAFTA*, edited by John Odell. Cambridge: Cambridge University Press.

Narlikar, Amrita and Diana Tussie. 2004. The G20 at the Cancun Ministerial: Developing Countries and their Evolving Coalitions in the WTO. *World Economy* 27(7):947-966, July.

Nye, Joseph S. 2008. *The Powers to Lead.* Oxford: Oxford University Press.

Odell, John S. 2005. Chairing a WTO Negotiation. *Journal of International Economic Law* 8(2):425-448.

Sally, Razeen. 2008. *Trade Policy, New Century: the WTO, FTAs and Asia Rising*. London: Institute of Economic Affairs.

Schott, Jeffrey J. 2008. The future of the multilateral trading system in a multi-polar world. Discussion Paper 8. Bonn: German Development

Institute. At: http://www.iie.com/publications/papers/schott0608.pdf, accessed on 4 November 2008.

Subacchi, Paola. 2008. New power centres and new power brokers: are they shaping a new economic order? *International Affairs* 84(3):485-498.

Warwick Commission. 2007. *The Multilateral Trade Regime: Which Way Forward?* Coventry: University of Warwick. At: http:// www2. warwick.ac.uk/research/warwickcommission/report/uw_warcomm_tra dereport_07.pdf, accessed on 27 April 2008.

Young, Alasdair. 2010. Transatlantic Intransigence in the Doha Round: Domestic Politics and the Difficulty of Compromise. In *Deadlocks in Multilateral Negotiations: Causes and solutions,* edited by Amrita Narlikar. Cambridge: Cambridge University Press.

Wolfe, Robert. 2008. Can the Trading System Be Governed: Institutional Implications of the WTO's Suspended Animation. In *Can the World Be Governed? Possibilities for Effective Multilateralism*, edited by Alan S. Alexandroff. Waterloo, Ont.: Wilfrid Laurier University Press.

Zoellick, Robert B. 2003. America will not wait for the won't-do countries. *Financial Times.* 22 September.

INDEX

CPSIA information can be obtained at www.ICGtesting.com
Printed in the USA
BVOW08s2314010914

365005BV00012B/332/P